Occasions And Protests

Occasions And Protests

John Dos Passos

Henry Regnery Company   1964

Contents

Occasions and Protests

I. Certain Fundamentals

The American Cause

Some years ago I received a letter from a bunch of German students asking me to explain to them in three hundred words why they should admire the United States. "Young people in Germany," they wrote, "as in other places in the world are disillusioned, weary of pronouncements on the slogan level. They are not satisfied with negatives, they have been told over and over again what to hate and what to fight. . . . They want to know what to be and what to do."

This is what I didn't tell them: I didn't tell them that they should admire the United States because we were first to develop the atomic bomb or the hydrogen bomb, or because we had bigger and shinier automobiles or more washing machines and deep freezes; or more televisions, or ran up more passenger miles of airplane travel a year than any other people. I didn't tell them to admire us for getting more productive work done with less backbreaking than any other people; or for our high wages, or our social security system. I didn't tell them to admire us because our popular misleaders had the sweetest smiles before the television cameras or because we lived on a magnificent continent that offered an

From *The Theme is Freedom,* by Dos Passos (New York: Dodd, Mead & Co., 1956).

unbelievable variety of climates, mountains, plains, rivers, estuaries, seashores. These are not things that would help them "to know what to be and what to do."

This is what I told them: I told them they should admire the United States not for what we were but for what we might become. Selfgoverning democracy was not an established creed, but a program for growth. I reminded them that industrial society was a new thing in the world and that, although Americans had gone further than any other people in spreading out its material benefits, we were barely beginning, amid crimes, delusions, mistakes and false starts to spread out what people needed much more: participation, the sense of belonging, the faith in human dignity, the confidence of each man in the greatness of his own soul without which life is a meaningless servitude. I told them to admire our failures because they might contain the seeds of victories to come, not of victories that come through massacring men, women and children, but of victories that come through overcoming the evil inherent in mankind through the urgent and warmhearted use of our best brains. I told them to admire us for our unstratified society, where every man still has the chance, if he has the will and the wit, to invent his own thoughts and to make his own way. I told them to admire us for the hope we still have that there is enough goodness in man to use the omnipotence science has given him to ennoble his life on earth instead of degrading it.

Selfgovernment, through dangers and distortions and failures, is the American cause. Faith in selfgovernment, when all is said and done, is faith in the triumph in man of good over evil.

The Workman and His Tools

An apologia at thirty-six. Thirteen years after writing *Three Soldiers,* I had to read it over to correct misprints for a new edition. It was not exactly a comfortable task. The memory of the novel I wanted to write had not faded enough yet to make it easy to read the novel I did write.

The memory of the spring of 1919 . . . Any spring is a time of overturn. But then Lenin was alive. We thought the Soviets were New England townmeetings on a larger scale. Socialism seemed a radiant dawn. The Seattle general strike seemed the beginning of a flood instead of the beginning of an ebb. Americans in Paris were groggy with new things in theatre and painting and music. Picasso was to rebuild the eye. Stravinski was cramming the Russian steppes into our ears. Imperial America was all shiny with the idea of Ritz. Currents of energy seemed breaking out everywhere as young guys climbed out of their uniforms. In every direction the countries of the world stretched out starving and angry, ready for anything turbulent and new. Whenever you went to the movies you saw Charlie Chaplin at his best . . . The memory of the spring of 1919 had not faded enough yet to make the spring

First printed in 1936.

of 1932 any easier. It wasn't that *today* was any finer in 1919 than in 1932, it was that in 1919 the tomorrows seemed vaster. Growing up is the process of pinching off the buds of tomorrow.

Most of us who were youngsters in 1919 had already, by the spring of 1932, made our beds and lain in them. You wake up one morning and find out that what was to have been a springboard into reality is a profession. The organization of your life that was to be an instrument to make you see more and clearer, turns out to be blinders made according to a predestined pattern. The boy who thought he was going to be a tramp turns out a nearsighted middleclass intellectual (or a tramp, it's as bad either way). Professional deformations set in. The freeswimming young oyster fastens to the rock and grows a shell.

Well, you're a novelist. Why? Why not? What excuse have you got for not being ashamed of yourself?

Not that there's any reason, I suppose, for being unduly ashamed of the trade of novelist. A novel is a commodity which fulfills a certain need; people need to buy daydreams the way they need to buy ice cream or aspirin or gin. They even need to buy a pinch of intellectual catnip now and then to liven up their thoughts, a few drops of poetry to liven up their feelings. All you need to do to feel good about your work is to turn out the best commodity you can, play the luxury market and to hell with doubt.

The trouble is that mass production involves a change in the relationship between the workman and his tools. In the Middle Ages the mere setting down of the written word was a marvel; something of that marvel got into the words set down. In the Renaissance the printing press suddenly opened up a continent more tremendous than America. Sixteenth and seventeenth century writers are all on fire with it.

Now we have linotype, automatic typesetting machines, phototype and offset processes that plaster the world from end to end with print. Certainly eighty percent of the inhabitants of the United States read a mess of print a day, if it's only the advertising on tooth paste or the Sears Roebuck catalogue.

The perfection of the machinery of publication ought to be a stimulant to good work. But first the writer must decide exactly what he's cramming all these words into print for; the Freudian gush about selfexpression that fills the minds of newspaper critics and publishers' logrollers, emphatically won't do. Making a living by selling daydreams, sensations, packets of mental itching powders, may be all right, but I think most people feel it's not much of a life for a healthy adult. You can make money by it, sure; but for a hundred reasons profit is a wornout motive, tending more and more to strangle on its own power and complexity. No producer, even the producer of the shoddiest of five and ten cent store goods, can do much about money; the man who wants to play with the power of money has to go out after it straight, without any other interest. Writing for money is as silly as writing for selfexpression.

What do you write for then? To convince people of something? That's preaching, and is part of the business of everybody who deals with words; not to admit that is to play with a gun and say you didn't know it was loaded. But outside of preaching I think there is such a thing as writing for writing's sake. A cabinetmaker enjoys whittling a dovetail because he's a cabinetmaker; every type of work has its own delight inherent in it. The mind of a generation is its speech. A writer makes aspects of that speech permanent by putting them in print. He whittles at the words and phrases of today and makes forms for the minds of later generations. That's history. A writer who writes straight is an architect of history.

On being invited to join a Communist writer's union. Anybody who can put the words down on paper is a writer in one sense, but being able to put words down on paper no more makes a man a professional writer than the fact that he can scratch up the ground and plant seeds in it makes him a farmer, or that he can trail a handline overboard makes him a fisherman. That is fairly obvious. The difficulty begins when you try to work out what really distinguishes professional writing from the average man's letters to his family and friends.

In times of rapid change when terms are continually turning inside out and the names of things hardly keep their meaning from day to day, it's not possible to write two honest paragraphs without stopping to take crossbearings on every one of the abstractions that were so well ranged in marble niches in the minds of our fathers. The whole question of what writing is has become particularly tangled in these years during which the industry of the printed word has reached its high point in profusion and wealth, and, to a certain extent, in power.

Three words which still have meaning, that I think we can apply to all professional writing, are discovery, originality, invention. The professional writer discovers some aspect of the world and invents out of the speech of his time some particularly apt and original way of putting it down on paper. If the product is compelling enough, it molds and influences ways of thinking to the point of changing and rebuilding the language, which canalizes the mind of the group. The process is not very different from that of scientific discovery and invention. The importance of a writer, as of a scientist, depends on his ability to influence thought. In his relation to society a professional writer is a technician just as much as an engineer is.

As in industrialized science, we have in writing all the steps between the complete belt conveyor factory system of production and one man handicraft. Newspapers, advertising offices, moving picture studios, political propaganda agencies, news magazines produce the collective type of writing where individual work is indistinguishable in the industrial synthesis. Historical and scientific works are often turned out by the laboratory method where various coworkers collaborate under one man's supervision. Songs and ballads are sometimes the result of the spontaneous efforts of a group working together. At present stories and poems are the commonest output of the isolated technician.

Any writer who has ever worked in any of these collective undertakings knows the difficulty of bucking the routine and the officeworker control that seems to be an inseparable part of large industrial enterprises, whether their aims are to make money or to improve human society or to furnish jobs for officeholders. It is a commonplace that business aims, which are to buy cheap and sell dear, are often opposed to the aims of the technician, which are, insofar as he is a technician and not a timeserver, the development of his material and of the technical possibilities of his work. The main problem in the life of every technician is to secure enough freedom from interference from the managers of the society in which he lives to be able to do his work.

As the era of free competition gives way to that of state monopoly, with the corresponding growth of officeworker control, inner office intrigue and the other maladies of bureaucracy, it becomes increasingly hard for the technician to get that freedom. The need for functional hierarchies on an enormous scale and the difficulty of keeping the hierarchies in check through popular control, makes the position of the technician extremely difficult; because, by his very function, he has to give his time to his work instead of to "organizational problems."

When you add to this disability the knowledge that the men behind the desks in the offices control the police power—indirectly in this country, but directly in the Communist countries—which can at their whim put a man in jail or deprive him of his life or of everything that makes life worth living, you can see that the technician, although the mechanical means in his power are growing every day, is in a position of increasing danger and uncertainty.

The only name you can give a situation in which a technician can do his best work, and be free to give rein to those doubts and unclassified impulses of curiosity which are at the root of invention and discovery and original thinking, is "liberty."

Liberty in the abstract is meaningless outside of philosophical chessgames. The word has taken on various misleading political colorations. In America it once meant liberty for the manufacturer to cut wages and throw his workers out on the street if they didn't like it; in labor union parlance it means liberty for the union leaders to force union members to strike whether they want to or not, and to vote as they are told.

But, underneath, the word still has a meaning that we all know, just as we know that a nickel is a nickel even if the Indian and the buffalo have been rubbed off. The writer as a technician must never, no matter how much he is carried away by even the noblest political partisanship in the fight for social justice, allow himself to forget that his real political aim, for himself and his fellows, is liberty.

A man can't discover anything, originate anything, invent anything unless he's at least morally free, without fear or preoccupation so far as his work goes. Maintaining that position in the face of the conflicting pulls of organized life demands a certain amount of nerve. You can see a miniature of the whole thing whenever a man performs even the smallest technical task, such as cleaning a carburetor, or taking a bead on a target with a rifle. His state of mind is entirely different from that of the owner of the car who wants to get somewhere, or of the man himself a second before he puts his eye to the sight, all of a fluster to win the match or in a cold sweat of fear lest his enemy shoot him first.

This state of mind, in which a man is ready to do good work, is a state of selfless relaxation, with no worries or urges except those of the work at hand. There is a kind of happiness about it. It is much nearer the way an ordinary daylaborer feels than it is the way a preacher, propagandist or swivelchair organizer feels. Anybody who has seen war knows the astonishing difference between the attitude of the men at the front, whose work is killing and dying, and that of the atrocity-haunted citizenry in the rear.

At this particular moment in history, when machines and institutions have so outgrown the ability of the mind to dominate them, we need bold and original thought more than ever. It is the business of writers to supply that thought, and not to make of themselves figureheads in political conflicts. I don't mean that a writer hasn't an obligation, like any other citizen, to take part if he can in the struggle against oppression, but his function as a citizen and his function as a technician are different, although the eventual end aimed at may in both cases be the same.

To fight oppression, and to work as best we can for a sane organization of society, we do not have to abandon the morality of freedom. If we do that we are letting the same thuggery in by the back door that we are fighting off in front of the house. I don't see how it is possible to organize effectively for the humane values of life without protecting and demanding during every minute of the fight the liberties of investigation, speech and discussion which are the greatest part of the ends of the struggle. In any organization a man gives up some of his liberty of action. That is necessary discipline. But if men give up their freedom of thought, what follows is boss rule, gang warfare and administrative stagnation.

The dilemma which faces honest technicians is how to combat the imperial and bureaucratic tendencies of the groups whose aims they believe in, without giving aid and comfort to the enemy. By the nature of his function as a technician, the writer finds himself in the dangerous and uncomfortable front line of this struggle.

In such a position a man is exposed to crossfire. He is as likely to be mowed down by his friends as his enemies. The writer has to face that. His only safety lies in the fact that the work of an able technician cannot be replaced. It is of use and a pleasure to mankind. If it weren't for that fact, reluctantly recognized, but everywhere and always recognized, the whole tribe of doubters, inventors and discoverers would have been so often wiped out that the race would have ceased to produce types with those peculiar traits.

It's an old saying, but a very apt one, that a writer writes not to be saved but to be damned. *Publico ergo damnatus.*

I feel that American writers who want to do the most valuable kind of work will find themselves trying to discover the deep currents under the surface of the opinions, the orthodoxies, the heresies, the gossip and the journalistic trivialities of the day. They will find that they have to keep their attention fixed on the simple needs of men and women. A writer can be a propagandist in the most limited sense of the word, or he can use his abilities for partisan invective or personal vituperation, but the living material out of which his work is built must be what used to be known as the humanities. The humanities— in the original sense of the word—are based on sharply whittled exactitudes about men's instincts and compulsions and hungers and thirsts.

There is no escaping the fact that you are dealing with all mankind, starting with all the readers of your language in your generation; with all the varied traditions out of the past and men's feelings and perceptions in the present. No matter how narrow a set of convictions you start from, you will find yourself, in your effort to probe into men and events, less and less able to work within the prescriptions of doctrine; and you will find more and more that you are on the side of the men, women and children alive right now against all the political organizations, however magnificent their aims may be, that regiment and bedevil them; and that you are on the side, not with phrases or opinions, but really and truly, of liberty, fraternity and humanity.

The words are old and dusty and hung with the faded bunting of a thousand political orations, but underneath they are still sound. What men once meant by these words needs defenders today. And if the kind of men who have, in all kinds of direct and devious ways, stood up for them throughout history do not come out for them now to defend them against the gangsterism of the political bosses and the zeal of the administrators, the world soon will be an even worse place for men, women and children to live in than it is at present.

The writer's liberty is indissolubly linked with the liberty of his fellowcitizens. There may have existed societies in the past where thinkers and painters could win their way into some privileged sanctuary where they would be comparatively free to express themselves as they pleased, but in the close-knit society imposed on us by the structure of mass production industry no such sanctuary exists. The writer is free to write and to publish what he believes to be true only insofar as the farmer is free to work his farm as he pleases, as the factory worker is free to move in search of better opportunities, as the bookkeepers or the merchants are able to make their livings as best they can without the supervision of some government's police.

For the ordinary citizen liberty means the freedom to make his own choices as to how he shall live his life, the freedom to be a complete man, instead of half a man. For the writer it is even more profoundly the essence of his being. It is freedom to search for the truth.

All writing which is in any way first rate is an effort to tell the truth. Good writing is useful to society because each first rate piece of work adds a little something new to truth. The old truths don't need retelling; first rate writing must always add something to man's knowledge of himself, of man's behavior when he runs in packs, of the world around him.

First rate writing—the casting of fresh ideas in new and

noble words—is true in the profoundest sense of the word. From Homer and Confucius to our own day the first rate writers have managed to bring to light, in a thousand different styles and languages, varying fragments of that basic knowledge of man's hopes and fears, of his strengths and weaknesses, which we have a right to call truth.

Truth is by its very nature painful.

Men are able to live with old truths because they have become encysted in the commonplace, but fresh truths are painful to come by, and even more painful to hear. Particularly do they cause acute agony to the political bosses of this world who make their living by trying to run the lives of their fellowmen.

In a tolerably free society the man who uncovers some tiny capsule of truth has to face the chance of being derided and ignored. If he insists too much he is likely to be lynched. It was the free Athenians who voted the hemlock for Socrates.

In a state managed by policemen a man doesn't even have the opportunity to assume the objective attitude which is the necessary preliminary to the discovery of truth. The race of policemen, throughout history, has been quick to notice the first flicker of enquiry in a man's eye that marks the beginning of the questioning or inventive mood. A trouble-maker: get him out of the way.

Without liberty the writer cannot even begin to entertain those first untoward inquisitive thoughts about himself or the people around him which are the seeds of invention. Unless he can forget everything else in the painful search for some few fresh fragments of truth his work will be of no use to the world.

First rate writing is hard enough to come by under the most favorable conditions. Without liberty it is impossible.

The Harvard Afterglow

Dean Briggs: In Memoriam. Looking back
on it years later I found myself remembering the time I spent
at Harvard as a period of afterglow. At nineteen and twenty I
was mighty impatient with that afterglow. No more ungrate-
ful brat ever ran for a nine o'clock across the old duckboards in
the Yard.

It was my fate to come in on the end of an era. Victorian
scholarship had fulfilled its cycle. William James was dead.
The afterglow of the great Transcendentalists had not quite
faded from the Cambridge sky. Graduate students were still
retailing awed anecdotes of Santayana.

There had been a young poet named Tom Eliot, an ex-
plosive journalist named Jack Reed. They had moved out into
the great world of hellroaring and confusion. I felt I'd come
too late. Some of my undergraduate friends were trying to re-
place the ardors of the past with Oscar Wilde and Beardsley's
illustrations and *The Hound of Heaven*: the mauve gloaming.
I wasn't satisfied with any of it. I guess I wanted Periclean
Athens right that day in the Harvard Yard.

It took me twenty years to discover that I did learn some-

From *College in a Yard,* by Dos Passos (Cambridge, Mass.: Harvard
University Press, 1957).

16

thing at Harvard after all. Cambridge wasn't such a backwater as I'd thought. There was Robinson's Chaucer course, Henderson's History of Science . . . But it wasn't a question of scholarship: only years later did I begin to understand the uses of scholarship; it was the acquisition of a sort of an inheritance—from "an age that is gone" just like in the song.

As for so many others, it was Dean Briggs who became for me the personification of that inheritance. Not that I appreciated him at the time. It wasn't that I didn't feel respect and affection for him as a man and, in the best sense of the word, a New Englander. The man was unashamedly himself. No one could help being moved by his lovely candor, his tenderhearted irony, the salty smalltown way he had of putting things. But I thought of him as a museum piece, quaint, in the way in these latter years we have come to admire American primitives; provincial. I was among his irreverent students who spoke of him as Aunt Betsy. Though we revelled in shocking him, we preferred most of the time to pretend that we were shielding him from the facts of life.

What horrid little prigs undergraduates were in my day; I suppose they still are. In our idiot sophistication we thought of the dear Dean and his English 5 as hopelessly oldfashioned.

Of course he was. It's taken me a second twenty years to discover that his great value to me as a student was his oldfashionedness. He had an oldfashioned schoolmaster's concern for the neatness of the language, a Yankee zest for the shipshape phrase, an oldfashioned gentleman's concern for purity of morals, to use a properly oldfashioned expression, and a sharp nose for sham and pretense which was neither old nor newfashioned but eternally to the point. As a professor he was perfectly accessible. After I graduated I often regretted I didn't take more advantage of his openheartedness.

The last time I saw him was in Paris in 1919, if I remember

right, during the sham and fustian of the Peace Conference. He had been induced to come overseas on one of the fast proliferating commissions that were being posed to distract the public from Woodrow Wilson's failure to make the world as safe for democracy as we'd hoped. The Dean and Mrs. Briggs were housed, somewhat incongruously as it seemed to me, at the Hotel du Quai Voltaire on the Left Bank. Who could imagine anyone less bohemian than Dean Briggs! I went to see them.

As I remember it I was still in uniform. The last time I'd seen him I'd been fretting and fuming because I was trapped in a backwater cut off from the main currents of life. Well, in the three years that had passed since I'd turned in my last theme in English, I'd seen some life and a good deal of death. War had turned out to be a great teacher. I'd lost all pretense of collegiate sophistication but I'd come out with a prime case of horrors. I had seen too many men in agony. I had the horrors too about the kind of world the gentlemen at Versailles were arranging for us poor buck privates to live in. All through those years in college I'd been honing for "the real world." By the time I went to call on the Briggses at the Quai Voltaire I already had a belly full of it.

There's a special musty smell about old Paris hotels, a mildewed grandeur; after all, Paris has so often been the capital of the world. At that moment it was again. I found Dean Briggs and Mrs. Briggs shivering under shawls as they hovered over an alcohol lamp that was heating water for tea. The high-ceilinged room with its spangled chandelier was wretchedly chilly from the raw breath of the Seine under the windows.

I never saw two people who looked so out of place. Although they had both aged noticeably since I'd last seen them, they had a fresh rustic look that delighted me. The Dean's eyes were as bright as if he'd just stepped off a New Hampshire pasture. Mrs. Briggs' cheeks were apple red. I've forgotten what we talked about—probably I was still shielding them from the facts of life—but I remember my delight in their country cousin look. "Provincial," "oldfashioned" had become words of tenderness in my vocabulary.

They were indeed travellers from another world. In the wartime bombarded Paris of a few months before they wouldn't have seemed so out of place, but in the Paris of the Peace Conference they had the innocence of new born lambs. A soldier gets pretty sick of Mademoiselle from Armentières and all that sort of thing. Here was home, something more like home than anything I had ever known. I stayed on with them as long as I could. Too long, I imagine. When I left to go out into the alluring treacherous streets of the city of light, to go out into the future, my future not theirs, a future where hope and disaster seemed about evenly matched and both seemed full of grime and bloodshed, I can still feel the wrench it took. I remember thinking as I went down the stairs, that if it were possible to change lives with another man the way people do in the old Welsh stories, Dean Briggs even at seventy was a man I would change with. He seemed so much younger than I and, in a way, more enduring.

Satire as a Way of Seeing

Introducing a portfolio of drawings by George Grosz. Your two eyes are an accurate stereoscopic camera, sure enough, but the process by which the upsidedown image on the retina takes effect on the brain entails a certain amount of unconscious selection. What you see depends to a great extent on subjective distortion and elimination which determines the varied impacts on the nervous system of speed of line, emotions of color, touchvalues of form. Seeing is a process of imagination.

From the first weeks after birth when the baby begins to make up for itself, out of bright and gloomy, warmcosy and scaring, a universe to live in, a framework for the classification of seeing is laid down. As the visible elements, lights, shadows, faces, hands, tables, chairs, colors are named and isolated they are pigeonholed into a conventional pattern by the child's mimicking the habits of seeing of the older people who raise it. Styles of drawing and representation create these conventions. Thus the visible arts shape the way we see just as the audible

From *Interregnum,* edited by Caresse Crosby (New York; Black Sun Press, 1937).

arts shape the way we hear; somewhere between them lies the mind, the whole complication of styles of seeing and hearing, and of habits of thought, phrases and concepts that somehow get transmitted from generation to generation to constitute the human heritage.

How you see depends upon what your parents were seeing when you were little, and on how and what you've seen since you've been out in the world on your own. It is by the arts that stimulate seeing and the interlocking keyboard of the senses of weight, touch, order, rhythm that you make up your universe. Taste and hearing have their importance but sight is the basic sense. It is not nature, but drawing and painting and photography that educate the eye. They furnish the frame of reference by which we invent nature as we look at it.

In the last fifty years a change has come over the visual habits of Americans as a group, something analogous to what must have happened to Winslow Homer when after half a lifetime grinding out stiffly drawn imaginings of current events as a newspaper artist, he suddenly broke out in his watercolors into the world of sunlight and clouds and ocean. From being a wordminded people we are becoming an eyeminded people.

As I remember how things were when I was a child, the sort of people my parents knew had hardly any direct visual stimulants at all. There were engravings on the walls, and reproductions of old masters even, but the interest in them was purely literary. The type of drawing current in the late nineteenth century had such meager conventions of representation that it tended to evoke a set of descriptive words instead of something seen. I am sure that my parents, enjoying a view from a hill, say, were stimulated verbally, remembering a line of verse or a passage from Sir Walter Scott, before they got any real impulse from the optic nerve. Of course there were a few oil paintings in the upstairs bathroom, those mysterious little works done by forgotten members of the family that you used to find in all the dark upper halls, little landscapes that people had been reluctant to throw away because they were "handpainted" oils, but that were shamefacedly kept out of sight in the less seen parts of the house. As I remember the paintings in my mother's house in Washington, they tended to have millwheels in them and a patch of woolly blue water towards the center of the canvas. Children used to enjoy looking at them but no grownup ever thought about them; the graphic arts consisted of illustrations to literature, in a magazine or a book or on the wall, and old masters.

I must have been well along in college before I looked at a picture directly as an excitement for the eye, and then it was because I'd been reading Whistler's *Gentle Art of Making Enemies* and went into the Boston Art Museum to see what his painting was like. It must have been at about the same time that I first heard the music of Debussy. My generation in college was full of callow snobadmiration for the nineties. I can still remember the fashionable mood of gentle and European snobmelancholy the Whistler pastels produced, so like that of Debussy piano pieces, little scraps of red and yellow and green coming out of the dovecolored smudge. At that I think the titles affected me more than the pictures. Still I must have been visually stirred because I soon got hold of a box of pastels and began to make dovecolored smudges of my own. The trouble was that it immediately became obvious that almost any combination of pastel blurs was as agreeable to look at as any other, and my enthusiasm for that sort of thing began to flag.

The Armory Show was a real jolt, though I can't remember

any picture I saw there, and it is mostly associated in my mind with a torn yellowbacked volume of Van Gogh's letters a friend lent me along with a terribly bad French translation of *Crime and Punishment*. In spite of all the kidding about the "Nude Descending Stairs," I didn't recognize it when I saw it again at the Museum of Modern Art in New York. The most I got from cubism at the time was the tingling feeling that a lot of odd things I didn't know about were happening in the world.

I imagine that I still thought Andrea del Sarto, of whose paintings we had photographs in the library at home, top notch in that line. Through George Moore I'd learned the names of the French Impressionists but thought of them as literary figments like the Goncourts. The first time I was in Madrid the Velasquez paintings gave me most pleasure. I remember being rather scared by the Goyas and Grecos in the Prado. One rainy day in Toledo I did take a good look at the "Entierro del Conde de Orgaz" and Greco began to bite in without my knowing it.

Right after that, in my short snatches of Paris during the first war, I found myself all at once spending time walking up and down the rue de la Boëtie and the little streets on the Left Bank looking at pictures in the windows of the few picture dealers that were still open, and really seeing them; but I can't quite remember when the transition from the old way of looking at them took place. Then, in Italy on leave, the frescoes on the walls became suddenly more important than anything else.

What started me off was going into Giotto's chapel in Padua one fine wintry day after an airraid. A big domed church was burning on the other side of town sending up one long straight plume of smoke. The chapel was all banked up with sandbags and the fellow I was with and I were both eating some sort of round sausage made of chocolate and filbertnuts, a Paduan specialty that seemed delicious to us at the time; and as we looked, shivering in the cellar chill, munching with our caps in our hands in spite of the appeal of the guardian to cover our heads as the chapel had been unchurched, we were stunned with the sense of the permanence of Giotto's perfectly imagined forms, colored and spaced with such sober magnificence. Perhaps the feeling was enhanced by the knowledge that the chapel might be blown to hell the next moonlight night.

After that the appetite for painting grew fast. On leave I did hardly anything but look at paintings in churches and museums, wherever I could get through the protecting sandbags, discovering Piero della Francesca and Paulo Uccello and the "Last Judgment" in the Orvieto Cathedral and the city hall in Siena and the cemetery walls in Pisa and the paintings in the catacombs at Rome. Back in Paris after the armistice there were Cézannes to see and Picasso and Juan Gris and the feeling that great days were beginning. Since then I think I tend to take a painting visual end first.

Something of the sort has happened to many of my generation, and even in a greater degree to the generations younger than ours, so that an appetite for painting has grown up in America. Display advertising and the movies, though they may dull the wits, certainly stimulate the eyes. In New York the visual attack of the show windows of Fifth Avenue stores almost equals in skill and scope that of windows of the picture dealers on the rue de la Boêtie in the heyday of the school of Paris. It was not entirely because we were considered the freest spenders that artists who found Europe during the period between the wars impossible to live in tended to settle in the U.S. There has grown up here—thirty years ago how we wise guys would have sniggered at the suggestion—the sort of previous atmosphere of taste and enthusiasm that might make great work possible, if any painters should be found who were men enough to do it.

Thus far, outside of whittling and ironwork and the naïve domestic painting of which those little bathroom pictures I spoke about were the last representatives, American art has been first English provincial—and darn good provincial when you think of Copley and his contemporaries—then French impressionist provincial, and finally School of Paris provincial. For a while it leaned towards becoming Mexican provincial, and now it might be described as international provincial.

We have produced some good honest painters who stand out amid the phonies but we haven't yet done anything really firstrate in that direction. Young Americans with a taste for painting have felt that they had to go abroad somewhere to do it and most of them have come home devout faddists, useless to themselves and to the culture of their country. But in the years between the wars Europe (due to the abundant sprouting of the dragons' teeth the old men had so sanctimoniously sowed round the green baize at Versailles), instead of being the land of liberty and art young middlewestern highschool students used to dream about, became so stifling to any useful and rational human effort that suddenly the tables were turned. In the arts as in science, America became the refuge of the skills and traditions of western Europe.

The fact that firstrate men who couldn't live in their own countries felt that they could breathe here made me feel happy about the U.S.A. It was a pleasure to see Léger in New York. The fact that George Grosz, the great German visual satirist, took out papers, and for a while considered himself an American, made me feel that, in the arts at least, we were coming of age.

It was in Paris on the Boulevard St. Germain some time during the Peace Conference that I first saw a German booklet of drawings by Grosz. It must have been in a bookstore I suppose, but I somehow connect it in my memory with a magnificent colored print of cirrhosis of the liver in the window of the Society for the Suppression of Alcoholism opposite the old abbey. I suppose it was because what Grosz was representing was cirrhosis of nineteenth century civilization.

It's hard to reimagine the feelings of savage joy and bitter hatred we felt during that spring of 1919. We were still in uniform. We still had to salute officers, to go into outoftheway bistros to talk to our friends who happened to be wearing goldandsilver bars. But with the armistice each one of us had been handed his life back on a platter. We knew what dead men looked like and we weren't dead. We had all our arms and legs. Some of us had even escaped G.O. 42.

The horsechestnuts were in bloom. We knew that the world was a lousy pesthouse of idiocy and corruption, but it was spring. We knew that in all the ornate buildings under the crystal chandeliers, under the brocaded hangings the politicians and diplomats were brewing poison, huddled old men festering like tentcaterpillars in a tangle of red tape and gold braid. But we had hope. What they were doing was too obvious and too clear. It was spring. The first of May was coming. We'd burn out the tentcaterpillars.

We believed we knew two things about the world. We subscribed to two dogmas that most of us have since had to modify or scrap. We knew that life in the militarized industrial nations had become a chamber of horrors, and we believed that plain men, the underdogs we rubbed shoulders with, were not such a bad lot as they might be. They wouldn't go out of their way to harm each other as often as you might expect. They had a passive courage the topdogs had never heard about and certain ingrained impulses towards social cohesiveness, towards the common good. Loafing around in little old bars full of the teasing fragrances of history, dodging into alleys to keep out of sight of the M.P.s, seeing the dawn from Montmartre, talking bad French with taxidrivers, riverbank loafers, workmen, petites femmes, keepers of bistros, poilus on leave, we young hopefuls eagerly collected intimations of the urge towards the common good.

It seemed so simple to burn out the tentcaterpillars that were ruining the orchard. The first of May was coming.

We felt boisterous and illmannered. Too many sergeants had told us to wipe that smile off your face, too many buglers had gotten us out of our blankets before we'd slept our sleep out. The only thing of value that had survived the war was this automatic social cohesiveness among men that seemed to come on whenever they slipped for a moment out from under the thumbs of their political bosses. If the old edifice crashed, the bosses who lived in all the upper stories would go with it. They had already pretty well shaken the foundations with their pretty war, their brilliant famines. Their diligent allies, typhus, cholera, influenza were working for them still. Now their peace could finish the job. All together boys. A couple of heaves and down she'll go. When the dust clears we'll see whether men and women are the besotted brutes the bosses say they are.

Finding Grosz's drawing was finding a brilliant new weapon. He knew how the old men, the fat men, looked. He knew their greeds and their murderous lusts. He drew them as they gruesomely were. Looking at his work was a release from hatred, like hearing a wellimagined and properly balanced string of cusswords.

May first came and went. And another. And another. Outside of Russia the edifice trembled but it still stood. Inside Russia a new autocracy took the place of the old. In the great halls generals and dignitaries clustered in front of the camera to pin medals on each other, seemingly unconscious of the rotten smell of corpses from the cellar.

At home we cynically embarked on Normalcy. The automotive boom began. Bitter laughter followed the breakup of the schoolbook illusions. America would fill the world with jazz and Ford cars and electric iceboxes. Americans poured into Europe to buy up artobjects cheap in the devaluated currencies. Americans still felt whole enough to make wisecracks about the bloody farce. We felt we had good comfortable seats for the last act of the European tragedy.

Those who didn't have any seats at all, who were actors in fact, felt differently. George Grosz's drawings will show the future how Europeans felt while their culture was dying of gas gangrene, just as Goya's drawings show us the agony of Europe a century before during Napoleon's wars. Their impression is not verbal (you don't look at the picture and have it suggest a title and then have the title give you the feeling) but through the eye direct, by the invention of fresh ways of seeing.

The impact of the disasters of the first war was naturally much sharper on Europeans who came of age during the war years than on Americans, and the sharpest of all on Germans. The generation of Germans who had begun their schooling in the nineties and were in their twenties when war broke out found themselves under a pressure almost unequalled in European history. They grew up in a respectable, easygoing, beerdrinking, sausageeating, natureloving world where everybody went to hear the band play in the tiergarden Sunday and was delighted to shine the shoes of his superiors, and if he didn't like it he could go to America. They had hardly begun respectfully and agreeably to occupy the situations to which God and the Kaiser had called them when they were goosestepping to the railroad station and in another fortyeight hours were being slashed to pieces by the French seventyfives.

George Grosz was born in Berlin in '93 and spent most of his boyhood at Stolp in Pomerania. His parents were Prussian Lutherans. His father failed as a restaurant keeper, and when things got bad for the family, his mother cooked for an officers' club. His life developed at the exact point of greatest strain in the European social structure, in the more impoverished section of the middle class. His drawing must have shown promise in school because he was sent to Dresden to learn academic pencil work and charcoal from casts of the antique. He started making his living by drawing for comic papers. He studied in Berlin. The summer of 1913 he spent in Paris.

Grosz had too much Prussian and too much Lutheran in his bones to feel at home in Paris, but he must have been stirred by the fact that the full tide of European painting was running through the less prosperous studios of Montmartre and Montparnasse.

Bohème was attaining real eminence under Guillaume Appolinaire, its last king. Out of student traditions of the cult of oddity, the romantic libertarianism of "les bourgeois à la lanterne," scraps of science and anthropology, and the pressures on sensitive young men, and the releases which resulted from a social system tottering to collapse, the whole modern point of view towards painting was coming into being. In spite of the romantic bohemian tradition of spontaneous artistic flareup (the sideshow charlatan tradition, in my opinion), painting suddenly became a matter of experiments and theories pursued with almost scientific rigor. Through all the fads and isms of the painters and writers of that time there was a core of real effort to cope with reality.

Grosz seems never to have espoused any of these causes but his work shows the influence of all of them, particularly of Italian futurism and of cubism. He used what elements he needed out of all the various styles of seeing that flourished and disappeared. His interests lay not in the studio or in the metaphysics of color and form, but in everyday life as he saw it, men and women sleeping, dressing, eating, going to work, drinking, making love. He followed them into their dreams. He spied out their wants, the grimace of desire. He was a satirist and a moralist.

Like Swift in another age, and working in another medium, Grosz was full of the horror of life. A satirist is a man whose flesh creeps so at the ugly and the savage and the incongruous aspects of society that he has to express them as brutally and nakedly as possible to get relief. He seeks to put his grisly obsession into expressive form the way a bacteriologist seeks to isolate a virus. Until that has been done no steps can be taken to cure the disease. Looking at Grosz's drawings you are more likely to feel a grin of pain than to burst out laughing. Instead of letting you be the superior bystander laughing in an Olympian way at somebody absurd, Grosz makes you identify yourself with the sordid and pitiful object. His satire hurts.

In a different environment Grosz might have been a Holbein or a Breughel. In fact in the comparative calm of his maturity in America, he did find relief from the satirist's nightmare in oils full of a quiet pleasure in the colors and shapes of things. But during the formative period of his life he was involved as actor and spectator in too many tragedies to take pleasure in anything. Like any firstrate pencilman he had to put down what he saw.

Certain hopes had survived the relapse into savagery of the European order. Out of the comradeship of the trenches had come a belief in some ultimate social cohesiveness more powerful than all the propagandas of hate. When Woodrow Wilson's dream of peace through a League of Nations proved a cheating illusion, masses of men who had lived through the war but who came out of it maimed in body and soul, turned to Marx in angry frustration. Jobless veterans, peasants, factoryhands, doctors, engineers, students training for the professions, came to feel that the only hope for civilization lay in a complete social overturn. This feeling furnished the emotional basis for Bolshevism in western Europe.

With the thwarting of these hopes, as much by the rise of a new military autocracy in the Soviet Union as by the failure of the Spartacist uprising in Germany, Europe turned back on itself in despair. Germany particularly fell prey to the delusions and manias of the psychopathic ward. Hitler was the revenge of the old Adam. The second war proved more hideous than anything the mind of man had conceived. As a limner of horrors Grosz felt himself the voice of outraged humanity.

As the passions and pains of those days subside, Grosz remains, like Goya, a great shatterer of complacency. Complacency is a fatty growth that stultifies intelligence. The satirist in words or visual images is like the surgeon who comes with his sharp and sterile instrument to lance some focus of dead matter. Without continually sharpening intelligence it is impossible to cope successfully with the intricacies of the changing world, or with the potential madhouse every man carries within him. Few complacencies can survive the bitter intensity of Grosz's pencilled line. When complacency fades intelligence finds room to grow.

The Use of the Past

Every generation rewrites the past. In easy times history is more or less of an ornamental art, but in times of danger we are driven to the written record by a pressing need to find answers to the riddles of today. We need to know what kind of firm ground other men, belonging to generations before us, have found to stand on. In spite of changing conditions of life they were not very different from ourselves; their thoughts were the grandfathers of our thoughts, they managed to meet situations as difficult as those we have to face, to meet them sometimes lightheartedly, and in some measure to make their hopes prevail. We need to know how they did it.

In times of change and danger when there is a quicksand of fear under men's reasoning, a sense of continuity with generations gone before can stretch like a lifeline across the scary present and get us past the idiot delusion of the exceptional. Now that blocks good thinking. That is why, in times like ours, when old institutions are caving in and being replaced by new institutions not necessarily in accord with men's hopes,

From *The Ground We Stand On,* by Dos Passos (New York: Harcourt, Brace & World, Inc., 1941).

political thought has to look backwards as well as forwards.

In spite of the ritual invocation of the names of the Founding Fathers round election time, Americans as a people notably lack a sense of history. We have taken the accomplishments in statebuilding of the seventeenth century colonists and of the thirteen states for granted as we took the rich forest loam and the coal and the iron and the oil and the buffalo.

We wasted and exploited our political heritage with the same childish lack of foresight that wrecked our forests and eroded our farmlands and ruined the grazing on the great plains. We have replanted the forests, we have fertilized the farms, we have established windbreaks on the plains; but we never have faced the problem of adapting our political system to the modern world.

Now that we are caught up short at the edge of the precipice, face to face with the crowded servitude from which our fathers fled, the question is how much is left; how much of their past achievement is still part of our lives? It is not a question of what we want; it is a question of what is. Our history, the successes and failures of the men who went before us, is only alive in so far as some seeds and shoots of it still stir and grow in us today.

The Americans of our time who have put their minds to work in this direction have come late, on the whole, to understanding the actuality of the American past. They had to get a lot of callow debunking off their chests first. Right from the beginning the line of American thinking has been twisted off the straight course by periods of backsliding into a provincial tone towards Europe.

The young men of my generation were set from childhood against looking with fresh eyes into our history by the lackluster apologetic tone of the voices that taught it in school. Romantic schoolteachers insinuated that proper history was something that had happened to lords and ladies and knights in armor in a cultivated never never land across the sea. In the colleges, instructors full of the unconscious yearning of the underpaid for an upperclass viewpoint told of the vulgarity and corruption of the American system and couldn't wait to unveil the fashionable beauties of the British Constitution. In the towns and cities they knew young men found the phraseology of our political heritage dribbling greasily from the mouths of wardheelers spellbinding the greenhorns, or else polished smooth and meaningless in the afterdinner speeches of the respectable starchedshirt candidates for office. Election time and the Fourth of July they saw the old bunting brought out and tacked on the political booths which the politicians operated with the cynical geniality of gamblers getting their shellgames and three-card tricks ready for the yokels at a country fair. It was inevitable that the first impulse of any fresh young intelligence was to throw the whole business overboard lock, stock and barrel.

In a rebellious frame of mind the young men of my youth listened to Woodrow Wilson. They had hardly time to get a deep sniff of the New Freedom before the first great disillusion came. From the business of reforming America they were distracted by the dream of making the world safe for democracy. In the face of the electoral mandate to stay out, they found the country at war and themselves conscripted into the army. Wilson's failure to pull anything worth while for America or for the world out of the peace finished the business.

To the minds of bitter young men, and we mustn't forget that we were right to be bitter, the American republic was just another piece of stage scenery, so crudely painted as to

deceive only the rankest suckers, that masked a slaughter-
house of industrial exploitation. We had seen the physical
power of lies to kill and destroy. To men who still had the
smell of blood and rotting flesh in their nostrils any chance
seemed worth taking that might lead to a better world.

It was against this stale murk of massacre and plague and
famine that, just as the early Christians had under somewhat
similar circumstances painted in the mind's eye a shining City
of God above the clouds, the social revolutionists projected
their magic lantern slides of a future of peaceful just brotherhood, if only the bosses of the present could be overthrown.
While the bulk of the American population settled back to
the wisecracks and the bootlegging and the cheerful moral
disintegration of Normalcy and the New Era, disillusioned
young men whose careers lay outside of the world of buying
cheap and selling dear, swallowed the millennial gospel of
Marx in one great gulp.

Marx was a mighty historical critic of the society he knew
and his voice had the ethical assurance of the old Bible prophets, but the trouble with Marxism as a religion was that its
principles had to be carried out on earth. Once the Russian
experiment got under way it was perfectly possible to go see
for yourself how it was working out in terms of misery or
happiness. The history of the political notions of American
intellectuals during the twentieth century is largely a record
of how far the fervor of their hopes of a better world could
blind them to the realities under their noses. Conversion was
followed sooner or later by disillusion; the process was useful in so far as it turned disinterested people to the study of
our own frame of society in pursuit of the deadly pressing
question: how to make the industrial setup fit for a man to
live in.

Meanwhile, in the years between the two wars, the gulf between Europe and America, that had once seemed so narrow and bridgeable, widened and widened. In Europe the police state the Bolsheviks had called into being under the delusion that they could use it to force men into the mould of a good society, ran its normal course towards tyranny, bloodshed and despair. In Italy and Germany the Fascist and Nazi regimes, after dumping the humanitarian baggage overboard, took over and improved the efficient machinery for driving the mass which the Bolsheviks had invented in their one party system. The businessmen and politicans of the oligarchic and even of the approximately selfgoverning states of Europe proved helpless to hold their divided nations together in the face of an incomparable industrial machine so skillfully rigged for the purpose of destruction.

In contrast to the agony of Europe, it became apparent during those years that our poor old provincial American order, whatever it was, was standing up fairly well. Maybe the republic was something more than a painted dropcurtain hiding the babyeating Moloch of monopoly capital. Maybe there was something more than campaign oratory and pokerplaying and pork and dummy bankaccounts behind those Greco-Roman colonnades.

While we can't get away from the fact that most everybody in the world believes in his heart that life is more worth living for the average man in North America than anywhere else, we still don't feel secure. Indeed we lack that minimum of security necessary to keep a human institution a going concern. Too many Americans have let in among their basic and secret beliefs the sour postulate that American democracy is rotten. In spite of the ritual phrases and the campaign slogans out of our national folklore, like the frogs in Aesop's fable, many of us are croaking that we are sick of King Log and that we want to be ruled by King Stork. "When fascism comes to America," said Huey Long, one of the smartest aspirants for the position of King Stork that ever stuck his head out of our frogpond, "it will come as antifascism." It won't matter what name we call King Stork by; if we let him in he'll eat us up just the same. Under the verbal pieties of democratic phraseology the state of mind of a good deal of the country is summed up by a man I heard cap a long irate political argument by shouting: "This man Roosevelt's got too much power: what we need's a dictator."

How are these doubts to be answered? I myself believe that we are going to stick to our old King Log, that our peculiar institutions have a future, and that this country is getting to be a better place for men to live in instead of a worse; but unfortunately just putting the statement down on paper does not make it true. How are we going to answer the angry young men of today? How are we going to reassure the great mob of secret subjects of King Stork? Are we sure that King Log isn't as rotten as they say?

The answer is not in speeches or in popular songs, but in the nature of our political habits.

One reason why the Communist cure in Russia has proved worse than the disease is that the only political habits the Bolsheviks had to work with were those of serfdom and subjection to a despot. In Germany the Weimar Republic failed for much the same reason. German history had been politically the opposite of English history: it had been the history of the successive subjugation of the more western and selfgoverning aspects of Germany by the despotism of the Prussian drillmaster. None of the Russian or German Marxists had any idea of politics as an art. The Englishspeaking peoples are heirs of the largest heritage of the habits and traditions and skills of selfgovernment there has ever been in the world. Politics is our whole history. If we fail to cope with the problem of adjusting the industrial machine to human needs it won't be for lack of the political tradition.

By politics I mean simply the art of inducing people to behave in groups with a minimum of force and bloodshed. That was the purpose of the tribal traditions on which our common law is based: the patching up of private and public rows without violence by the opinion of a jury or the counting of heads at a meeting.

Under the stresses of the years between the wars we saw nation after nation sink to its lowest common denominator. Naturally it was easy for us to see the mote in our brother's eye. The question we still have to face is: What is the content of *our* lowest common denominator?

If, in the bedrock habits of Americans, the selfgoverning tradition is dead or has been too much diluted by the demands of the industrial setup or the diverse habits of the stream of newcomers from Europe during the last century, no amount of speechifying of politicians or of breastbeating by men of letters will bring it back to life. We so easily take the word for the thing anyway, that even if what we consider our way of life were gone, we wouldn't quite know it. It's part of the way the human mind works that the verbal trappings of institutions linger on long after the institutions they referred to have faded away. We can study the past but about the present there are times when we can only state our hope and our faith.

What we can do is give that cantilever bridge into the

future that we call hope a firm foundation in what has been. We can, without adding to the cloudy masses of unattached verbiage that make any present moment in political life so difficult to see clear in, at least point out that, so far in our history, habits of selfgovernment and the use of the art of politics towards increasing rather than decreasing the stature of each individual man, have survived.

Often it's been nip and tuck. Our history has been a contest between the selfgoverning habits of the mass and various special groups that have sought to dominate it for their own purposes. So long as that contest continues the nation will remain a growing organism.

On the whole the struggle has been carried on thus far without destroying the fabric of society. In any cross section of our history you can find the political instinct running a binding thread through the welter of interests, inertias, impulses, greeds, fears and heroisms that make up any event. Without overconfidence we can say that our people and the people of England, in their long career, first embracing and later supplementing and paralleling our own, have used the art of politics with more skill and have upheld the dignity of the citizen as a man better than the peoples of continental Europe, who at frequent intervals have gotten sick of King Log and called in King Stork and have been properly eaten up by him for their pains.

When we wake up in the night cold and sweating with nightmare fear for the future of our country we can settle back with the reassuring thought that the Englishspeaking peoples have these habits engrained in them. The reason so many angry young men were all for calling in King Stork in the form of the socalled dictatorship of the working class (we know now whose dictatorship it really is) was that they confused selfgovernment as a political method with a particular phase of the economic setup of production. It is fairly easy to demonstrate that uncontrolled government of monopolized industry and monopolized labor by irresponsible men is headed for ruin, and that that ruin might carry a good deal of the social fabric down with it; but it doesn't follow that the self-governing republic, as a method of enabling people to live together in groups without conking each other on the head every minute, would necessarily go by the board too.

If all the monopolies folded up overnight, or if their bosses converged on Washington and seized the government, as they've occasionally been on the edge of doing in one way or another, the next morning we would still face the problem of politics. Would the men who held power want to induce the others to behave in groups with a minimum rather than a maximum expenditure of force? At the minimum end of the scale would still be selfgovernment and the need to argue, cajole, and bribe their fellowcitizens into doing what they wanted them to; at the maximum end would be the sort of military bureaucracy and personal despotism that has so often been the style of government of the world outside of the Anglo-Saxon family of nations.

In the last analysis, to be sure, the continuance of self-government will always depend on how much the people who exercise that liberty will be willing to sacrifice to retain it. A man in power will push his subjects around just as much as they'll let him. But even in a riot the members of the mob and the members of the police force will behave as they have been brought up to behave.

We must never forget that men don't make up much of

their own behavior; they behave within limits laid down by their heredity, their upbringing and their group background. That is why individual men feel so helpless in the face of social changes. Modifications in the structure of any organization of men can't ever really take effect till the next generation. A revolution can keep people from behaving in the old way but it can't make them behave effectively in the new way. That is why a political system elastic enough to allow drastic changes inside of its fabric is one of the greatest boons any people can possess. Our occasionally selfgoverning republic has proved itself capable of bending without breaking under the terrific strains of the last years. The question is whether there is enough will to freedom in the country to make it keep on working. Social machinery, no matter how traditional, left to itself runs down; men have to work it.

Our history is full of answers to the question: How shall we make selfgovernment work? People like ourselves have been making it work with more or less success for centuries. And history is only dead when people think of the present in terms of the past instead of the other way round. The minute we get the idea that the records can be of use to us now, they become alive. They become the basis of a worldpicture into which we can fit our present lives, however painful they may be, and our hopes for the future. We have never been told enough about the worldpicture which the founders of the American republic held up to the men who followed them.

We need to look into that worldpicture to see how it has changed with the years and whether enough of its brilliance is left to outshine the hopes which in the second war led millions to conquest and destruction in Europe and which, in its aftermath, are subjecting the peoples of a rash of new nations to the exploitation and tyranny of their upstart leaders.

In our past we have whatever hope it was that kept Washington's army together the winter at Valley Forge, but today have we anything left of that worldpicture of 1776? The Communists used to tell us we had only the Almighty Dollar and the degradation and sluggishness that came from too much property on top and too much poverty below. Now they specialize in racial tensions. To answer them we don't need to fill ourselves up with the hope of another historical illusion like theirs, but we do need to know which realities of our life yesterday and our life today we can believe in and work for. We must never forget that we are heirs to one of the grandest and most nearly realized worldpictures in all history.

If we can counter the illusions of the Communist world with practical schemes for applying the selfgoverning habit more fully to our disorganized social structure, to the factories, labor unions, employers' associations, chains of stores, armies that are imposed upon us by today's methods of production and destruction, then the croaking doubts will be quiet. Even if it means reversing the trend of our whole society in order to make it continually more selfgoverning instead of less so, the trend will have to be reversed. The alternative is destruction.

If, then, what we aim to do is to work towards increasing the happiness and dignity of every man, just because he is a man, that is what the founders of this country wanted too; in their lives and writings is a great storehouse of practical information on how to go about it. Our machinery has changed, but the men who run it have changed very little. That the republicans of the seventeenth and eighteenth centuries succeeded in starting something mighty in the world I don't think even the most despairing black advocate of tyranny can deny. If the first builders succeeded against great odds, why should we who have their foundations to build on, necessarily fail?

It's worth trying to imagine, to take an example, how the problem the little group of Virginians round Jefferson and young Madison had to face at the beginning of the Revolutionary War must have seemed to them, to imagine it without any of the assurance of hindsight.

They had first of all to carry on against the most powerful nation on earth. To do that they had to induce the scattered farmers and plantation owners and country gentlemen of English origin, and the wild Irish and Scotch pioneers of the region beyond the Blue Ridge to work together and to risk their lives and property in the enterprise of independence, to forget their religious bigotries with the disestablishment of the Anglican church, to drop their local prejudices and interests for the sake of cooperating with the states to the north and south, and at the same time to concur in a radical rationalization of legal and governmental procedure: all that sounds easy when you read it in a history book, but imagine how hard it must have seemed to the men of the time, continually hampered as they were by the difficulty of communication and of transporting themselves and their goods across a country that had only muddy tracks for roads.

In spite of the immense increase in the complexity of organization, our problem is not so very different now: again in order to survive in a warring and hostile world we have to induce the weak and the powerful of all sections of our population to drop prejudices and bigotries and to pool their efforts in the common cause. Our problem is more difficult than the problem of the men of 1776. In order to tackle it we must have what those men had, besides the selfgoverning habit: the will.

But will and energy cannot be directed without an aim. The aim that moved them was the attainment of a world that could be pictured fairly sharply in the mind's eye. Of all the great mass of material that has come down to us from that day, the letters and notes Jefferson wrote and particularly the buildings he designed, which we can still see and walk around in, are of paramount interest because he had this world-picture so clearly in his mind that the imprint of it was sharp on everything he did. It was as if his clear musing mind had reduced the main conformations of the thought of his time to a design as plain as a seal on a ring.

When Jefferson as a young man used to scramble up the steep trail among the oaks that took him up in half an hour to the top of the hill he was later to name affectionately "Monticello," what kind of a world was it that he saw, looking thoughtfully at the densepacked trees of the valley of the Rivanna and the little raw village of Charlottesville and the long ranges of the Blue Ridge beyond?

What he saw depended on what he was. He was a frontiersman, first, and always felt the great continent, stretching ridge after ridge to the west, opening out into the grasslands, rivers, plains, a boundless store for the generations growing up, the promise of a future that like a great convex mirror magnified every act and gesture of the men working their fields and building their farms in the tiny settlements along the eastern seaboard. Then he was a Virginian who shared the traditions of the highflown gentry that came to him through his mother's family, and, through his father's, of the pushing country stock forced westward by the hardening stratification of Tidewater society. He had had the best eighteenth century education, through his good luck in finding in Williamsburg, when he went to study law there as a boy, a small group of brilliant men, from whom he had eagerly absorbed the vanguard intellectual outlooks of Europe. His philosophic and religious bent was impressed on him by early and thorough training in the Greek and Roman classics; it was the stoicism of Cicero and Seneca, strained through the *noblesse oblige* imperative that the English gentry had inherited from the chivalry of the feudal landlords, combined in the best Englishmen of the century with an intensely practical flair for experimental knowledge, the heritage of Newton and the Royal Society. Although he never went abroad until middle life he somehow managed to absorb even the literary fads and accomplishments that were the trimming on the sound broadcloth of the age, the taste for Ossian, the Gothic sensibility to landscape, the fondness for Italian music. Somewhat unique, because those were the directions in which his mind pushed out towards original discoveries, was his sense of the common law as a code of human rights rather than as a code for the protection of privilege, and his intense and inventive interest in architecture. Already as a young man he was planning with the help of a volume of Palladio to build on that very hill above Charlottesville a homestead that would make manifest in brick and stucco his own adaptation to the Virginia frontier of an antique Roman sense of the dignity of free men.

A set of ideas, a point of view, a frame of reference is in space only an intersection, the state of affairs at some given moment in the consciousness of one man or many men, but in time it has evolving form, virtually organic extension. In time ideas can be thought of as sprouting, growing, maturing, bringing forth seed and dying like plants. To make sense of the tangled jungle of men's thoughts and impulses that makes up the history of a culture we have continually to invent sequences which we can follow like footpaths through the thickets of what was.

Into the antecedents of the American republic, I think it is useful, at the moment, to trace two main trails. One is the trail I have been speaking of that leads back through the Low Church and the traditions of the plantation families of Virginia to the country gentleman republicanism of the seventeenth century in England. The other leads back to the roundhead townspeople and the Protestant sects. While the gentlefolk and parvenu planters and the country lawyers of Virginia were quite unconsciously laying the foundations of Monticello and of *The Federalist,* the New England towns, each one a little City of God, were developing townmeeting, building public schools and town homes and libraries and volunteer fire departments and perfecting that intense municipal organization that made it possible for the Englishspeaking settlements out in the great riversystem of the Mississippi and in the West to stick fast where the French and Spaniards who preceded them lasted no longer than the buffalohide villages of the wandering Indians.

In the seventeenth century Commonwealth of England the two currents had merged and fused, but after its collapse the English social system had become stratified and set under the pressure of reaction, and the setup we think of as characteristically English in distinction to American, had come into being. But in New England, on a small provincial scale, the English republic went on. The political and religious life of Boston, Plymouth, Hartford, New Haven, Providence, Newport had much more in common with the life of the British Isles under Elizabeth and James and Cromwell than it had with the various transformations of the developing maritime empire. During the High Church reaction and the counter-reaction that brought in the house of Orange and saw the beginnings of the Old Lady of Threadneedle Street and of the plundering of India, the settlements of Englishspeaking peoples on the east and west coasts of the Atlantic were already drawing apart. In England social stratifications were setting hard: in America they continually tended to break up.

In distinction to the absolute liberty of the Virginia planter, who had only to pay his tithes in tobacco to the local clergyman to be undisputed king of his acres and his bondservants and his slaves, the New England townsman was walled up in the exact limits of a theocracy. But the New England towns stayed alive and kept breaking out of the narrow shells their clergy kept tracing for them; first, because there were vast open lands to the west to which energetic men who couldn't stand the tyranny of the local pulpit could move with some certainty of bettering their condition; and, second, because Protestant theocracy rested on the conscience of every man alone, instead of being vested in an organized priesthood.

Continually the divines tried to organize themselves into a ruling caste, but they never entirely succeeded on account of the fundamentally libertarian bias of Protestant Christianity. Almost from the first moment of the first Puritan settlement the conflict between the clergy and the consciences of their church-members began. As the towns developed it became complicated by the long struggle between the proprietors of the lands and the voting inhabitants of the towns which foreshadowed the later social history of the United States as the federal arrangements of the New Englanders foreshadowed the form of political organization for the nation.

Of all the men who stood boldly up to the denunciations

of the pulpit, and so helped keep the towns alive, and made possible their growth into the singularly beautiful and successful social units they became, Roger Williams stood tallest. He best exemplified the fruitful side of English Protestantism, the side from which grew the Quakers and all the rational and irrational sects and humanitarian movements that we think of as peculiarly American. As Jefferson was the second, Roger Williams was the first great leader of the tendency in American life that has striven to keep the roads open instead of to close them, that has fought for selfgovernment instead of for government by a privileged group, and that has defended liberty against the oligarchy of the various privileged groups who have at one time or another tried to impose themselves upon the country. Without his influence and the success of his rash enterprise at Providence Plantations, other men in New England would hardly have had the courage to call their souls their own in the face of the convinced autocrats of the pulpit and the bench. The New England towns, instead of being the seedbed of the nation, would have shriveled into grim little lamaseries in the granite inlets of their chilly coast.

Like Jefferson's, Roger Williams' mind was the ancestor of the mind we, for want of a better word, used to call "liberal" in America, when we still used the word in its nineteenth century sense. With the world drift back into an epoch of wars and savage persecutions, we suddenly find ourselves very near the seventeenth century. Fifty years ago we could hardly have understood the fervors or the ideological jargon of the Cavaliers and Roundheads. Our time has in common with theirs the manly revolt that was once behind the labor movement, the fanaticism of the Marxist and nationalist cults and the sullen hatreds that have become the stock in trade of political upstarts the world over. Accustomed to the doubletalk of

Marxist ideology, it is easy for us to translate into our own terms the religious jargon of the Roundheads. We too have seen men and women dying for righteousness' sake. As they did, we live in a time of danger when life is cheap. Then as now a man who writes has to weigh his words. They had to train themselves not to be afraid of the scaffold and the brandingiron; even in America with the great oceans between us and the worst of it, we can feel across our windows as we write a shadow of barbed wire.

The men of those times lived through and brought through with them the bundle of notions that is the culture of the western world; what has been done once can be done again.

If ever a man crossed the ocean bringing the seeds of a whole civilization in his head, like the culture heroes of the old legends, it was that preacher, explorer, trader, negotiator, linguist, Roger Williams. Just as it's hard to imagine the Democratic-Republican party overthrowing the special interests of the Federalists, without Jefferson's leadership and the variety and dignity of his life, so it is impossible to see how toleration of religion and thought, or indeed selfgovernment at all, could have taken root on this continent without the firey preaching and canny negotiating and the goodnatured hardihood of Roger Williams, the great Seeker.

The side they fought and worked and lived for hasn't won by a long shot. Perhaps it never can win. Liberty is something men don't understand till they lose it. Yet it has been this struggle between men who have managed in one way or another to get hold of the levers of power and the people in general with their vague and changing aspirations for equality, for justice, for some kind of gentler brotherhood and peace;

which has kept that balance of forces we call our system of government in equilibrium. Sometimes one scale is up and sometimes another. Sometimes the conflict is acute and at other times barely visible under the prosperous surface of eras of good feeling. In these days of the greatest diffusion of material prosperity the human race has ever known, the struggle is muffled and confused by the unfamiliar terrain of everchanging systems of production. But when we rack our brains for understanding, it does us good, I think, to remind ourselves that in spite of hell and high water, Americans in the past have managed to live for and to establish some few liberties.

A Question of Elbow Room

Individuality is freedom lived. When we speak of individuality we refer, of course, to a whole gamut of meanings. Starting from the meanings which pertain to the deepest recesses of private consciousness, these different meanings can be counted off one by one like the skins in the cross section of an onion, until we reach the everyday outer hide of meaning which crops up in common talk.

When we speak commonly, without exaggerated precision, of an individual, don't we perhaps mean a person who has grown up in an environment sufficiently free from outside pressures and restraints to develop his own private evaluations of men and events? He has been able to make himself enough elbow room in society to exhibit unashamed the little eccentricities and oddities that differentiate one man from another man. From within his separate hide he can look out at the world with that certain aloofness which we call dignity. No two men are alike any more than two snowflakes are alike. However a man develops, under conditions of freedom or conditions of servitude, he will still differ from other men.

From *Essays in Individuality,* edited by Felix Morley (Philadelphia: University of Pennsylvania Press, 1958).

The man in jail will be different from his cellmates but his differences will tend to develop in frustration and hatred. Freedom to develop individuality is inseparable from the attainment of what all the traditions of the race have taught us to consider to be the true human stature.

Fifty years ago all this would have been the rankest platitude, but we live in an epoch where the official directors of opinion through the schools and the pulpits and the presses have leaned so far over backwards in their efforts to conform to what they fancied were the exigencies of a society based on massproduction in industry that the defense of individuality has become a life and death matter.

It is a defense that a man takes on at his peril. The very word has become suspect. Even to mention individualism or individuality in circles dedicated to the fashionable ideas of the moment is to expose oneself to ridicule. "Listening to papers on individualism—how boring!" exclaimed the wife of a scholarly scientist to whom I tried to explain over the phone what I was doing in Princeton in September, 1956, at the symposium where this paper was first read.

Casting around for some examples which would bring home the essential characteristics of individuality, without seeming too boring, even to heads full of the fashionable negations of the moment, I found myself falling back on the storehouse of English literature which awaits us on the library shelves.

I'm thinking of the magnificent series of imaginative writings in modern English that began with Chaucer five hundred years ago. You can make out a very good case for the notion that there runs through it all a unifying thread which is the measure of its difference from other literatures. The entire literature is dedicated to the description of man not only as an individual but as an eccentric. Naturally it is colored throughout by the peculiar eminence the traditions of English law and of English thought generally gave to individual rights and individual responsibility, but it is flavored, furthermore, by a real enjoyment of idiosyncrasy. Perhaps English literature will continue to be the conduit through which our now so discredited passion for personal liberty will be freshened and stimulated by impulses from past generations. The belief in the uniqueness of each human being is, after all, not of yesterday. To the Athenians this belief was incarnate on earth. Primitive Christianity turned it inside out and established it in heaven. Our practical English forbears managed to bring it down to earth again.

Their earthy individuality is the heart of our literary inheritance. To root that inheritance out of our minds you'll have to pull the English classics off the shelves of our libraries. The American educational process, with its bias towards conformity on the basis of the lowest common denominator, has not managed to do quite that, at least not yet; but it has succeeded in letting the classical literature moulder in innocuous desuetude in the dust of the unvisited stacks. Scrape the mildew off the backs of the books and you'll find them as ready as ever to fill the imagination with a rich spawn of cantankerous human beings.

Chaucer is the fountain head. Right at the beginning, in the earliest days of the formation of the language, you'll find in the *Canterbury Tales* the characteristics which are to be the special earmark of English literature for the next five hundred years. The minute you step into that Tabard Inn at Southwark in the first few lines of the Prologue you find yourself part of the pilgrimage of all the great characters of English fiction. Right away the poet starts describing people, individuals he enjoys for their own sake. Already he shows the downtoearth knowledge of vulgar reality, the gift for jocose narrative, the appetite for freedom and elbow room, the sharp satire mellowed by fellow feeling for a great many varieties of men which are to characterize the whole literature to come. You feel behind every word and phrase the driving force of Chaucer's enthusiasm for individuality, for idiosyncracy even.

Not only the men but the women are individuals. It is in Chaucer that there first appears a certain special attitude towards women. The women have as much private and personal individuality as the men. Compare them with the women in the French romances of the period. In the Prologue to the *Canterbury Tales* and in the marvelous interludes between, you meet real women, humorously and tenderly and understandingly described, women who stand up in their own right and say their own say in the world. The Prioress and the Wife of Bathe are the first of a long line of large scale portraits of women: the women of Shakespeare's plays from Mistress Quickly and Juliet's nurse to Hamlet's mother and Lady Macbeth; the hapless solitary figure of Vittoria Corombona in the Duchess of Malfi, the pert matrons of Restoration comedy, the aware young ladies walking on the lawns of Jane Austen's country houses, Dickens' female gargoyles out of the London slums, and the inimitable Becky Sharpe.

Chaucer's men are a zestful crew. They have the high spirits of people with elbow room in the world. The foulmouthed innkeeper, the scoundrelly pardoner, the miller and the reeve, the cynical merchant, the wealthy franklin in whose house it snowed of meat and drink, who foreshadowed Squire Western and Mr. Wardle the genial landlord of Dingly Dell, the lawyer who was such a very busy man and yet seemed ever busier than he was, the mild spoken knight and his wellbred son, the squire who left half told the story of Cambuscan bold.

And through it all the feeling of the road. A man is never more his single separate self than when he sets out on a journey. A man is on his own on the road. This excitement of adventuring from place to place will reappear in some of Defoe's narratives and in Tom Jones's burlesque adventures and in the tribulations of Smollett's rascally heroes and in the preposterous travels of the Pickwickians and the contemplative excursions of Thoreau and George Borrow.

From the *Canterbury Tales* on there is a certain amount of understanding to be gained by thinking of the main stream of English literature as a continuation of Chaucer's pilgrimage. With the coming of the English Renaissance there appear, to be sure, the towering figures of leaders of men painted with breathless haste on the huge canvasses of Marlowe and Shakespeare; individuality on a superhuman scale facing the dilemmas, the crimes, the failures, the glories of the untrammeled will.

The comically sketched lowlives are pushed into the shadow. But even in Shakespeare the Chaucerian preoccupation with the laughable idiosyncracies of all sorts of men has kept on developing as a contrasting background to the romantic passions and the bombast of the tragic roles that fill the center of the stage. Though Sir John Falstaff seems to have been invented as a foil for Prince Hal, he soon became, in response to the audience's demands, a protagonist in his own right. The fat knight and his rowdy crew would have found themselves thoroughly at home among the Canterbury pilgrims. As their story evolves through four plays it becomes one of the precursors of the English novel.

While the gaudy romanticism of the age of Elizabeth tears itself to tatters, the Chaucerian sort of comic naturalism subsists in the dramatists who are trying to reproduce the Greek and Latin comedy of manners. With the reopening of the theatres the comedy of idiosyncracy will dominate the stage. With the emergence of prose narrative in Swift's satires and in Defoe's commonsensical tales the depiction of individuals will become the main business of the writer. As the modern novel is born out of Fielding's Gargantuan amusement at Richardson's attempt to turn the art of fictional narrative into an apology for the ideas and prejudices of the rising shopkeeper class, the Chaucerian naturalism and the Chaucerian satire become its very substance.

With *Tom Jones* the novel is established as the chronicle of individuality. By the time Sterne writes his Tristram Shandy the scheme is so thoroughly established that he can treat his reader to endless whimsical variations on it. In the nineteenth century, when novel writing will become the passion of the age, Sterne's whimseys will reappear in more Chaucerian form in Charles Dickens' portraitgallery of comic characters. Somehow the English of the great tradition managed, no matter from what low caste they sprang, to maintain enough elbow room about them to cherish this appreciation of individuality as the central pleasure of their lives.

It is certainly no accident that the political institutions which grew up in the society that produced this literature of individualism should have been individualistic too. When all the discussions of the position of man in the framework of government which had obsessed so many of the best minds of the century came to a focus in 1776, the chief preoccupation of the statebuilders in America was to establish institutions in their new country that would allow each citizen enough elbow room to grow into individuality. They differed greatly on how best to bring about that state of affairs, but there was no disagreement on fundamental aims. Protection of the happiness and health of the individual was the reason for the state's existence.

Thomas Jefferson and Gouverneur Morris held very differing views on the problems of government. Jefferson was an agrarian democrat who believed that every man was capable of taking some part in the government of the community. Morris was a Hudson River aristocrat who believed that only men to whom wealth and position had given the advantage of a special education were capable of dealing with public affairs; but when Morris wrote George Washington his definition of statesmanship, "I mean politics in the great Sense, or that sublime Science which embraces for its Object the Happiness of Mankind," he meant the same thing by the word "happiness" as Jefferson did when he wrote it into the Declaration of Independence. To both men it meant something like elbow room. Elbow room is positive freedom.

Consult any sociologist today as to the meaning of "happiness" in the social context and he'll be pretty sure to tell you it means "adjustment." Adjustment for the individual is the opposite of elbow room.

To Morris and Jefferson the "sublime Science" consisted of building a government which would allow the greatest possible amount of elbow room to its citizens; to the political leaders and theorizers of today the "sublime Science" consists in teaching the citizen to adjust himself to the demands of the state. He is supposed to learn to put up with an everincreasing lack of elbow room.

We are hardly conscious of the immensity of the change which has taken place in the aims of statebuilding because we still use the vocabularly of our individualist tradition in literature and politics. The change has been so gradual through the years that we have failed to notice that the words don't apply any more to the facts they are supposed to describe. This lag in definition makes it extremely difficult to project our traditional notions of individuality, which are still thoroughly cogent in their own context, into the twentieth century society we have to live in. Perhaps the reason why we are so uncomfortable with the very term "individuality" is that its redefinition will bring us up against a set of realities highly unpleasant to face.

It's startling to remember that only a hundred and thirty some years, merely the span of a couple of lifetimes, have gone by since Jefferson died at Monticello on the same Independence Day 1826 when his old friend and political opponent, John Adams, died at Braintree near Boston, whispering, so the old tradition has it: "Thomas Jefferson still survives."

These years have seen such a transformation in the shape of American society that the age of Jefferson and Adams and Washington and Madison and Hamilton and the rest seems as far away as the age of Confucius.

People in late eighteenth century America tended to live out their lives grouped into one of two kinds of social organization. There was the New England type town where social standing depended on a combination of godliness with that possession of this world's goods which was the outward expression of divine favor. The tendency towards social stratification in at least the eastern Massachusetts towns was well expressed by the fact that at Harvard College students were listed according to their social standing instead of according to their scholastic ability. That doesn't mean that literacy wasn't highly regarded. The New Englanders were people of the book. Nor does it mean that they were not politically democratic. Their government was town meeting where every man had his say. The society which produced the Adamses was a democracy tempered by aristocracy.

To the southward there was the plantation society, where men were rated according to the acreage of their lands, which produced George Mason and Jefferson. In the Virginia county governments, as in rural England, the landowners were the law. Both of these systems were subject to the sometimes disturbing influence of the ebb and flow of the continually renewed pioneer enterprises of the new settlements, where the skill and courage and push necessary for survival were the most admired qualities and where universal manhood suffrage was the political rule. The best brains right along, tended to be attracted to the frontier. The educated men, the men of book learning, of all these differing communities were steeped in the spirit of *noblesse oblige* which had been the noble obverse of the greed and selfseeking of the British ruling gentry.

The thing the Americans—townsmen, fishermen, and sailors of the New England seaports; planters and merchants from the Chesapeake; hunters and furtraders from the Ohio—had in common was that they throughly understood the world they lived in. The technology was simple. From the age of the Hebrew prophets to the time of the American Revolution the basic operations by which men sowed crops for food and produced clothing and shelter had changed remarkably little. Since the Renaissance period there had been improvement in tools, but production was still based on the skill of the hand and the arm and the eye. Manufacture meant making by hand.

The family was still almost everywhere the central productive unit, as it was the central social unit. Manufacture, trade, farming and the professions were conducted on a family basis. The work of apprentices, indentured servants, Negro slaves on the plantations in the South, all meshed into the framework of a man and his wife and his sons and daughters coping with life as a group.

Any tolerably bright individual knew from personal experience how wheeled carriages and sailing ships worked, understood the processes of agriculture and manufacturing, the use of money and the technique of buying and selling on the market place. Much more important, they all knew by direct personal experience how the different kinds of people worked who made up their society.

They took human cussedness for granted.

The outstanding fact you learn from reading the letters of the men of that day was that none of them had any illusions about how men behaved in the political scheme. A radical idealist like Jefferson allowed for the selfinterest (real or imagined) of the average voter or the vanity and ambition and greed of the officeholder as much as a cynical conservative like Gouverneur Morris. The difference was that they applied their knowledge according to different theories as to what sort of government would most desirably influence human behavior. Jefferson thought that under proper institutions people could be indefinitely improved. Like his Scottish contemporary Adam Smith, he trusted to the workings of enlightened selfinterest.

Both parties understood the common man as well as any of the more desperate demagogues we have with us today. They allowed for the common man's selfseeking, for his shortsightedness, his timidity, his abominable apathy, his only intermittent public spirit. The difference was that the statesmen of the early republic used that knowledge, "the sublime Science," in the service of their great statebuilding aims. Using men as they found them, they managed to set up the system of balanced selfgovernment which made possible the exuberant growth of the United States.

In Jefferson's day the average citizen had a fair understanding of most of the workings of the society he lived in. The years that stretch between us and the day of his death have seen the shape of industry transformed in rapid succession by steam power, electric power, the internal combustion engine and now by jet propulsion and the incredibly proliferating possibilities of power derived from nuclear fission and fusion. Any social system of necessity moulds itself into shapes laid down by the daily occupations of the individual men who form its component parts. The mass production methods of assembly line industry have caused a society made up of individuals grouped in factories and officebuildings for whom family life has been relegated to the leisure hours. And now, before the population has managed to learn how to live in the present framework, automation threatens to bring new and drastic changes.

Life in our changing industrial world has become so cut up into specialized departments and vocabularies, and has become so hard to understand and to see as a whole that most people won't even try. Even people of first rate intelligence at work in various segregated segments of our economy tend to get so walled up in the particular work they are doing that they never look outside of it. Even if they remember that every man has a duty to give some of his time and some of his energy to the general good, they don't know how to go about it.

Enormously complicated political institutions have grown

up in response to the exigencies of the industrial framework. Instead of the farming communities which Jefferson expected to be the foundation of selfgovernment we have a population concentrated in cities and suburbs. Instead of living under the least possible government, most of the American people are living under an accumulation of often conflicting sovereignties.

A man working for General Motors in Detroit, for an example, is subject to the management of his corporation, and to the often arbitrary government of the United Auto Workers. He is subject to the traffic police on the road on his way to and from work, to the taxes and regulations of the town where he lives, to the taxes and regulations of the state of Michigan and to the authority of the federal government. Each of these sovereignties has the power to make itself extremely disagreeable if he crosses its bureaucratic will. To hold his end up against this panoply of disciplinary powers, the man's only answer is the precarious right to hold up his hand in the meeting of his union local, and the right to put his cross on the ballot in an occasional election, opposite the name of some politician he has only heard of in the confusion of electoral ballyhoo.

Is it surprising that the common man is hard to coax out of the shell of political apathy he has grown to protect himself from the knowledge of his own helplessnesss? The first step towards restoring to this man a sense of citizenship would be to explain his situation to him in terms which had reference to the observable facts of his daily life. A fresh political vocabulary is needed before we can try to reset the individual cogs so that they mesh into the wheels of government.

None of this means that Thomas Jefferson or John Adams' aspirations to build a state which would afford the greatest possible amount of elbow room to the greatest number of its citizens are obsolete. Their "sublime Science" was based on an understanding of factors in human behavior which haven't changed since the beginnings of recorded history. Newton's basic principle of gravitation has not been superseded. It has been amended and amplified by Einstein's formulae. Newton's still remains one of the explanations through which mathematicians cope with the observable facts of physics. In a somewhat similar way, if men could be found to apply to political problems the sort of first rate rigorous thinking which we have seen applied to physics in our lifetime, new statebuilders would discover that the great formulations of the generation of 1776 were as valid as ever.

It is always well to remember that the commonest practice of mankind is that a few shall impose authority and the majority shall submit to it. Watch any bunch of children playing during a school recess. It is the habit of individual liberty which is the exception. The liberties we enjoy today, freedom to express our ideas if we have any, freedom to jump in a car and drive any place we want to on the highway, freedom to choose the trade or profession we want to make our living by, are the survivors of the many liberties won by the struggles and pains of generations of English speaking people who somehow had resistance to authority in their blood. Their passion for individuality instead of conformity was unique in the world. What the generation of 1776 did was to organize those traditions into a new system.

When the British troops marched out of Yorktown to surrender to Washington's army one of their bands played a tune called "The World Turned Upside Down." In the long run the United States have managed to make the promise of that tune come true. Underdog has come mighty near to becoming topdog. The underside of that medal is that the cult of the lowest common denominator has caused brains, originality of mind, quality of thought to be dangerously disparaged. Conformity has been more prized than individuality.

All the same we can write in the credit column of the ledger that there has never been a society where so many men and women have shared a fellow feeling for so many other men and women. With every change in economic organization new class lines and stratifications have appeared, but they have hardly outlasted a generation or two. The old saying about three generations from shirtsleeves to shirtsleeves has turned out profoundly true. Compared to the rest of mankind, we have come nearest to producing a classless society. Ask any recent immigrant. Nine times out of ten he will tell you that what struck him first in the United States was that feeling of the world being turned upside down. The question today is whether for all its wide distribution of material goods, this classless society offers the individual enough elbow room to make his life worth living.

Right from the beginning the wise men have said that democracy would end in the destruction of liberty. Washington in his last years, and John Adams and the whole Federalist faction thought universal suffrage would end in demagogery and despotism. Their reasoning was the basis of the lamentations of the school of Brooks Adams and Henry Adams at the beginning of this century. Hamilton's "your people is a great beast" was echoed by Chief Justice Holmes in his explosion to Carl Becker, "Goddamn them all, I say." Since the earliest days only a small minority have at any time really believed in the privacy of their own consciences that American democracy would work. This conviction among the learned and the wellborn was admirably expressed in a letter Macaulay wrote to H. N. Randall when Randall was putting the finishing touches on his biography of Jefferson in the eighteen-fifties.

"You are surprised to learn," Macaulay wrote Randall, "I have not a high opinion of Mr. Jefferson and I am surprised at your surprise. I am certain that I never wrote a line and that I never, in parliament, in conversation or even on the hustings,—a place where it is the fashion to court the populace,—uttered a word advocating the opinion that the supreme authority in a state ought to be entrusted to the majority of citizens told by the head; in other words, to the poorest and most ignorant part of society. I have long been convinced that institutions purely democratic must, sooner or later, destroy liberty or civilization or both.

"You think that your country enjoys an exemption from these evils. I will frankly own to you that I am of a very different opinion. Your fate I believe to be certain, though it is deferred by a physical cause. As long as you have a boundless extent of fertile and unoccupied land, your laboring population will be far more at ease than the laboring population of the old world; and while that is the case the Jeffersonian policy may continue to exist without causing any fatal calamity." (Macaulay is launching the theory of the last frontier which is now popular among certain historians.) "But the time will come," Macaulay went on, "when New England will be as thickly populated as Old England. Wages will be as low and will fluctuate as much with you as with us. You will have your Manchesters and Birminghams. Hundreds and thousands of artisans will be sometimes out of work. Then your institutions will be fairly brought to the test. Distress everywhere makes the laborer mutinous and discontented and inclines him to listen with eagerness to agitators who tell him that it is a monstrous iniquity that one man should have millions, while another cannot get a full meal. In bad years there is plenty of grumbling here and sometimes a little rioting. But it matters little for here the sufferers are not the rulers. The supreme power is in a class, numerous indeed but select, in an educated class, in a class which is and knows itself to be deeply interested in, the security of property, and the maintenance of order." (This is the type of government Gouverneur Morris and Alexander Hamilton wanted.) "Accordingly, the malcontents are firmly yet gently restrained. The bad time is got over without robbing the wealthy to relieve the indigent. The springs of national prosperity soon begin to flow again; work is plentiful, wages rise and all is tranquility and cheerfulness.

"I have seen England three or four times pass through such critical seasons as I have described. Through such seasons the United States will have to pass, in the course of the next century, if not of this. *How* will you pass through them? I heartily wish you a good deliverance, but my reason and my wishes are at war and I cannot help foreboding the worst. It is quite plain your government will never be able to restrain a distressed and discontented majority. For with you the majority is the government and the rich, who are always a minority, are absolutely at its mercy. The day will come when, in the State of New York a multitude of people, none of whom has had more than half a breakfast or expects to have more than half a dinner, will choose the legislature. Is it possible to doubt what sort of legislature will be chosen? On one side is a statesman preaching patience, respect for vested rights, a strict observance of public faith. On the other side is a demagogue ranting about tyranny of capitalists and usurers, and asking why anybody should be permitted to drink champagne and to ride in a carriage while thousands of honest people are in want of necessities. Which of the two candidates is likely to be preferred by a working man who hears his children cry for bread?

"I seriously apprehend that you will in some such season of adversity as I have described do things which will prevent prosperity from returning; that you will act, like people in a year of scarcity who devour all the seed corn and thus make the next year not one of scarcity but of absolute distress. The distress will produce fresh spoliation. There is nothing to stay you. Your constitution is all sail and no anchor. As I said, when society has entered on this downward progress, either civilization or liberty must perish. Either some Caesar or Napoleon will seize the reins of government with a strong hand or your Republic will be as fearfully plundered and laid waste by barbarians in the twentieth century as the Roman Empire was in the fifth; with this difference, that the Huns and Vandals who ravaged the Roman Empire came from without, and your Huns and Vandals will have engendered within your own country by your own institutions.

"Thinking this, of course I cannot reckon Jefferson among the benefactors of mankind."

Macaulay's practical experience in Parliament gave him a particularly sharp insight into political behavior. This letter is an early statement of the underlying theme of Ortega y Gasset's *Revolt of the Masses,* and of many more recent expositions of the danger of the cult of the lowest common denominator. If there should grow up in this continent a generation of men and women ready to give their lives to defending the last strongholds of the practice of individual liberty, their first duty would be to prove, by word and deed, that Macaulay and Ortega y Gasset were wrong. The imperative need of our time is to prove to ourselves first, and to the rest of the world after, that the methods of selfgovernment can assure elbow room to the individual man in an industrial society.

A solution to the problem would be seemingly hopeless if new factors had not appeared which Macaulay had no way of foreseeing. One is the immense increase in productivity. Another is the massdistribution of massproduced goods which has resulted from high wages. Macaulay had no way of knowing that the American industrialist and the American farmer would be producing within a hundred years such a profusion of goods that the questions facing our political economy would be those of surplus rather than scarcity. Whenever we get a breathing space from the waste of war, we start to pile up such mountains of wheat and corn, such rivers of crude oil, such avalanches of automobiles, washing machines, hedge clippers, of everything you can think of, that the economy gets the blind staggers.

Franklin Roosevelt's New Deal revolution had all the earmarks of the sort of uprising Macaulay looked forward to with so much dread. We had our hundreds and thousands of artisans out of work. We had our mutinous and discontented labor. "Spend, spend, spend. Tax, tax, tax. Elect, elect, elect" was the watchword. The sufferers marched to the polls and elected and re-elected Franklin Roosevelt, who sure ranted plenty about the tyranny of capitalists and bankers. The rich were despoiled through the income tax. The poor were to a certain extent subsidized. But the end result, instead of the republic's being laid waste by the barbarians from below, was that everybody got richer, at least in material things.

Nobody who remembers what these United States looked like in the twenties can drive across the country today without seeing the spread of electric power, the improvement in roads, in school buildings, in the health of the children you see in the playgrounds, in all kinds of housing, in all the facilities for more comfortable living. The people of this country are immensely richer in material goods than they were thirty years ago and that wealth is very much more evenly distributed.

Events have disproved Macaulay's theory that wealth is unsafe in any hands but those of the rich. It is as untenable as the complementary theory that taking the wealth away from the rich adds to the wellbeing of the poor. Wealth, in modern industrial society would seem to lie in the full use of technology and knowhow to produce goods and in seeing to it that the men who produce them get enough return for their effort to be able to buy and to enjoy the goods they help to make. At the same time the intellectual levelling which has come about through mass communication would seem to have left the working man, in an industrial structure so cut up into segments that no man can see beyond the end of his nose, neither more nor less capable than the business man or the farmer of dealing with political problems.

Though the first results of mass communication, as of mass education, have been to level thinking to a lowest common denominator set pretty near the idiot level, it is possible to hope that the eventual results will be immensely to broaden the educated class "deeply interested in the security of property and the maintenance of order" to whose hands Macaulay wished to entrust the supreme power.

On the other hand future historians are going to puzzle over the fact that just at the moment when American industrial society was showing how youthful and elastic it was, and how adaptable to changing conditions, so many well educated young men threw overboard the whole idea of selfgovernment within a framework of law, and turned to the Communist Party. They are going to puzzle about our failure as a nation to draw any advantage for ourselves or the world from a series of military victories in the course of two world wars. At the moment when our traditional social values were proving their practical effectiveness the ethical structure behind them was showing every sign of coming apart at the seams.

Somewhere along the way we lost our conviction that the best government was selfgovernment. In our enthusiasm for turning over every social problem to the administrative bureaucracy for solution, we forgot that democracy was based on the maxim that the solution of the problems of social life was the business of the people themselves. Neither Macaulay nor Jefferson, when they scanned the horizon for dangers threatening American democracy, foresaw this prodigious growth of a bureaucracy armed with police powers, a bureaucracy which has become a vested interest in its own right.

The whole subject has been confused, of course, by the doubletalk of the zealots for total bureaucratic rule, a doubletalk where the old vocabulary of democratic liberties is made to mean something quite different from what was originally intended; but the fact remains that Americans are finding it harder and harder to apply the words and phrases that fitted so well the society that Jefferson and Madison lived in, to the pyramidshaped social structures of today.

Man is an institution building animal. The shape of his institutions is continually remoulding his life. Every new process for the production of food and goods, or for their distribution, changes the social structure. Careers are tailored to fit each new process. People's lives become intertwined with the complicated structures of vested interests. With every institutional change adaptations are demanded.

Adaptation is slow and difficult and painful. The symptoms of insufficient adaptations are maladjustment, frustration and apathy. The bureaucratic social structure which has grown up round the present type of industrial production has developed so fast that we are finding it hard, perhaps harder than we realize, to operate the system of checks and balances against inordinate power which the English speaking peoples built up through centuries of resistance to authority.

It was Jefferson's sarcastic young friend from Orange County, little James Madison, who set down, in the often-quoted number 51 of the *Federalist,* the basic hardheaded rule on which all the men of the generation of 1776, radical and conservative alike, based their political theories: "In framing a government which is to be administered by men over men, the great difficulty lies in this; you must first enable the government to control the governed and in the next place oblige it to control itself."

The problem which men will face, when they try to make elbow room for themselves and for their fellows, in the new type of society now coming into being, will be the problem of bureaucracy. Bureaucracy has become dominant in government, in industry and in the organizations of labor. The first interest of these bureaucracies, as of all human institutions, is in their own survival. If these bureaucratic hierarchies, which seem unavoidable in a mass society, can be harnessed to the dynamic needs of selfgovernment, the task of reversing the trend towards individual serfdom into a trend towards individual liberty may not be as hard as it seems at the first glance.

The first prerequisite is a fresh understanding, untrammeled by prejudice or partisan preconceptions, of the institutions we live in. Such a view is unlikely to result from the labors of research teams or sponsored surveys. The prime discoveries are more likely to be made by solitary individuals, who have managed by hook or crook to find the elbow room they need to look about them, and the selfsufficiency they need to observe their world objectively.

Observing objectively demands a sort of virginity of the perceptions. A man has to clear all preconceived notions out of his head in a happy self-forgetfulness where there is no gap between observation and description.

There's a description of a variety of cuttlefish in Darwin's *Voyage of the Beagle* that gives a notion of the delights of first hand observation:

Although common in pools of water left by the retiring tide these animals are not easily caught. By means of their long arms and suckers they could drag their bodies into very narrow crevices; and when thus fixed, it required great force to remove them. At other times they darted tail first, with the rapidity of an arrow, from one side of the pool to the other, at the same instant discoloring the water with a dark chestnut brown ink. These animals can also escape detection by a very extraordinary chameleonlike power of changing their color. They appear to vary their tints according to the nature of the ground over which they pass; when in deep water, their general shade was brownish purple, but when placed on land their dark tint changed into one of yellowish green. The color, examined more carefully, was a French grey, with numerous minute spots of bright yellow: the former of these varied in intensity, the latter entirely disappeared and appeared again by turns. These changes were effected in such a manner that clouds, varying in tint between a hyacinth red and a chestnut brown were continually passing over the body.

The sensitivity of a man's perceptions is in no way increased by the squinting of eyes and the straining of ears. The state of mind of the dispassionate observer is somewhat analogous to the hunter's. An expert hunter in a duck blind, or walking behind his dogs round the edges of a cornfield or waiting by a deerpath in the woods, thinks of nothing. He forgets himself. He lets all his senses come awake to respond to the frailest intimations that come to his ears or his eyes of the movement of game. Really good shots, the fellows who really bring down the quail, are people who are able to forget who they are and become for the moment just an eye and an ear and a gun.

To report objectively some scene, some situation, the movement of some animal, the shape of some organism under the microscope, a man has to fall into a state of unpreoccupied alertness very similar to the state of a sharpshooter stretched out under cover to take a bead on an enemy.

This hunter or sharpshooter knows what to look for. For years he has been building up a bank of experience. A good ornithologist can give one glance into a thicket. Where I see only some English sparrows he can pick out a wren sitting on her nest and three different kinds of warblers. As a result of a lifetime of observation a good hunter can tell, from the slightest disturbance of twigs and pinetags on a path through the woods whether it was a deer or a raccoon that just passed that way.

The trouble with most classroom education is that the emphasis is on the name of the thing instead of on the thing itself. Classroom education teaches men to believe that if they have labelled and pigeonholed something they have disposed of it. So the educated man is liable to start to apply the label before he has really seen the object. To describe something objectively you have to see the individual thing before you name it.

Of course where the uneducated man falls down is in integrating what he has seen into some rational scheme. He's likely to try to fit the picture into some purely superstitious frame. Still, before you have an experience or an event fresh and new and individual enough to be worth integrating into your rational scheme, you've got, just for a slice of a second, to let yourself fall into the uneducated man's naïve and ignorant frame of mind. Astonishment is a wonderful stimulus to thought.

You have to meet each new phenomenon with a clean slate as if you had never heard of it before. Most of the time we live in a shut-in universe of labels and classifications and verbalisms. It's only in brief glimpses that we have the luck to see things as they are, instead of as we were told they ought to be.

I wonder sometimes if the curiosity that makes a man want to see clearer and clearer isn't related to the hunters' or trackers' alertness which might well have been one of the qualities most needed for survival far back in the history of the race.

The state of mind that makes for objective description, like every state of mind in which you forget who you are, has a sort of primeval happiness about it. You look out at the world with a fresh eye as if it were the morning of the first day of creation.

There is a lucid little paragraph in an English translation of William Harvey's *Circulation of the Blood.*

We have a small shrimp in these countries, which is taken in the Thames and in the sea, the whole of whose body is transparent; this creature, placed in a little water, has frequently afforded myself and particular friends an opportunity of observing the motions of the heart with the greatest distinctness, the extreme parts of the body presenting no obstacle to our view, but the heart being perceived as though it had been seen through a window.

Before we can start even to suggest the readjustments needed to assure fresh elbow room for the individual we must manage to see the shape of our society as clearly as Harvey saw the heart of the shrimp.

II. The Leaders and the Led

The Education of Leviathan, 1943-45

The protocol. Mrs. Frankfurter had said to come "around fiveish." Through a tall narrow window green light poured up into the room reflected from the brilliantly sunlit grass and dense shrubbery of the garden in back. It was a high narrow dark room with a moulded gesso ceiling in an old brick house that smelt cosily of books and waxed parquet. My hostess sat on a couch in the shadow against the wall behind a beaded pitcher of iced orangeade. She was an awfully nice woman, the model of the nicest kind of Harvard professor's wife. She was listening with a small indulgent smile to a question I kept presenting to her in various soggy shapes. How much did she suppose social life really counted in Washington?

Justice Frankfurter came in the door and stood with his head cocked on one side for a moment. He was a small ruddy brighteyed man with a sharp nose. His posture was alert and birdlike. "Are you entering into competition with Lucius Beebe?" he asked sarcastically. Before I could answer he went out of the room to fetch some whiskey.

From *State of the Nation*, by Dos Passos (Boston: Houghton Mifflin Company, 1944).

When he came back with a pint of rye, I tried to explain that since it happened that society, like golf, was a sport I knew very little about, I had to go around asking questions about it. If you didn't play the game yourself you had to get information from people who did. The difficulty was to find anybody sufficiently detached to admit they played it at all.

"Of course we don't have any choice," whispered my hostess thoughtfully. There was some dismay in her tone.

"The ladies really understand that subject because they never take it seriously." Justice Frankfurter turned towards the couch. "Speak up as an entity in your own right," he said.

"Sometimes . . ." she began. But the Justice was already talking again: "For one thing the protocol is stricter than in any other capital in the world. Even people who knew St. Petersburg and Vienna under the old regime say the same thing. It's often struck people as odd."

"I suppose you know," Mrs. Frankfurter said with her small smile, "that there are still great unsolved problems. There are people the Chief Justice can never eat dinner with because the problem of precedence has never been worked out."

"Problems that await the solution of some Beebe yet unborn," cried out Justice Frankfurter with a shrill laugh.

He spoke of Jefferson's effort to introduce what he called the rule of pêle-mêle. When dinner was announced every gentleman should take the lady nearest him into table and seating should be accidental or arranged as in an ordinary Virginia gentleman's house. This procedure at the White House had horrified Anthony Merry, who was then British ambassador and a great stickler for the etiquette of the Court of St. James's, and he had written copious memoranda complaining about it to the Foreign Office. In the long run it had been the British ambassador's idea that had prevailed, not Jefferson's.

"At least people still pursue good food," Mrs. Frankfurter said, smiling. "I've never seen people pursue food and drink so frankly as they do in this town. It's not a dressy town, as you know. People don't care what they wear. The money goes into catering. You have to have good things to eat if you want to have a crowd at your afternoons at home. You know there are certain officials whose wives have to have afternoons at home whether they want to or not. Even the day of the week is set for them. It's one of the laws of the Medes and the Persians."

Did a man's social rating affect his career in government? I asked.

Well, there were the wealthy young men who gave big parties. There was the embassy crowd. There were the hostesses of great wealth who liked to have the latest celebrities. There were certain embassies whose invitations had a political intent. But on the whole social life was mechanical.

Wasn't one reason why so many people cracked up there that there was so little social relaxation? Didn't the town lack any real society?

We talked a little about what was meant by society. We decided it might mean, in a good sense, a sort of republic of equals. Once you were admitted into such a group competition and social climbing ceased. The nourishment and relaxation of such a society came from the fact that people inside it could exchange ideas, gossip, jokes—could feel at ease among equals. Jefferson's dinners had aimed at a republic of entertaining conversation where good breeding was taken for granted. Perhaps people would use their heads in their jobs if they had that kind of refreshment in the evenings.

There was the moral check on a man that came from feeling that he belonged to a group whose judgments he had respect for. Ethics depended in some degree on your respect for the judgment of your peers.

We fell to talking about various mutual acquaintances who had come to Washington. Some had struggled hard to go out to dinner with the right people and not to be seen with the wrong people. Some had drifted innocently. None of them had gotten much nourishment out of it. In the long run it made very little difference one way or the other, not so much as it would in London, say. It was a man's position on the political or bureaucratic pyramid that determined his value as a dinner guest rather than the other way around. The halo of celebrity hovered fitfully about this or that man's head for a while, then it vanished and left no trace.

But hadn't the new population that had come in during the last ten years changed things? Some of the best brains in the country had poured through Washington. Hardly. Washington wasn't a city where people had much curiosity about why they behaved as they did. New Deal or old deal, Justice Frankfurter suggested, the same dignitaries still had to invite their opposite numbers to dinner. Maybe the protocol was an accommodation. With the protocol you didn't need to think. It was the unexamined life, he said with a smile, which Socrates had not thought worth living.

"We haven't any Socrates," Mrs. Frankfurter made a little face, "and now the war has put a stop to formal entertaining anyway. And to tell the truth," she added heartily, "it's been quite a relief."

A passion for anonymity. It was late afternoon. Coppery clouds were building up over Georgetown, giving a reddish glow, as if it were heated from within, to the asphalt on the Avenue. Bill Hassett met me at the door of his apartment. He apologized for his bathrobe. It was so damned hot he couldn't keep his clothes on. Though he'd worked many years in Washington, first as a journalist and now as one of the devoted little band with a "passion for anonymity," that did most of Franklin Roosevelt's writing for him, his speech still had a little Vermont twang.

After he'd settled me on a couch opposite the window, he handed me a dripping glass of beer.

"I had to bring this in on my back. You can't get anything delivered," he said, and we started chatting about the District.

Did I know that the old gentleman who ran the brewery this beer came from was still alive? He was over a hundred. A living advertisement for his produce and for the healthiness of the city. Maybe people complained about the Washington weather too much. If people lived to be a hundred it couldn't be too bad.

Did he feel, I asked, that the war had cut the President off from the country?

"Every time he takes a trip," he answered a little aggressively, "he comes back very much refreshed. Maybe he's a little like the Greek mythical giant who lost his strength as soon as he ceased to touch the earth . . . I think he's quite conscious of the importance of keeping that touch."

"Can he do it? Can he get away from official channels enough to do it?"

"Well, he still sees his old friends . . . all sorts of people turn up who have no connection with politics or business of any kind—family friends, legal friends from New York, casual acquaintances. He can't give them quite as much time as he used to. But he certainly sees them. Some people feel that he gives them too much time . . ."

"It must be hard for President Roosevelt to keep in touch with reality," I insisted. "It's so much easier for people to tell him what he wants to hear. I should think the longer he stayed there, the harder it would be for anybody to tell him any bad news."

Bill Hassett's face took on a look of almost ferocious devotion. "That would be true of an ordinary man," he said tensely. "A man has naturally to be a genius at that kind of thing. I think this man is . . ." He caught himself short. The soul of discretion, he couldn't let himself show so much emotion. He regained his offhand sociable manner. "How about another glass? A bird can't fly on one wing, you know."

Only a handful of men. When you have an appointment with someone in the East Wing of the White House you have to go first to a little glass sentry box set up in the middle of the short barred-off street that divides the White House grounds from the Treasury Building. The secret service men check your name with their list. When you have been identified, you walk past the barricade and up the low steps to the porch. In an airy corridor a few men in khaki are lounging on a rushbottomed colonial bench. A sergeant ushers you into a little office where a blue-eyed girl with a pompadour tells you that Mr. Hopkins has been detained, won't you please wait a minute. She hands you the morning's *New York Times.*

It's quiet and cool there in the small modestly furnished office. You read through the news columns that interest you, and then you read the book reviews, and then you read the financial page, and at last you turn back to the editorials. You've read all the letters and are starting in on the sports when the young lady, who from time to time has encouraged you with accounts of how things are progressing in the inner office, at length tells you with a smile that you can go in now.

Harry Hopkins is sitting at a desk in another small office. The window is behind him. He is a tall stooping man with a high forehead and nose glasses. For a flitting instant there's a recollection of Woodrow Wilson's long pale stubborn face. You can see that he has been ill. There's a waxy, almost transparent look about his skin. At first he has a little difficulty finding his words as he talks. He stammers a little. There's no side about him. He doesn't talk like a man who's holding back half his mind. You feel that he trusts your respect for the seriousness and selflessness of his purpose, that he feels that if it is his purpose it must be a good one.

The place has an air of seclusion like a den in a large house in the country. It's quiet in the office. Perhaps you only imagine the faint hum of energy like a generating plant. Is it real or imagined, the feeling like terror that comes from being close to a source of power over the destinies of many men? As Harry Hopkins talks, he keeps looking away from you across the green sheltered lawn towards the pedimented main building of the White House.

You have to start him off with questions. They are the old clumsy questions. Is there a rift appearing between the White House and the country? Is it possible for the commander-in-chief in a global war, the man a southern senator has said his dearest wish was to nominate for President of the United States of the World, to keep in touch with the picayune unglobal needs and aspirations and reactions of the people of the forty-eight states of the Union on this segment of a continent? The questions aren't very well put. You don't have much confidence in questions anyway. Nobody ever learned anything by asking questions.

Harry Hopkins is patient about the questions. He doesn't evade them or bristle at them. You feel that he doesn't hear them. Some time ago he made up his mind and closed its windows on the world.

He starts talking about how the running of the war is necessarily in the hands of a few men. Only they know the facts. The President knows things nobody else knows. A great deal of his time, a great deal of his thinking, has to be on the level of the four leaders of the United Nations—Roosevelt, Churchill, Stalin, Chiang Kai-shek. There are decisions that only these four men can make. Below that is the level of general staffs, of coordination of campaigns, the world-wide allocation of munitions, Lend Lease. The facts upon which these decisions were based are known only to a handful of men.

Several times Harry Hopkins used the phrase "only a handful of men."

I mentioned Congress and strikes and food production. He frowned. A lot of that was politics. The press was always puffing up the importance of domestic problems. Problems made a great splash at first and gradually they were solved and people forgot them. In the White House they were bored with domestic problems. If the war were brought to a successful issue, all these troublesome things would fall into line. Did I realize how much work had to go into every separate decision as to what munitions were to go to what front, for an example, how much time had to be taken up on the level of the four leaders? Only a handful of men had the information on which to base an opinion. It was boring to come back to the petty misunderstandings of domestic problems. They should wait until victory. With the victory all these things would fall into line.

"How?" the small question was in my mind but I didn't ask it. It was time to go. He had talked pleasantly and patiently and he was a very busy man. I said goodbye.

As I walked out, past the limp guards, enjoying the civilian-in-uniform look these young men still had in spite of years of military training, and past the broadfaced secret service men in the little glass shelter and out onto the hurrying noontime crowds and cars and taxicabs of the street that the flailing sunshine lashed like rain, I pictured Harry Hopkins walking back with long unsteady strides across the secluded lawn to President Roosevelt's office in the central part of the White House. There life went on on the level of the four leaders.

Dr. Win-the-War. About the only change war has brought to the procedure when you go to the President's press conference is that the secret service men have to find your name on a list at the gate before they let you walk across the drive to the entrance in the West Wing. If you are not a regular attendant, you are ushered into the long panelled room filled up with the great mahogany table Aguinaldo gave. You sit there remembering old bronze Andrew Jackson on his rearing horse taking off his hat to all the world, and the sailors talking to girls on the benches of Lafayette Square, and the pigeons drinking at the fountains, lifting their pink bills and puffing out their rainbow-colored breasts and stretching their necks to let the cool water run down their gullets. You sit there remembering the stately simplicity of the main porch of the White House, the spacing of the trees, the box bushes in tubs you had a glimpse of as you passed, the Augustan afterglow in the ornament of the portal you came in by. It's still the sort of thing Jefferson meant. In this long room where you sit, the panelling has dignity; there's a Hellenic reminder in the dentated cornice. The minutes pass. You sit on a red couch, one of a row of men who don't know each other. From the hallway outside comes a faint babble from the regular newspapermen in the hall. You go over your notes. You jot down appointments, you try to remember your expenses, that taxicab, the check at dinner last night. The minutes drag on.

All at once the newspapermen start pouring down the hall. A suave tall gentleman in a cutaway has his arm across the door. As the crowd thins, he lets it drop. We follow the tail end of the procession into the oval blue-gray office. The brownish velvet curtains are new. The pictures of boats are the same, the flag and the eagle. Across the shoulders, past the ears of the newspapermen who got there ahead of you, you look down on Franklin D. Roosevelt seated at his desk.

On either side behind his chair stand secret service men. One of them is burly, middleaged, with a red beefy face; the other is a square-jawed expressionless young man who might be a floorwalker in a department store. Beyond you can see the green lawn sloping down the hill to the great enclosing trees. Lustrous in the crosslights behind President Roosevelt's head, shines a large globe of the world. It is against the blue Pacific Ocean that you see his head uptilted.

As always he's handsomer than he appears in his photographs when you see him face to face. He hasn't changed so much since I saw him seven years ago in the early days of greensickness and accomplishment of the New Deal. His hair is grayer. He still has the fine nose and forehead, the gray eyes blandly unabashed under the movable eyebrows.

Looking down from this angle you don't notice the broad stump speaker's mouth, the heavy jowl.

Today he looks well rested. He's in high good humor. At breakfast they brought him the news of a Japanese retreat on Guadalcanal. The reporters shoot questions up over each other's shoulders. So long as it's on the foreign wars it's fun. The President's manner is boyish and gay. He shoots the answers back with zest, blowing out his cheeks the way he does when searching for a word, lifting his eyebrows to make the questioner feel he has all his attention, man to man, for just that one moment; cosily scratching an ear or the back of his head as he formulates one of his sparkling improvisations. The boys are being made to feel at home in the headmaster's study.

It's only when rationing, the coal strike, price control, come up that a frown appears on his forehead. He begins to talk about deep water. His manner becomes abrupt and querulous. A note of vexation comes into his voice. He won't talk about these things. Congress will have to decide them, he says. His face begins to take on an air of fatigue. There's a sagging look under the eyes of having been up late at his desk, of sleepless nights.

"Thank you, Mr. President," a voice pipes up. The President's gray face is hidden by the younger fresher unworried faces of reporters turning to shove for the door. The press conference is over.

Departure. It's dark under the great soap-colored Roman vaults of the Union Station. Not much daylight gets in through the grimed windows. The electric bulbs have the redeyed look of having been up all night. So many people have absorbed all the light. The floor, the benches, the entrances are dark with shifting masses of people. About half of them are young men in uniform. Negro families are spread around the benches. Queues fan out in shifting tentacles from every ticketwindow, from the information booths, from the newsstands, from the telegraph offices. In the telephone room men sitting on upended suitcases wait glumly for a chance at the booths. In the dim blurred light of the glass train shed sailors in whites with their heavy canvas seabags on their shoulders are being mustered into ranks. A stream of men, women and children flows sluggishly down the platform towards the New York train. No seats in the coaches. Everything booked in the Pullmans. Just as I'm sliding into a place at a table in the diner, I see a man I know.

"Hello," he says, as he shakes hands. "You ought to have called me up sooner. I bet you've seen nothing but liberals." He grins. He has protruding brown eyes and a brown round face with a big jaw in it. We sit down side by side. "I used to think I was a liberal once. But they've turned out no good." He made a downward gesture with his hand. "I don't mean they don't mean well. But they've proved themselves unable to put their ideas across. They don't stick together. They're not coherent. They aren't tough enough to survive in the battle of Washington. They're too yellow to slug it out man to man. They're not efficient. My quarrel with a lot of these New Deal agencies is they don't deliver. I been in all of them. I'm working for the army now, thank God . . ." He suddenly rubbed his hand across his forehead. "Here I am spilling my guts and I haven't even had a drink yet. Here, waiter!"

We ordered some drinks and lunch. "Well, go on!" he shouted above the thumping of the train. "What have they told you? You spill something now."

"For sheer human suffering the foxholes of Bataan have nothing on the foxholes of Washington."

" 'Don't cheer, men, the poor fellows are dying.' " He threw back his head and laughed uproariously.

"In all the conversations I've heard for and against this man and that man," I was trying to draw him back, "nobody has ever mentioned whether he was doing a good job. Efficiency never seems to come up in Congress or in any of the pow-wows I've listened in on at all. It's all—Is he right politically? Has he the right ideas?"

"Hell, that's natural. This town's a vast clearing house. There's no real work done here."

"But there must be some people doing an efficient job of paper work."

"The country does the job. Washington is no place for brighteyed idealists, even if their ideal is efficient work."

"Why not?"

"The stakes are too high. . . Has there ever been a time since Cleopatra's barge when the stakes were so high?. . . Ever read about the Roman Empire? Since the days of Caesar and Crassus and Pompey there's never been a time when so much direct power was within the grasp of a few men's hands."

"All the more need to work in the public interest."

"Interests in the plural is the thing in this town. Lately, I've had a good deal to do with the British. The difference between our boys and the Britishers is that the Britishers always put England first and the old firm second. With our boys, it's the other way around."

"Do you honestly think so?"

He nodded vigorously over his plate. "Look at your idealist. Look what happens to him. He comes down here in the public interest. That's what he thinks, anyway. If he has any brains

91

he's probably had theories and spouted them around at some time in his life. The Dies Committee gets on his trail. Right away he's a Red. Maybe he's been a tulip fancier or gone in swimming without any clothes on. He's a crackpot. He's a nudist. The Kerr Committee makes him miserable digging up his past. He either runs to cover and stops trying to do anything or else his boss puts him in cold storage. . . He's not a party man. Say he's just out to save American people some money. The first time anybody needs to be fed to the wolves, out he goes on his fanny. What comeback has he? A letter to the *Nation.* If he's a real conspiratorial Communist the party protects him. He sits pretty. If he's a crook he's got partners in crime. An unattached individual citizen has no more chance than a man trying to fight a tank with a croquet mallet. We live in the world of machines. Some machines are made of steel; others are made up of men."

"Isn't a good deal of the government machinery antiquated?" I asked. "I don't mean that selfgovernment is antiquated. It hasn't really been tried yet."

"Antiquated! They've got an engine built for a side-wheeler, one of those old excursion boats, and they're trying to fly an airplane with it. What do you expect?"

From the train whenever the line passed through a town or near a group of houses we could see Victory gardens, carefully tilled plots rich in curling ranks of corn, stately poles of beans, fat cabbages, lacy patches of potatoes in flower.

"Look how well we cultivate gardens," I cried out. "I bet half the people growing vegetables this year never had a hoe in their hands. They are doing a hell of a good job."

"Sure, but don't forget that the knowhow exists. Any fool can read a book and plant a garden. The science of government ain't."

"What about the Constitution?"

He suddenly looked tired. "This is over my head. . . I'm a realist," he muttered in a shaky voice. "All I meant, I guess, was that the present gang has shot its bolt. We got to have a new outfit, new leadership, new ideas."

Beyond Baltimore when we came out into the sunlight after the tunnel, the train passed between vast low factory buildings prettily camouflaged with clouds and hills and pictures of trees and houses.

"Now that's a good job," he exclaimed. "My work's part of that; that makes me feel good."

Across immense runways new fighting planes stretched in ranks as far as you could see. "I don't care whether it's just for war or not," he went on in a tone of explanation. "It's wonderful. . . I was born in the old country and I know it's freedom we are fighting for. You can't separate any of it from freedom here and in England. . . If freedom could find a way of running its own affairs. . . that would be democracy."

An Old-fashioned Progressive

Noontime a sunny Sunday in New York. The tall office buildings of downtown Manhattan and the glittering midtown pinnacles stand up in the hazy sunlight, immense and empty of life as eroded rock mesas in the Painted Desert. In the deep streets a few buses start and stop and start again as the traffic lights blink red and green. Men and women in their best clothes move slowly away from the doors of churches. In the parks there's more life. Couples stroll, push baby carriages, drag small children along cement paths. Old people sit drowsing on benches. Boys with baseball mitts run yelling out on the trodden green grass.

Indoors people come sluggishly to life, raise shades, open hall doors to gather up newspapers, grope sleepily for milk-bottles, loaf over their breakfast at tables littered with the funnies and the Sunday supplements, or sit on the edges of overstuffed living room chairs waiting for Sunday dinner. Out of every apartment, eddying back through every open window, out of every court and airshaft comes the clamor of radio voices. When it gets to be one o'clock people tune in on the city station to hear the Mayor.

Liberty magazine (1943).

94

Fiorello La Guardia's voice is low and chatty. It's like having a well informed and slightly fussy uncle come to call. He is disturbed about the family's welfare. He can't quite conceal the feeling that people aren't doing as well for themselves as they should. He's anxious about them. He talks along in a low casual voice as if he were sitting there in the room with his glasses pushed back on his forehead. He's full of advice about marketing.

He's concerned with mother's shopping: lamb chops will be scarce and high this week; there's plenty of nice crisp lettuce; fish is reasonable. Be sure you get it fresh. Don't forget variety meats and not to pay more than the ceiling price. There's plenty of cream. You don't have to take half water ice any more unless you want it. Don't let them tell you anything different. Pure icecream is nourishing and good for the children. Let them eat plenty of it. It won't hurt them. . .

The Mayor has had letters complaining about uncivil bus drivers. He reads a couple out. . . Well we must all do our best to get along with each other at a time like this when everybody's overworked and working under strain. He himself is willing to admit he blows up in his office sometimes and says things he wishes he hadn't. He regrets it afterwards. Most of the city employees are doing their best. With the present manpower shortage we can't always get the class of people we'd like. . .

A threat comes into his voice: all complaints will go on the record. We won't forget any complaints when the time comes. He goes on to talk about how the war is going and the current bond drive and the magnificent concert there's going to be this week for the benefit of the Red Cross. . . He's telling us what's what but with an undertone of understanding of what it means to raise kids in a cramped apartment, to

95

make both ends meet on a small salary, to get to work every morning. When the admonishing voice goes off the air people are left with the feeling that Mayor La Guardia really cares.

Of course, if you go around town asking questions, his enemies will tell you that the radio talks are all political window dressing, that Fiorello La Guardia is as coldhearted as only a hotheaded Latin can be. "Well, isn't he efficient?" you will ask. "Didn't he clean up Tammany?" Most of them admit that; they'll even tell you that his first administration was the best the city has had in the memory of man including Reform's past golden age under Mayor Mitchel. But they'll hasten to add that La Guardia can't get along with first-rate people, that since he was blocked in his ambition to step out on the national stage he has been an embittered man who can't keep down his bullying temper, but to keep in office he's had to compromise with organizations as corrupt as the Tammany he rooted out. As a progressive, they'll say, he's washed up.

You ask a philosophical politician, who is a friend of the Mayor's, what about it? He answers that it's not so bad as all that. Maybe the Little Flower doesn't get along with individual people very well, but he gets along marvelously with people in general. He's got the common touch.

This man I am talking to puffs thoughtfully on his cigarette and goes on to explain in a drawling voice that La Guardia is the most representative mayor the city has had for a long time. "You fellows mustn't forget," he says, "the change there's been in the makeup and geography of this town. Never forget that there are five boroughs."

Manhattan wasn't the center of population any more. The city was a third Italian now, a third different kinds of Irish, Germans, Jewish, Scandinavians, Negroes and all the rest; old stock Americans could be lumped into the smallest third.

The lace curtain Irish who'd run the town in the last days of Tammany Hall didn't represent it any more.

It wasn't for nothing that Fiorello started his life in New York as interpreter at Ellis Island. He'd learned there to talk to the people in their own languages: Italian, Yiddish, German, south Slavic dialects. His father was a musician. He was brought up in a musical family. He had a good ear. That made learning languages come easy. As a young man in the consular service he found out a lot about where all these people's fathers and mothers came from in the old country.

"But foreign languages are dying out in New York."

"Sure, but Fiorello's Johnny-on-the-spot there too. He's more thoroughly American than most people in this town because he was raised in the West. His old man was regimental band-master at an old-time army post in Arizona. Could anything be more grassroots? That frontier beginning gave him something to stand on a little outside of the immigrant community he represented when he opened his law office and barged out into politics as champion of the underdog. There was something self-respecting in his background," this man says, picking his words carefully, "that saves him from two of the worst vices of men who slug their way up from the ranks: greed for money and social climbing."

The man glanced up at the clock on the wall and the thoughtful searching look went off his face. "I'm just rambling on. . . The thing for you to do," he says, "is to go talk to the man himself."

When I came sloshing up through the dripping park to the Gracie Mansion, early one rainy summer morning, a tall cop in a rubber coat stepped in my path to ask if I had an appointment and led me up to the front door under the high white porch of the old-time country house. There he turned me over to a maid. Right away she ushered me through the whitepanelled hall into a side room that looked spacious and empty in the gray light that came in off the river through the tall window.

A small broadshouldered chalkyfaced man buttoned into a doublebreasted blue suit with a red Memorial Day poppy in his buttonhole sat behind the desk at the end of the room. He was smoking a long cigar while he went over a pile of papers. He had the look of a man who had enjoyed his breakfast. His dark eyes set in dark pouches of skin behind blackrimmed horn spectacles were eating up the typewritten sheets.

When he got to his feet to say "How do you do?" he pulled off his glasses. I could see that his eyes were spaced rather far apart in his head. After a sharp glance in my direction they settled into a thoughtful stare ahead of him. His manner was absolutely without pretension.

The room was quiet except for the tiny hiss of the rain beating against the window. He offered me one of his cigars, saying a friend had sent them from Jamaica. A marvelous place for a quiet talk I was thinking to myself as I lit it, turning over in my head the topics I want to bring up, children, city housekeeping, postwar planning. The first question was just forming on my lips when the Mayor hopped to his feet. "Well, it's time to go to work," he said in a snappish tone.

On the way out I mumbled something about what a handsome old house the city had given him to live in. He stopped in his tracks and looked up on the elaborate mouldings of the ceiling. "It's tough on my wife," he said, "keeping it up. The Metropolitan Museum fixed up these lower rooms in good taste. They gave me a rare old antique carpet for the hall. When the king of Greece came to call he dropped right down on his knees to feel it with his hand and said it was so valuable it ought to be hung on the wall."

The Mayor acted out the visiting king's gesture and the connoisseur's expression of a man putting on his eyeglasses to got the habit of running down the stairs and jumping on it."

We duck into the driving drizzle and squeeze in beside the driver of a single seated police roadster. As we shoot down the East River Drive past the tall grouped chimneys of power plants and the sprawling buildings of the hospitals on the islands we talk about children.

The Mayor likes to talk about children. One thing he feels he can boast about, he says, was that the children of the city are better fed, better clothed, cleaner and healthier today than they were ten years ago. Speeding towards the old bridges, humming with traffic, he pointed out parks and playgrounds and the staggered blocks of the new housing.

I say something about missing the old East Side that used to be so much part of New York. "You never had to live in it," he answers dryly.

The car turns in through a brick street of warehouses with green shutters and gilt lettered signs that give you a momentary flash of what the Port of New York looked like in the days of the clipper ships, rounds the slick soaring walls of the new high buildings that house the lawcourts of the city and the state, and draws up in the middle of the park before the arched entrance so stately and so carefully designed to the human scale, of the old City Hall.

The Mayor jumps out of the car and trots up the steps into the vestibule. Reporters in raincoats converge on him there and hold him in a huddle. He breaks away and darts off past the desks of the receptionists, bolts into a narrow passage clogged with typewriters, hands his hat to a tall man in uniform with gilt braid on his shoulders, and before you know it he is at work. Three girl stenographers who have followed him into the office sit alert and smiling on the edges of their chairs along one side of his enormous desk.

Immediately there's a hush of concentration in the room. There is no sound but the jangle of downtown traffic filtering in, muffled, through the closed windows in their high arched embrasures. From the walls portraits of former mayors in silk stocks look down out of their gilt frames. Under a great crystal chandelier, that gleams reflected in the dark of the window beyond, the Mayor sits pouting over a set of folders stacked with correspondence. In front of him is his calendar. On either side, the desk is piled with reference books and folders full of documents. A small gavel lies handy.

On the settee behind, a tin hat and two pairs of army boots, and some civilian defense apparatus stand waiting for an air raid. On the wall opposite there's a large scale civilian defense map of the city with a diagram of an enemy bomb bursting in Brooklyn and the resulting action.

In the corners of the room potted palms give the grave official air. On one windowsill stands a large piece of petrified wood. Around the walls chairs and settees wait for visitors. Over to the right of the desk a group of armchairs still hold the attitude of respectful attention of those who last sat in them the afternoon before.

The Mayor looks up from the pile of various colored sheets, white, blue, green, pink, in front of him, pulls on his half-smoked cigar and starts dictating replies in a low quiet voice. The topics range from airport problems, and inquiries for missing persons, through buses, sewers, ferries, motor-driven sand spreaders, pet dogs threatened with rabies in the Bronx, to open air concerts. Now and then a serious-looking man comes in with an old-fashioned black ledger under his arm and opens it under the Mayor's nose to check on an appointment, or a young fellow, with pencils stuck in beside the point of the handerchief in his breast pocket, shows him clippings pasted on cardboard.

When there's someone on the phone he ought to speak to, a young woman secretary comes out and whispers in his ear. He trots out into the other room and is back in an instant at his dictating again. This secretary has black attentive eyes and moves silently around the big office with the vigilant air of a stage manager superintending the shifting of scenery between the acts. The people who work in the Mayor's office call him "Major."

At ten-thirty the stenographers slip out with their pads held against their chests. Several city officials have moved into the room and twisted the group of armchairs to the right of the Mayor's desk into fresh attitudes of consultation. Two small dark men have slid silently onto the settees in the back of the room. The Mayor starts reading a document in a rapid perfunctory voice. The words "statutory public hearing" stand out of the hurried ritual. It's something about changing the name of a street somewhere in Queens. In three minutes it's over. The little men in black vanish as silently as they came.

The period of conferences has begun. "What have you got?" the Mayor will ask sharply as the visitor settles in his seat. A greyhaired man can't seem to disentangle himself from the details of the problems surrounding an easement for a sewer. The Mayor's voice goes shrill as he cuts him off in the middle of a sentence. "All right. That ends that."

Two men and a woman chat about how the Borough Presidents are going to vote in the Board of Estimate. The Chief of Police reads a report. A redfaced man in uniform goes over the Fire Department's troubles in getting enough men to man the stations at the beaches where, he explains, every shack and doghouse has been taken for the summer. That means more fire hazard. A brisk young man is asking whether they shouldn't plant apple trees at the reform school. "Cooking apples mostly," says the Mayor, "but a few eating apples to keep the boys interested."

A young lady with glasses is talking about relief clients, caseloads, limited employability. The Mayor pushes the black hornrimmed spectacles up on his forehead and leans back in his chair to listen. "Nobody ever sees these people. Are you sure they are unemployable? Why I'm so worried is one morning we are going to wake up and be hit between the eyes. That's why I want to save every cent I can to be ready when the time comes."

When he talks he gestures with the hand that holds the cigar.

Often there's a coaxing whine in his voice as he ends a conversation. "We've got to go in with one eye open and know what we're doing." Or a sharply phrased question: "Is it on the level?" Admonishingly he shakes the square forefinger of a stubby hand. "Be alert on this, won't you please?"

Each time the group round the desk changes there lingers a mute overtone from the last conversation in the attitudes of the armchairs. As the morning goes on the feeling of pressure rises. The hands of the clock seem to move faster. Business has to be speeded up, decisions hastened. More and more items have to be squeezed in among other items. Secretaries and assistants run in and out. The Mayor looks down, pouting at papers laid down in front of him. He pulls off his glasses and chews on the earpieces. Wisps of black hair begin to shake down on his forehead.

At twelve o'clock the secretary brings him black coffee in a heavy white porcelain cup. The visitor gets a sandwich with his cup of coffee. A newspaper is laid on the Mayor's desk. A typewritten copy of a speech is handed him. His eyes run over it fast as he sips his coffee. "Sure, give it out."

All morning there's been talk about the leakage of city employees into war jobs. The Mayor's assistant comes in with an armful of lawbooks. He has been looking up authorities to see whether or not it's a crime for a man to use another man's social security card. Passing my chair he whispers, "I've been with five mayors. On all questions of law I was the authority. Now he knows more about it than I do."

As one o'clock approaches the pressure of conferences relaxes. The Mayor starts to dictate, in Italian, a letter of congratulations on the advance of the Fifth and Eighth armies. Until he gets going he occasionally stumbles over a word. The dark girl who is taking it down in shorthand occasionally corrects him over the form of a verb.

As he warms up he begins to talk fluently with very little accent. He gets to his feet and walks back and forth behind his chair as if he were addressing a meeting. Meanwhile the secretaries are fussing about a letter that's been lost in the files. Folders are hurried in and out. Documents rustle impatiently. A young man comes in with a Bible and reference book. The Mayor wants to look up something to use in the speech he is scheduled to make at a luncheon. The secretary starts a rambling explanation. "I don't want any explanations. Give me the passage, will you?"

"And this is a quiet day," whispers the assistant as he brushes past my chair. "You ought to see a busy day."

Five young soldiers in summer khaki are ushered in. "Well we didn't know whether you'd remember us or not," says the redheaded sergeant who leads the way. "Makes us feel better about government when a man like you can find time for guys like us."

The Mayor says sure he remembers that talk in Kodiak in Alaska. How are things out there anyway? Stationed down in North Carolina now they said. They had a couple of days leave and had come to take a look at New York. As they all lived west of the Mississippi they'd never been here before. Tomorrow they were going to Washington to sit in the gallery of Congress and hear the ifs, ands and buts in the G.I. Bill of Rights they'd heard so much about.

"Going overseas soon?" the Mayor asks. They shrug. "Well," says the Mayor cheerfully, "if there's one sight prettier in the whole world than steaming out of the port of New York it's steaming in again."

Suddenly it's time to go to the luncheon. The officer with the gold braid on his shoulder runs after the Mayor with his broadbrimmed hat and catches up half way down the steps. City Hall reporters crowd around asking if there's anything cooking.

Two women are standing by the steps of the City Hall. "Sure that's the Mayor. Everybody knows what he looks like," one of them shouts excitedly.

"I'm the only executive in the whole country," the Mayor says with some pride, as we squeeze into the single seated police car again, "who hasn't got a car of his own."

Driving uptown through crowded midday streets the Mayor is recognized on every corner. Men on trucks, people in cars, taxidrivers, groups at crossings waiting for the traffic lights smile and wave to him as he passes. They know him. He's their Mayor.

The luncheon is on Park Avenue. Sitting on gilt chairs amid

a profusion of potted palms and not a little encrustation of diamonds and real lace, women dressed for the afternoon and elderly men are listening to a rambling toastmaster who has become entangled in a long speech that never seems to end. When the little Mayor takes the microphone he brings a breath of city streets and tenements into the stuffy room. We mustn't forget the girls we are trying to help are real people like their own daughters, he tells them. He talks indulgently and understandingly about the need for romance these girls feel, about their craze for uniforms and for the young men who may not have very long to live. To help these girls we must look to the heart more than the head.

While they are still applauding, while the photographers' bulbs are still flashing, he is already making for the door.

Back at the office appointments have piled up. The other speakers at the luncheon took up so much time that the Mayor was late getting started. Now everybody's hard at work speeding up the schedule. A delegation from Harlem has been waiting, a colored clergyman, a lieutenant, several neatly dressed women, photographers. They are posed in a jiffy. Bulbs flash. The Mayor is photographed exchanging checks with the clergyman.

"To take care of the kids not handled by other organizations," he says. Handshaking.

Before they are out of the room he has settled down for a long talk with a nautical looking man about the employees of the city's ferries and sludgeboats. The Maritime Commission is luring them away to the Merchant Marine.

The assistant is standing by the desk smiling with his finger in a lawbook. "Major I've got a statute for you," he whispers as soon as there is a pause in the conversation.

The talk switches from the question of manpower to plans for a new ferry station on Staten Island. They are all on their feet studying the big maps of the five boroughs against the wall opposite the desk. It is all about the flow of traffic, tunnels after the war, appropriations.

Back at his desk, the Mayor plays with a gold pencil case frowning with pursed lips. "That's money in a different order of magnitude. . . Can't you do it in two or three bites. . . I'm a little timid. . . I'm a little scared of it."

There's less routine in the afternoon. Conferences are more conversational. There's time for general matters. There's talk about medical insurance, about the Board of Education, about a truck-drivers' strike; there's a long session about the budget.

"Gee Whiz, Thursday's the first of the month," the Mayor blurts out in the middle of it. Secretaries flutter around the desk. The black ledger reappears. "I've got to change my whole schedule. Tomorrow I'll do my thinking. Cancel everything from one o'clock down Monday and don't crowd me in the morning so I'll be all tired out. Call off everything else Monday so I can do that."

A man from the Department of Health sits in the front armchair talking about research, the need for an expert personnel director, the incidence of measles, the quarantine against rabies in the Bronx.

"Now about dogs. I think I'm going to make this clear Sunday. If your pooch is at large there's a chance that he'll get it. People don't understand the seriousness . . . they must not take risks. The effects of the Pasteur treatment are pretty bad aren't they? Fever, swelling, headache pain, even some deaths. I'm going to picture that."

At four-thirty he's signing his mail while the secretaries who have brought it in hang over his shoulders. He grumbles over the letters as he turns them over. "Are you sure they are feebleminded? Missing persons . . . after all there are a lot of people in New York. The police'll do the best they can. What's this? Where did you get those facts? I won't sign that one . . . Let me look at that. I think they are playing politics with that. It's just an outrage to play politics with that. . . Cheap bastards."

The man with the gold braid comes in to report that the Mayor's late for his appointment in Brooklyn. We go charging out, somebody breathless running after with the Mayor's broadbrimmed hat. He talks over his shoulder with the newspaper men as he runs down the steps. On the pavement outside we tangle with an elderly man with blank eyes with a suitcase under one arm and a paper parcel under the other arm who announces in a loud voice that he is waiting to remind the Mayor that he's promised that today he'd appoint him Commissioner of Bugs and Poisons Dropped From the Air.

"Tomorrow!" shouts the Mayor and ducks into the police car. "He's always there," he says, puffing and grinning. "Been going on for years. He's bats. He even followed me out to the World's Fair when we had the summer City Hall out there. He's a peddler. Seems to have enough sense to make his own living. He peddles socks and neckties in office buildings."

Outside the brick building newly converted into a firehouse on a back street in Brooklyn the firemen are all lined up. There's a band, a chorus, admirals from the nearby Navy Yard, a small crowd of neighbors standing across the street. Some small boys have got into the firehouse and are scampering around among the shining engines. The band strikes up. The chorus sings "God Bless America." There are some speeches. Bulbs flash for photographs. There's a double-quick inspection while the small boys duck in and out among the legs of the admirals and off we go, charging through Brooklyn in the police car, to a clubhouse where drinks and canapés are laid out to celebrate the occasion on a long table bordered with asparagus fern under the beaming glance of many a pink face traced with the landscape of Eire.

A couple of gulps and we are off again across the bridge to Manhattan. We stop for a quiet drink at the Engineer's Club. There in the empty bar we sit blinking at each other over our glasses. I'm supposed to ask him questions, but I find myself nonplussed by the sudden solitude.

We talk reminiscently for a moment about the Italian Front in the last war, about languages and music. He's fond of Wagner and operatic singing. I'm hoping he'll talk about himself, his early life, but it soon becomes obvious that he has no time to recall those things. He's alive only to the present, to the decision to be made, the speech to be delivered, the objection to be answered. He has taken the hurdles of today; already his mind is full of tomorrow's difficulties thronging toward him. There's no time for the past. A man paddling a canoe through the rapids can think only of the rocks ahead. The rush of business never lets up. Before we have started to talk our time has run out. He hands me a ticket to the concert that night, offers to drop me off at my door and we are off again, charging uptown in the white police car.

Walking out onto the floor of Madison Square Garden with its tiers and tiers of faces blurred blue under the reds and whites of the flags of the United Nations and the crisscrossing spotlights, through the hollow rumor of voices muffled by the hugeness of the hall, and the strains of the double symphony orchestra tuning up in front of the choir of children banked behind them waiting to sing Verdi's Hymn of the Nations, it strikes me that this is the culmination of the sort of life that Fiorello La Guardia probably dreamed of for himself. This was the world he had dreamed and made for himself when he was a child.

There he sat, a small man in a business suit, in his box beside his wife and a modestly dressed group of friends—no uniforms or white shirtfronts or ermine—just a medium New Yorker, conspicuous only, among the gaudy crowd in evening dress the Red Cross had filled the hall with, by that look of modesty, that look of being a modest New Yorker among millions of other modest New Yorkers. You wouldn't know where he was sitting if you came casually into the hall, and yet he was the skipper, very much so. He was the man who was running the show.

Applause beat about Toscanini's old white head as it rose above the ranked violins. He tapped with the white baton which the Mayor was going to auction off later for the benefit of the Red Cross. The Maestro's arms waved. The long strains of Lohengrin, immensely amplified by the augmented orchestra, filled the huge hall. The Mayor was quiet. His face was in repose. He was drinking in the music and the feeling of expectation in the crowd. This was his life as he liked it.

After the concert I met a newspaper friend in a bar across the street. He wanted to know what I'd been doing all day. "Well, did he jump down your throat?" he asked sarcastically.

"No. He was very pleasant. He didn't lose his temper once. He didn't blow up all day."

"I know what that means," my friend said laughing, "he's going to run again. He's going to run for a fourth term for Mayor."

Labor at the Grassroots

"As I was tellin' you," E. K. Bowers was saying, "I was a farm boy raised on Sand Mountain. Well I never knew nothin' about unions nor nothin' like that, but in July 1936 I'd gotten married. I was running a little crop on halves. There was nothin' to it but to come back to work down in Gadsden. . . My daddy told me I'd better not come down but times was bad and I was desperate."

E. K. Bowers was a longlimbed blackbrowed young man of the old black Scotch-Irish mountain stock. As he talked he stretched his legs out on two chairs. Then he tumbled off the chairs onto the bed.

"A feller can talk better if he gets hisself comfortable," he apologized in a smiling drawl.

"In them days you couldn't hardly get in the rubber plant unless somebody recommended you."

He lay flat on the bed and addressed his reminiscences to the ceiling. "There was a highway patrolman who was a friend of mine and when he carried me over there he said, 'First thing I want you to go in there and work. I know you'll do

From *The Prospect Before Us,* by Dos Passos (Boston: Houghton Mifflin Company, 1950).

that . . . but I want you to promise me you won't mess with no union.' At that time I didn't know what a union was. I made him that promise. It was the only way to get a job. That was the time the United Rubber Workers was just tryin' to get a start. They'd set up Local #12 with twenty or thirty guys. Well I went to work there but conditions was terrible. I hired out at 32 cents an hour. Every day or so they'd run somebody out of the plant. A big bunch of thugs would come down the aisle after him akickin' his ass as fast as his feet hit the ground. Well I just kep' my mouth shut. I was inspectin' tires then. We just had three or four days work a week and as soon as I finished I'd light out for home up on the mountain. There was a man I knowed right well got nearly beat to death. That was gettin' close to home. Then the man I rented rooms from joined the union. That was closer yet. Still I'd made that promise and I didn't join up. I was caught between a shit and a sweat. I got a big blackjack and kept it in my toolbag just for protection. In 1936 when Sherman Dalrymple—he was president of the international union they organized in Akron—came down he tried to address a meetin' and they beat him nearly to death."

E. K. Bowers raised himself on one elbow. "The law didn't do a thing to help him. He had to drive clear to Birmingham before he could get any medical help. Well they beat the union down."

E. K. Bowers got to his feet and began to stride with uneven steps up and down the room. "It went plumb out of the picture in 1938. . . They layed off any man had anythin' to do with the union. Well in 1941 the Rubber Workers tried again. They beat that organizer nearly to death. The town was just flooded with people. The company thugs raided the union office and threw the typewriter out of the window. I stayed out of the way. In 1943 the Rubber Workers sent in another organizer. By that time I'd been through a whole lot. Every time a man seemed to be makin' too much money they lowered the piecework rates. They'd fire a man for being late twice. It was bondage, that's what it was."

He let himself drop into a chair. "I decided we needed somethin'. The steel union was already organized so when I heard there was an organizer for the rubber workers in town I went in to see him right here in this hotel. 'Boys,' I said when I come in the room, 'I'm not sure I want to join the union but I want to talk about it. . .' Well there was twenty-three on my night shift and next morning I had seventeen signed up. I carried them cards in next day."

He banged his fist on the bureau. Then he unlimbered his long legs and got to his feet. "Those organizers just about went crazy. Now it only takes eighteen members to form a local. They brought back the original charter and you'll see it on the wall. I was one of the charter members of the restored local. An election was held in 1943 under the War Labor Board and we won three to one."

E. K. Bowers folded his arms and leaned against the bureau staring at me out of narrow black eyes. His mouth broadened out in a slow triumphant grin. ". . . Well I better show you around town." He yawned. "I was up half the night," he said to explain his yawn, "trying' to ketch some little pigs."

We went down in the elevator and climbed into his light gray Nash. "They froze wages the next day," he went on. "Everything we got was through the War Labor Board. Management and the union set up grievance committees to handle problems for the people. Meanwhile the company was expanding. They started building tractor tires down here. They brought in a sole and heel plant. . . The union was expandin' too. The Rubber Workers had an educational program. They sent me up to the Highlander Folk School for a four weeks term in labor relations. Then in '46 I went to the University of Wisconsin for a two weeks course. That was the year the local elected me president. I served till last May."

We were driving up the broad main street of Gadsden with its bus depot and its filling stations and its lunch rooms and glaring moving picture houses and its jimcrack clothing and furniture stores. Bowers pointed out the hall where Dalrymple was so badly manhandled when he tried to hold that meeting thirteen years ago.

Crossing the bridge over the slow green winding Coosa River we found ourselves abreast of a police car. The policeman raised his hand and looked our way and grinned. Bowers smiled back.

"Looks like there had been a change in people's attitude," I said.

"There's been a change all right. . . If we have a problem we call up the Chief of Police. If he has a problem he calls us up. We'll go around to see him later."

"What do you think caused it?" I asked him.

"I'm just a farm boy," he said and winked. "I wouldn't know. . . But there's been a change all right. Some people date it from the time we began askin' the mayor and local business and professional leaders to come to our union's anniversary banquets. They began to see that we didn't have horns and a tail. Then from nineteen forty-six on we began to take a real active interest in civic affairs, the Community Chest, and Red Cross drives and the like. The way we figured was that anythin' that was good for the community was good for us. . . We done our best to show 'em that we wanted to do our part and

I guess they figured that we were here to stay. . . We have a hundred percent union membership. Some of those very men that helped nearly kill Sherman Dalrymple go along with us now. Gadsden is a workin' people's town. They tell me one in every six inhabitants belongs to the C.I.O. but we get along fine with the A.F. of L. locals. We've never had a jurisdictional strike."

We were over in the industrial suburb of East Gadsden. We had been driving along a street of small new white houses in neatly trimmed lawns and shrubberies. "Mostly rubber workers here," E. K. Bowers was saying. "The plant's just a few blocks."

He drew up to the curb in front of a row of yellow brick stores. The local was in the corner store. An elderly man was sweeping cigarette butts and chewing gum papers off the cement floor. There were a few vending machines and a soft drink counter. The inner wall was plastered to the ceiling with posters advertising local merchants. One corner was full of piled up yellow chairs to be used at the meetings.

In the office we found a quietspoken slender man with glasses, named Thompson, the present president. Proudly he pointed to the framed union charter hanging on the wall. He said he had been in the plant from 1933 when the A. F. of L. had made its first efforts to organize rubber. There'd been a change all right. The worst time in his opinion had been between the passing of the Wagner Act and the Supreme Court decision. The hearings before the La Follette Committee had helped. The government had brought pressure on the rubber industry during the war. But the company didn't really call off its dogs till a cease and desist order was served on them by a federal court.

"A lot of them people was misled," said Bowers. "There's

been a complete reverse among the people of this community in about four years. . . Of course we've got eighteen hundred voters now. In the old days only two or three hundred took the trouble to vote. We put on a big campaign and got up a fund to pay back polltaxes so that the boys could vote."

A substantial-looking square built man with close cut light hair had come in the office. His name was Jim Huey. I asked him if he noticed any change in Gadsden. He smiled. "I surely can see it," he said, "because I've just come back after an absence of several years."

He'd first gone to work in the rubber plant for twenty-five cents an hour. He'd gotten interested in the union way back when the A. F. of L. was trying to organize rubber under the N.R.A. "Many a day I didn't know whether I'd go home to my wife and children or end up in the hospital. . . Finally I got laid off along with everybody else who had talked union. I went out of town and got jobs in construction work during the war. When I came back after we had a union and some sort of security I went up to the superintendent and asked him 'Do I look like an outlaw to you?' 'No,' he says. 'Well I'm the same man now as I was in 1936.'"

Had there been much change in the management of the plant?

No, company management was about the same, explained President Thompson, but policy seemed to have changed. There was a new labor relations man. In the old days what they told you was "if you don't like it there's a barefoot boy waiting at the gate to take your job." Now they behaved like reasonable men.

As we talked other men strolled into the office and added a phrase now and then: people in town looked up to Local #12 now instead of looking down on it. The working people had credit with the local merchants. In 1933 five percent of the rubber workers owned their own homes. Today certainly over half did. Wage rates down here were still under the national average for the industry. Had I heard about the sign some of our boys found in a carload of scrap rubber that came down from Akron? "We get 65 cents to load this stuff and you sons of bitches are only getting 35 cents to unload it." Well that wasn't so true any more but the gap hadn't been closed up. In Gadsden they averaged somewhere around twenty-five cents an hour less than in Akron but the takehome was about the same because here they worked eight hours and there they only worked six.

"The bankers and merchants and businessmen think somethin' of us now that we've got money to spend and the politicians talk sweet as sugar now that we're usin' our votes," said a tall young man in a red hunting cap who had just come in.

"We tried to show 'em that we were responsible citizens of the community," E. K. Bowers summed it up. "We cut out wildcat sitdowns. We showed the company that if they'd stick to their word we'd stick to ours. The company and our international union sign a master contract that's nationwide, and we put in some local amendments. If the foreman and the shopsteward can't settle a complaint it goes to the grievance committee. If the grievance committee can't settle it it goes to the arbitrator who is paid jointly by the international union and the company. So far nothin' has come up that the arbitrator couldn't settle."

Jim Huey drove us over to the plant that stretched in long oblongs of glass and concrete and brick under the sparkling winter sunlight. Four huge chimneys let out coils of black smoke into the blue sky of the Alabama foothills. When we went inside a hot sick spicy smell hit our nostrils. "That's the rubber smell," said Bowers. "You get used to that the first thing."

In the vestibule was a box marked "suggestions." Was there much interest in the suggestion program? I asked.

There was during the war, they answered, but now any good suggestion meant men laid off. Not much interest in that.

We walked through the plant; huge well lighted spaces threaded with overhead conveyors. Some carried strips of rubber on their way to the tirebuilders, or bulky half-built tires towards the ranks of hot moulds. On others the crisp finished product moved in a long slow line towards the inspectors. We stopped now and then to chat with some man E. K. Bowers knew particularly well. Each time I'd ask him to tell me how things had changed in the last ten years.

"It's a different place," said an elderly man who was trimming the little ends left on the finished tire when it came out of the mould. "It's not the wages. It's working conditions are so much better. Now the foreman treats you like a human being. Before he acted like a slave driver. I wouldn't go back to the way things was not for any amount of wages."

"I know what it used to be," said a youngish man trimming the edges of a black slab of rubber that was being pressed out by a shining steel roller, "because my Daddy told me. Things seem pretty good in Gadsden since I come back from the army. Wages aren't so bad. Town's growing all the time. I think things look pretty good."

We found a black smudged Banbury operator sitting on a truck eating a sandwich from between waxed paper. The Banburies, he explained, were the huge hot chopping machines where the rubber was melted and mixed. "There just ain't no comparison," he went on, his blue eyes flashing in his lean blackened face. "Before we had a union it was just simply hell. Now workin' in a rubber plant may not be heaven but it's all right. A man can feel some self respect."

In the tube department we found a burly popeyed colored man operating an electric truck. E. K. Bowers explained that the colored people and the women were all in the union. "It's nicer now," the colored man said, "we make better money. About a third of our people own their own homes. Before the union hardly any of 'em did."

"We haven't quite closed the gap in wages yet, but we hope to do it," E. K. Bowers explained in an apologetic tone. "Equal pay for equal work all down the line is what we're workin' towards."

"Yessir Mr. Bowers," said the colored man cheerfully.

On our way out we stopped in to say goodbye to the people in the labor relations office. "If you people will give me a job, I'll go to work inspectin' tires first thing Monday morning," said E. K. Bowers.

A company man looked up from his desk in surprise.

"Sure enough?" he asked. E. K. Bowers nodded.

"Well, I'll be damned."

As we left the plant he went on talking out the side of his mouth in a half apologetic tone. "I been away from home on different kinds of union business for the better part of a year. I've got to get back in the good graces of my wife and kids and I've got a farm to look after. Sure enough I'm goin' back to work."

He drove the Nash fast out a broad highway, crossed over red dirt roads through new developments and went back into town by another highway. Everywhere he pointed out the homes of rubber workers. Most of them were one story or story and a half houses, small but sparkling new. Some had gardens or a peach orchard or a couple of cultivated acres off which cotton had recently been picked. He told me some rubber workers owned filling stations or grocery stores.

About fifteen miles out we turned in beside some new fencing and drove up to a white newpainted house on a hill. We found a friend of his out on a freshly cleared sloping pasture. His son was helping him load freshly cut saplings onto a truck. He and E. K. Bowers kidded back and forth. This man hadn't been so strong for a union at first, it came out, but now he wouldn't go back to the way things had been, not for a million dollars. He worked on the midnight shift because that gave him some daylight to work on his farm. From where we stood he pointed out with the sweep of an extended arm how he was filling his gullies with brush, and his new fencing, and showed us the cattle he'd bought cropping the new green pasture and another field where he was feeding his neighbor's horses. He had only owned this place a few months. He had two hundred acres along the highway and up the wooded hills. It would take a pile of work to get that place productive and paid for.

As the man stood there beside us in his leather jacket with heavy work gloves on his hands with his legs apart bracing himself a little against the chill winter wind you could see in his eyes under bent brows the fields of alfalfa he was talking about for next year, the fattening calves, the new barns, the hog lot, the future full of hard independent work, and private personal satisfaction. "I guess I like farmin'," he wound up.

"Me too," said E. K. Bowers.

In the limousine driving into Akron in a cold drizzle from the airport on my way to visit the international office I met a tire salesman. "Lord what a dump," he was grumbling. "I have to come here once a year and I always dread it. The climate's terrible. There's nothing to do in the evening but go to hear hillbilly evangelists . . . The company does its best to make us happy while we're here, but I sure don't look forward to Akron."

I asked him where his home was.

"Florida," he answered proudly, "where the labor unions don't run everything and there's sunshine all the year."

I found the international office of the union—its full name is the United Rubber, Cork, Linoleum and Plastic Workers of America—in a small up-to-date building which the union owns and operates. I asked the men I met there the same question I asked in Gadsden: How are the Rubber Workers fitting in with community life?

"Well," answered the first man I met, "things sure have changed since the days of the great sit-down when we put out the longest picket-line in history in the zero cold. That was a real nasty fight with the community against us, but now we're in the City Council and the Community Chest, we're in about everything in this town except the Portage Country Club . . . We feel the Rubber Workers are part of Akron now."

I spent the afternoon talking to two young men from Buckmaster's brain trust. One was a scholarly skinny individual from the University of Chicago, who was Research Director. The other was built like a football player. He said he was only two years out of Harvard. He had no labor background at all. He had come out and found himself a job in a rubber shop and then had gone to work for the union because he wanted to learn what kind of a country he lived in. He said he was continuing his education.

When I told them I understood the Rubber Workers had no history, both men got belligerently to their feet. History hell. History had been popping all summer. Mr. Buckmaster had just come out of a knockdown and dragout political campaign. Mr. Buckmaster hated so to play politics he'd come near losing the International. The average labor leader spent as much time mending his political fences as any ward boss, but Mr. Buckmaster was the sort of man who believed if he did what he thought was right, the rank and file would understand and back him up. In the long run it had worked out that way but it sure had been nip and tuck. For a while the opposition had managed to unseat Mr. Buckmaster as president.

A radical faction—Communist-influenced supporters of Henry Wallace's Progressive Party—grouped round the president of the Goodrich local, had captured the executive board at the national convention the year before. They passed a resolution removing Buckmaster from the presidency. They came within an inch of taking over the leadership of the International. All the summer of 1949 was spent in desperate electioneering in the locals. Then at the September convention Buckmaster's supporters won a clean sweep. Since then they had been busy weeding out the Communists and near-Communists who had taken advantage of what was basically a political fight staged by ambitious personalities trying to get into positions of power. Communists were something Mr. Buckmaster was learning about. This time he learned the hard way.

The next day I met Mr. Buckmaster at his office. He turned out, as he'd been described, to be a tall quiet-spoken retiring man with glasses. His manner of talking was that of the principal of a good rural high school. He'd pause a long while before he'd venture an opinion. There was a certain amount of deadpan Hoosier humor in the way he put things. He was not a man given to generalizations. One of his favorite ways of turning off a question was to answer in a low slow tone, "I don't know enough about that to say."

He took me out to lunch, with some union officials, at the Portage Hotel, explaining that it was an old hangout of folks from the Rubber Workers' office. Although the coffee shop was crowded, the waitresses hovered solicitously about the long table we occupied in the middle of the room. It was obvious that they thought the world of Mr. Buckmaster and his friends. He was explaining that it was in this Portage Hotel that the convention was held that switched the Rubber Workers over into the newly formed C.I.O. He told how William Green sat there at a table with tears running down his face. He pointed out the circular seat in the apse-like depression at the end of the room where John L. Lewis used to plant himself when he came to Akron during the strenuous days of the sit-downs. Getting the rubber workers into the C.I.O. was one of John L.'s great victories.

Going down in the elevator, when I left the office, I asked an elderly man who had the burly look of a rubber worker whether Akron was a good place to live and raise a family. "It didn't used to be. Everybody thought they'd come here and make big money in the rubber shops and go along home. The companies used to threaten that if we brought in unions they'd move out and turn Akron into a ghost town, but now it looks to me as if workin' people get along better here than they do in most places."

As I walked along the main streets between the broad show windows of department stores, well stocked with goods that had quite a metropolitan air about them, I kept thinking of what the man had said; and particularly when I drove out through the residential districts where there seemed to be no dwellings worse than the big old frame houses with broad porches set on lawns along tree-lined streets which were considered a prerogative of the middle class a quarter of a century ago. These were nearly all houses of rubber workers. Nearly seventy per cent owned their own homes, I'd been told. There was an air of space and ease about them that expressed very patently the fact that the average hourly wage of their owners was a dollar seventy-three.

In one of these houses, on one of those suburban streets on the wooded edge of town, I sat in the parlor talking to a baldheaded man in his shirtsleeves. He worked as a tirebuilder in a rubber shop. When he apologized for the appearance of his house and yard, explaining that he'd been so tied up with community business recently that he'd let everything go to pieces, I couldn't help telling him that his house looked better than most of the places my friends lived in. He laughed and said he guessed he was persnickety. Maybe it was because his dad was a Scotchman. His dad had worked for thirty-five years at the Goodyear plant, as a foreman, and had never seen any need for a union. "If we could only get our people out to the meetings. Our local has thirteen thousand members and we consider it a good turnout if we can induce two hundred and fifty to come to a meeting . . . We should do more to sell the union to the rank and file and to the community at large . . ." He was almost tearful he was so earnest. "I put us down as a sales organization," he explained.

Suddenly he looked at me and grinned. "You've guessed it by this time. I'm a Republican in a Democratic town . . . but they let me live."

Next afternoon I sat in on a session of grievance committees at a mediumsized tire plant on the other side of town. At one end of a T-shaped table sat a slender young man who did time study work for the company and a big sallow Syrian with black brows and a mop of curly black hair who was assistant to the Labor Relations Director of the plant. He had a voice like the bull of Bashan. He had worked his way up to be an official of the union local and had been hired away to be a spokesman for the management, so it was explained when I was introduced to him.

At the other end of the table sat the negotiating chairman for the union, a tall bulky darkhaired Swede with a quiet judicial manner that would have done credit to the Supreme Court. Beside him sat a young fellow who was the union's time study man. Leaning back in their chairs against the opposite wall were several shop-stewards and the president of the local, whom they addressed as "Shorty."

The union men all wore their workclothes. It was a slate-gray afternoon of sleet and rain lashing against the windows. The steampipes hissed and rattled. There was a good deal of yawning.

The lights were on in the darkpanelled office. The discussion proceeded drowsily, enlivened by gusts of heavyhanded kidding. Most of the men were smoking and seemed to be enjoying the warmth and comfort of the conference room, and the feeling of sitting back and stretching out their legs on the company's time.

The cases under discussion nearly all involved seniority. There had been cutbacks in the labor force during the summer and now men were being rehired. As each man came back there had to be some reshuffling of jobs to conform with seniority rules. Other arguments were over pay rates on new machines and over how much work men ought to do who were back in the shops doing light work after accidents or illnesses. The union men brought up a couple of safety problems, a leaky steampipe, floor clearance in front of an elevator.

An argument was going on about some man who was getting slack in his work. "I'll bring my little boy in tomorrow," roared the company spokesman. "He can make that much money standing on one foot."

"What happened to this guy?" asked the Labor Relations Director, laughing.

"It's a new type machine," explained the union president.

"You can't run a farm and do a job in here at the same time," shouted the company spokesman.

"Last Tuesday we explained that what a man did outside didn't count," replied the union chairman in a tone of exaggerated patience.

They couldn't seem to decide this case so they went on to the next. This was a case of job selection by a man being rehired. The man wasn't satisfied with his rate.

"What do you want me to do, pay him six hours for an hour's work?"

"I'll tell you what's happened," said the Swede at the end of the table. "The job has changed since we put the rate in."

"All right," said the Labor Relations Director. "We'll check the rate."

"Now there's this fellow doing light work over in the tube room. He thinks he ought to be paid at his old rate before he got hurt. Now he's just getting the day work rate."

"He can make more money stayin' home," roared the company spokesman.

"But he wants to make a little money to buy crockery to sell for Christmas."

"Next thing he'll come over here with a tin cup."

Everybody burst out laughing.

"All right. All right, here's another. Let's get this one before anything else," said the president of the local in a pleading tone. He added ruefully, "We get a lot of hell from the people outside that isn't working."

This seniority business was as much of a headache for the union boys as it was for management, explained the Labor Relations Director as we settled down in his office again. It cost the company a lot of money every month changing men around, training them for new jobs. It was a headache but they had to live with it for the life of this particular agreement. The truth of the matter was that a lot of problems were coming up in labor-management relations that just couldn't be handled like a game of poker. Take pensions, for an example. That big Swede, the negotiating chairman, was as levelheaded and fair-minded a man as you'd hope to find. He wouldn't run for president but he did a grand job on the grievance committee. If only there were more like him. Some of the union officials were torn between their own good judgement and the fact that they had to bring home the bacon to their constituents. They forgot things weren't like wartime any more when the sky was the limit. Now competitors were cutting prices. Management had to keep down costs. Still he guessed it was better to have this grievance machinery if it worked a little raggedly, than to have no machinery at all. At least it helped build up a spirit of cooperation.

When the Syrian came back to the office I asked him if the

men didn't resent his switching to the management side of the fence.

"Well, they do and they don't," he said. "We've gotten to the point where we can kid about things and not get so mad at each other. To tell the truth in Akron there just ain't the bitterness there was."

An Unreconstructed
Jeffersonian

"Mr. Davis, what did you think of Eisenhower's election?"

Pushing eighty, John W. Davis is still at his desk. When he's not arguing a case, on working days you'll find him in the law office of his firm of Davis, Polk, Wardwell and Kiendl on Broad Street in New York. He sits in the middle of a large bare room at a rather small desk cluttered with papers piled on worn old blotterpads. Before he answers the question he starts to smile. He speaks slowly, with the faintest hint of a mountaineer drawl.

"As we used to say in West Virginia, I'm recuperated up."

His smile broadens as he pauses. He's a man who likes to think before he speaks.

"Suits me as well as any election I ever took part in."

The light that pours in off Broad Street through the tall open windows behind him fringes with silver his closeclipped white hair and throws his face into shadow. In spite of the wrinkles there is still a pink freshness about his complexion. His eyes are clear. They look out with a level steady gaze, a young man's eyes, except for a certain haunted thoughtfulness

New York Herald Tribune (1952).

that can only come from the experiences, sour and sweet, of a long long life. There is something leisurely, unemphatic, almost retiring about the way his body is poised in his chair as he sits at his desk. His voice, hardly rising above the hum of noises that drift in through the window, is full of quiet.

"I sat up till about one o'clock," he says, suddenly treating his visitor like an old friend. "It was sure, but Stevenson hadn't conceded. I was so excited I couldn't sleep when I went to bed . . . I just lay there thinking of one thing and another . . . It isn't the first time," he adds, "that the parties have changed sides. So far as you can read Eisenhower's speeches he's a good old-fashioned Democrat . . . I think I can call myself a Jeffersonian Democrat by inheritance as well as by conviction. In my opinion Jefferson remains the greatest political philosopher of all time."

"Even in your own rockribbed Democratic state of West Virginia the vote was close, wasn't it?"

He rummages on his desk for a newspaper. "According to the latest count Stevenson carried the state by a little less than thirty-five thousand . . . that's not quite complete. It's not a very large figure when you think of how industrialized we are."

"Do you ever go back to Clarksburg, Mr. Davis?"

Clarksburg is where he was born on April 13, 1873. He likes the idea of having the same birthday as Jefferson. The coincidence has always pleased him. There he first practiced law in his father's office. His father was described as a tall thin bearded man with a long threatening forefinger, and a perfervid Democrat.

"Clarksburg," John W. Davis says. The shadow seems to deepen on his face. He picks up his pipe. "When I do go back after so many years," his voice is almost a whisper, "I'm not fit company for man or beast . . . The streets are full of ghosts."

"The decision you won last June from the Supreme Court when they voided President Truman's seizure of the steel industry, that and the Eisenhower election, do you think they establish a trend against centralizing power in Washington?"

He smiles quietly: "One is always permitted to hope."

This Supreme Court decision, I am thinking, might prove the most important case John W. Davis ever won in his long career as constitutional lawyer. Historians might well find there the first real check on the expansion of presidential powers which began under Woodrow Wilson.

It was oddly fitting that he should be the man to make the argument before the Supreme Court which resulted in the Court's ruling against President Truman's seizure of the steel properties. It was John W. Davis, a young Democrat from West Virginia, whose work on the Judiciary Committee of the House caught Wilson's eye when he was looking for a Solicitor General. In a series of successful arguments before the Supreme Court of that day Davis helped establish as the law of the land the Federal Reserve Act, the Income Tax, Selective Service and other measures, which, whatever else they did, added greatly to the domain of the executive branch. If the steel decision turns out to have set an abiding limit to the President's powers, John W. Davis will, in his own lifetime, have rounded out an era in the constitutional development of the United States.

"I wish I'd seen you in action, Mr. Davis."

Smiling he spreads both hands out over the mound of letters, briefs, typewritten material which encumbers his desk. "I'm in action now," he says. In his tone there is a hint of apology for his cluttered desk. "I used to tell people I was just a country lawyer come to town. I guess it's still true."

Even at the time, some thirty years ago, when he first settled in New York to practice law with some of Grover Cleveland's old partners, the term "country lawyer" would have been a manner of speaking. He had already come a long way since he'd left his father's law office to take his seat in the House of Representatives in the first wave of the Democratic upsurge which was soon to elect Woodrow Wilson to the Presidency.

As Solicitor General he so impressed the Supreme Court by the pith and soundness of his arguments and the genial coolness of his mind that Chief Justice White went specially to the White House to suggest his name as a suitable appointment. Instead Woodrow Wilson sent Davis abroad on the commission for the exchange of prisoners with the Germans, and then, induced him, although he knew the expense would ruin him financially, to accept the post of Ambassador to London. So it was, as one of the leading figures of Wilson's retiring administration, blocked off from Washington by Harding's victory at the polls, that Davis resumed the practice of law in New York. All his life the lawyer was to prove stronger in him than the politician.

"I try to instill in the young men who come into my office," he is saying while his face fills with smiles, "the thought that there is more fun in practicing law than in anything else they can do. I try to make them feel it's a grand game to be in."

There's an almost boyish warmth about the way he speaks of the law. His father was a lawyer before him. The law is his profession and he's proud of it.

His attitude sets me to thinking: of course it's fashionable to disparage the law and lawyers in this country, but we have to remember that such liberties as the individual man has been able to preserve in an age unfriendly to freedom, have been maintained by lawyers spinning a framework of words, argument laid on argument, linking brief to brief and plea to plea, until the words tie into the old plain phrases of the Constitution.

A letter John W. Davis wrote to a supporter, at the time when his name was being considered as a possible Democratic candidate for the Presidency, expresses so well the faithful lawyer's attitude towards the law, that although it was written in 1924, the words still have a fresh sparkle. His correspondent had been suggesting that he would have a better chance if he cleared himself of the "taint" of Wall Street. First, answering facetiously, he quoted Mark Twain's crack that money had a double taint, "Taint mine and taint yours," but in a second letter he put down the essence of his code as a constitutional lawyer.

"You offer me a chance," he wrote, "to be the Democratic nominee for the Presidency, which carries with it in this year of grace more than a fair prospect of becoming President of the United States. In exchange I am to abandon forthwith and immediately a law practice which is both pleasant, and within modest bounds, profitable; to throw over honorable clients who offer me honest employment; and desert a group of professional colleagues who are able, upright and loyal. If this were all, I would think your figures pretty stiff, but you are really asking something still more.

"I have been at the bar nearly thirty years, and, with the exception of ten years spent in public life I have enjoyed during the whole of that time a practice of an extremely varied character.

"At no time have I confined my services to a single client and in consequence I have been called upon to serve a great many different kinds of men; some of them good, some of them indifferently good, and others over whose character we will drop the veil of charity. Indeed some of my clients—thanks perhaps to their failure to secure a better lawyer—have become the involuntary guests for fixed terms of the nation and the state. Since the law, however, is a profession and not a trade, I conceive it to be the duty of the lawyer, just as it is the duty of the priest or the surgeon, to serve those who call on him, unless indeed, there is some insuperable obstacle in the way.

"No one in this list of clients has ever controlled or even fancied he could control my personal or my political conscience. . . . I am vain enough to think that no one ever will. . . . What is life worth, after all, if one has no philosophy of his own to live it by? If one surrenders this to win an office, what will he live by after the office is won? Tell me that!"

Today, looking back over his very long life, he states again the essence of his code: "The law is a rule of conduct; the lawyer expounds the rules . . . Of course," he adds with a mischievous twinkle in his eye, "I don't tell my young men, because I don't want to discourage them, that with the present tax system they won't be able to put by enough to take care of their families and provide for their old age. An old age pension, that's a chilling prospect."

There is a long pause. He is looking across his desk with something very like resentment in his eyes. He rouses himself suddenly. "Why did you come to stir all these embers?"

"Mr. Davis, this is a time when we need divergent opinions."

"I speak," he says, selfpossessed and smiling again, "as a Democrat in exile . . . I am not willing to concede defeat yet. I mean defeat of the Jeffersonian principles. I still believe he was our greatest political philosopher. Either we have been dead wrong all the time or we are right now . . . The aim of government is to protect the freedom of action of the individual man. The urge of a man to better himself is what has dragged us forward through the centuries. I expect to go to my grave believing in pretty much what I started with . . . The lag between cause and effect in government is so slow that people don't connect them. They do not see the connection between policies and results so they are always looking for some new devil to whip . . . The mental contagion of statism gathers strength year by year. Perhaps the only way out is through . . . Government subsidies and contributions act like a narcotic. The more you give the more is demanded. What the final result on the patient is going to be no one can predict. I fear the fever will have to run its course."

"You never had it so good, is what they tell us."

"I used to say to my Republican friends, campaigning on the full dinner pail, that they would wake up one morning and find it empty. That was what happened in '32 . . . The voter has been debauched by handouts. He has been taught to rely on the government check and to take it as the donation of the party in power. It is permitted to hope that this can go on but I don't believe it. Two engines have been used in my lifetime by which any economy can be betrayed: the degradation of the currency and confiscatory taxation . . . Most of our government policies have been framed on the idea of what will get us by the next election, which is a poor way to run a railroad. I'm afraid there is a rough time ahead. One fine day there'll be nothing on the breakfast table."

Mr. Davis is smiling again. "I am reminded," he says, more in the tone of one of the afterdinner speeches he used to be so famous for, "of what Adam Smith told his class when somebody said a certain policy would surely bring the country's ruin. 'There's a lot of ruin in every country' . . . I believe the American people are still sound in the core. I don't despair of the country by any means."

"If half the world weren't organizing to destroy us."

"It breaks my heart to see this country militarized, although I know it has to be. When I was a boy I never saw a soldier. I was well along in manhood before I saw the U. S. army uniform. Listening to old men telling about the Civil War I used to think it was too bad I would never have those experiences. Now one can't help a certain nostalgia for those days of peace . . . We started in this country with an established body of principles. They were Jefferson's principles. One day I believe we will go back to them. The country isn't going to dissolve. We have an immense protection, which the British lack, in our written Constitution."

When John W. Davis says the word "Constitution" there is a vibration in his voice that sets the old plain phrases to echoing through your mind. "Of course the Constitution changes," he goes on, "and it should; but gradually, giving us time, perhaps, to understand what causes have produced what effects, and to be warned. The state governments are a protection. If someone dropped a bomb on Washington the state governments would go on . . . The real danger is that our political opposition will lose zeal. Men say to themselves what's the use? I can spend my life to better purpose. It is the lesson of all dictatorships."

Sometime back a young man in a gray suit has appeared in a door in the back of the room. There is business to transact. John W. Davis gets to his feet. Behind him on the wall between the windows hangs a small engraved portrait of Jefferson. He turns and points to it. There is something almost boyish in his tone and manner as he says: "There's my idol."

Labor at the Level
of the Leaders

"My name is James B. Carey. I have been Secretary of the Congress of Industrial Organizations for fourteen years and Secretary-Treasurer of the Congress of Industrial Organizations for nine years."

A slender young man in a neat blue business suit reads purringly off a mimeographed sheet from the witness' end of the long table in the senatorial committee room.

"Since 1950 I have been President of the International Union of Electrical, Radio and Machine Workers, C.I.O."

Under a comb of crinkly hair, he has stony dark eyes set above high cheekbones. His face narrows to a resolute knob at the end of the chin.

He pronounces his words carefully with full lips: "I have served and still serve on numerous official and semi-official government bodies, and I have travelled abroad on assignments dealing with international labor affairs and governmental programs."

His voice falls on the stale air of the hearing-room with the resentful intonations of a college student who knows he has his subject pat but feels he's up before a hostile panel of ex-

Written in 1952.

aminers. The scattering of newspapermen, lobbyists, labor lawyers, sightseers in the seats against the wall listen with respectful inattention. A light drowsy mechanical noise comes from the clerk's electric typewriter.

Senator Humphrey in the chair has a very bad cold. His head is all stopped up. He's preoccupied with his handkerchief but through his sniffles his manner is sympathetic. Occasionally he interrupts with a question.

Mr. Carey is saying that labor is opposed to any new legislation to deal with Communists in the unions. Let the unions clean house for themselves. As an illustration he sketches out the story of the war, in his own electrical products industry, between his anti-Communist union which has the blessing of the C.I.O. and the faction still run by the Party.

His voice rises to resonance when he accuses General Electric of favoring the Communists because since they are intent on politics and propaganda they make fewer demands in behalf of the rank and file. Favoring Communists in a sensitive industry amounts to collusion with traitors. His voice becomes tense with suppressed anger.

When the chairman asks him a question he lashes out suddenly "Yes Senator I would say there was a growing attitude in the ranks of labor that labor was being kicked around."

He ends his testimony by suggesting a procedure by which the Munitions Control Board should cancel government contracts with plants whose workers are proved to be under the thumb of a Communist union. When he finishes he clears his throat and rises stiffly to his feet. The Senator wheezily adjourns the hearing. An assistant helps James B. Carey stuff his documents into his briefcase. With a trace of a bantam strut he walks out of the room.

Back in his office, as President of the International Union of Electrical Workers in a building stuffed with C.I.O. agencies a little up Fifteenth Street from the Treasury, he pulls off his coat and settles back into the armchair behind his mahogany desk. He smiles a sudden Irish smile when his secretary, a pretty tall girl in a red dress, reads off the list of people waiting in the outer lobby. There's the representative of a presidential candidate, an economist, a Scandinavian trades union representative, a reporter, a couple of boys from the locals. "Of course," the secretary adds knowingly, "I told them you were detained on the Hill."

Meanwhile Al Hartnet, his Secretary-Treasurer, a longlegged young man in shirtsleeves and suspenders, strides in to continue an argument that's been going on for a long time: Jim's asking the Russian Embassy for a visa for the Soviet Union. If he decides to attend that Trades Union Congress in Berlin he has a plan to fly in to talk to some of his opposite numbers in the Russian Trades Unions. He claims they have influence with the Kremlin. Maybe he could get them to use it to help bring peace in Korea. Al Hartnet keeps shaking his head "No Jim no." James B. Carey finally leans back in his chair yawning. "And they say I surround myself with yesmen."

He picks out a cigar from a box of coronas on his desk. "They're real Havana," he says, defiantly. "A labor leader is supposed to smoke good cigars, isn't he? It's my only expensive habit. . . But no kidding you can get things out of those Russians if you hit 'em on the head with their own Marxist clubs. Who was it found out that when the Russians went to work to build themselves an airraid shelter at the embassy here in Washington, they looked all over town till they found a scab plumber. Have I razzed them about that? It's not easy to find a nonunion plumber in Washington. I won't let 'em forget it. I've been three times to the Soviet Union to talk to trade union officials. Kutznetzov and Tarasov and Madam Popover. . . I couldn't remember their names till I started calling them the mayhem brothers. Lord that had amused Mrs. Roosevelt when I told her about it coming home on the boat. . . No kidding this country needs workshirt diplomacy. The State Department people, now, they are highsouled gentlemen and polished lawyers but they aren't suited to the rough and tumble. I grew up as a labor leader fighting the Communists in the U.S."

Jim Carey's face glows with amusement as an idea strikes him: "American employers like U. S. Steel and General Electric, they've trained us labor leaders to negotiate the hard way. Believe you me, they are tougher than the Russians. . . We ought to give labor leaders a chance to negotiate. Who was it broke up the Communist celebration in Italy on May 1 in '48 but American labor? Harry Read and I—he's an old newspaper man who works for the C.I.O.—we jumped a plane, landed at the Rome airport just before day. The customs officers let us right through because Harry told 'em we were friends of Al Capone. We got the labor attaché of our embassy up out of bed and went around to see Di Vittorio. He's the powerhouse of the red trade union movement. We found him in the middle of a caucus planning a general strike. In those days it was nip and tuck whether the Communists would take Italy. I said let's join in the proceedings. I got up on the rostrum and addressed the meeting. When I didn't think the interpreter was interpreting right I gave him a shove and he went ass over teakettle over some folding chairs. That got a big laugh. When they tried to talk back I hit the gavel. I just talked plain English. Most of 'em had worked in America anyway. It was my line that if they wanted the Marshall Plan they'd have to take the whole of it. The Marshall Plan wasn't just a fruitcake they could pick the nuts out of. No more general strike."

The secretary stands over the desk frowning. "They are all still waiting," she says mock-severely.

Jim can't get off his subject. He raises his hand to quiet her. His eyes have a stony shine. His cheeks glow.

"Great balls of fire," he cries out. "If we really turned loose the revolutionary tradition we've got in this country we could make the Communists look like a lot of reactionary punks. Would we have fun?" He gets to laughing. "I'd like the popcorn concession."

"I'm going to start them in," the secretary says as she walks on her high heels out of the room. "I suppose you know you've got a luncheon appointment in twenty minutes."

The restaurant of the Lafayette Hotel on Sixteenth Street is frequented by labor officialdom. The portentous eyebrows of John L. Lewis himself occasionally bristle from a corner table. But today the place is crowded with fresh-faced boys and girls. Right away Jim Carey asks the waitress who they are.

"It's the graduating class of Southern Defiance High School from Ohio, Mr. Carey," says the hostess who hovers over the table.

"It's on one of those high school trips," Jim explains grinning, "that I first came to Washington."

At forty-one Jim Carey is still a very young man. Sitting there talking over his steak he doesn't look too much older than the boys and girls who keep up a subdued racket at the tables round about. His complexion is as fresh as theirs. His eyes are as eager. He's talking about something that interests him very much. He's telling about one of the most skyrocket careers in the American labor movement, his own.

"I came out of a radical Catholic atmosphere. My old man

was all for the Irish Republican Army. It wasn't until I was well up in the labor movement that I found he'd been a labor leader too. He was driving me in to Philadelphia from Glassboro. . . That's where I graduated from high school. I was fourth of a family of eleven but the first one to graduate. . . I was catching the train to Chicago for an A. F. of L. convention and on the way to the station I suggested he come up to meet the boys at the local office."

"The secretary looked up at my father and said, 'Carey, where have you been all these years?' They tried to organize government employees back in 1915. He was paymaster at the Philadelphia Mint."

"Pretty early I decided I was going to be a labor leader. First I'd been planning to be an electrical engineer and study at Drexel Institute. I was born in Philadelphia but my father moved the family out to a farm in New Jersey while I was still in parochial school. When I got a job at Philco I went on studying nights. My mother used to get up to get me breakfast in time to catch the five-fifty morning train. It would be after midnight before I got home. Didn't get much sleep weekends either. Too fond of dancing. I still love to dance. Ought to have seen me dancing with the Russians. My wife and I go out dancing by ourselves sometimes. Well when I made up my mind I was going to be a labor leader I switched to the U. of P. to take courses on industrial management. I've met several fellow students sitting on management's side of the table. The funniest thing was when I'd made a name as a labor leader one of the professors wrote to me to Washington asking me to speak. He couldn't make it out when I turned out to be the same Jim Carey that had sat in on his course. You see after we organized the Philco plant the boys sent me as a delegate to the first national convention in New York and I got elected president. I went right on working and studying nights. It wasn't till 1934 that I went fulltime on the A. F. of L. payroll. My first contact with the big league labor movement was at an A. F. of L. convention at the Willard Hotel. The delegates were all walking through a picketline into the fashionable Occidental Restaurant. I sure took the hides off them for that. out of the A. F. of L. into the C.I.O. ours was the third largest union in the country."

His old associates will tell you how hard he was hit when the Communists took over his union at the Camden convention in '41. Up to then it had all been easy. Labor was all white. Capital was all black. "Jim 'B for Boy' Carey" shouted the cheering delegates when he addressed a convention. When Jim Carey led the picket line the police took extra precautions. He was the fighting Irishman, trespassing, disturbing the peace, speaking without a permit. Twenty-seven convictions. A leader in the great New Deal drive to organize labor. Prospective heir apparent to Phil Murray. All this before he was thirty. The year the Communists captured U.E.'s half a million dues-paying members and left him a labor leader without any labor to lead the Jaycees voted him one of America's outstanding young men. The *Parents' Magazine* gave him its award for service to youth.

His home is in Washington. Besides being president of the anti-Communist electrical workers, he still has his niche as secretary-treasurer of the C.I.O. He's labor member on various government agencies. The New Deal created boards enough for everybody. Franklin Roosevelt could always find a job for a personable young labor leader, particularly if he had the prettiest little Irish wife you ever saw and two pretty darkeyed children with strawberry and cream complexions, who photographed beautifully. Mrs. Roosevelt asked them to the White House. They were written up in slickpaper magazines.

"People seemed surprised," he says scornfully, "that a labor leader should have a wife, and children and a dog, like everybody else. . . Suppose we go out to see the family. . ."

He drives a new dark blue two door sedan. The car has a good polish. The upholstery is carefully brushed. He lives on a pretty street in Silver Spring, just outside the District Line. In the spring sightseeing buses detour through that section to show off the flowering trees. It's a pretty house with picture windows, a green lawn in front and a view of a willowtree in a little valley out back.

Mrs. Carey is prettier than in her pictures, big dark eyes and lashes and a beautiful complexion. The little girl looks very much like her. No, they are explaining, she mustn't come home from school through that little path through the back lots. It isn't safe.

They call the dog. He's a well plucked Irish terrier. Jim mixes himself a gin and tonic. He tries to get the little girl to take a sip of the tonic water. "Too bitter, Daddy." She makes a face.

She brings out a pretty little chest neatly packed with costume dolls with clean faces and clean dresses. The boy James B. Jr. comes barging in. He has the pert tongue, the big dark eyes, the rosy Irish cheeks. He's going to be taller than his father. He attends the best Catholic schools, camp in summer. He teases his parents. He's planning to study law.

The little girl starts talking about ice cream. The boy promises he'll do his homework when they get home. The dog starts jumping up and down. They set out, youthful parents, bigeyed children, eager dog in their new two door sedan through the rosy gloaming over the smooth asphalt of the well-to-do residential streets, the typical American family of the automobile advertisements on their way to Howard Johnson's for some ice cream.

Science Under Siege

In the entrance hall to the office of the Director of the Institute for Advanced Studies at Princeton, housed out among green fields, away from the town and the university, in a modest red brick building in the standard neocolonial style of the academic groves, there hangs a hat. Round, brown, with a tucked-in crown, it is unmistakably a Harvard man's hat, but it has the look of having been worn in the open and gnawed by friendly dogs and sat on by children.

It is not a proud man's hat. There is something Franciscan about it; a wandering friar might have worn it in the middle ages. It is a hat that has seen history. It has sheltered the atomic secret.

The gray man who sits on guard at a small desk opposite the coatrack is unmistakably a plainclothesman from Washington. The minute a visitor sees the brown hat hanging on the coatrack he knows that Dr. Oppenheimer is in his office.

When Dr. Oppenheimer meets you at the door you are struck by the fact that there is little trace of Harvard in his accent. You know that he was brought up in New York, in that rather special New York that reflected so many of Europe's

New York Herald Tribune (1952).

best aspirations in the years before the twentieth century wars began, and which, since then, has furnished America with many good brains and much humane sensitivity; but there's little of the New Yorker in his manner. He speaks a clear, rather fastidious English without the accent of any group or region. His good manners are his own. There's a special private grace about his courtesy.

He's a lean man with large gray eyes and hair close-cropped over a rather slender skull, with a lean expressive face, more like the faces the Italian engravers of the Renaissance liked to engrave on their medallions, than the jowly countenances typical of presentday Americans. Could it be that the rigorous mental discipline of the physicist trains the muscles of the face into a different expression than the expression you find on the faces of even thoughtful people whose thinking follows a less exigent routine?

It is very quiet in Dr. Oppenheimer's office. There's a well polished conference table set about with taffy-colored chairs. From behind his ample desk a bank of windows lets in the cold light of a wide green lawn, with a few young willows set out on it, which stretches to a dense woodland beyond. The visitor glances apprehensively over his shoulder at the blackboards. No symbols or formulae on them today. Only a few incomprehensible syllables. The two little signs that hang from hooks beside them are set at *erase*.

"I'm not too happy about being interviewed," Dr. Oppenheimer is saying. "I feel that a little too much has been written about me."

"Personalities are a journalistic mania," his visitor admits. The physicist winces at the word "personality." He smiles to make sure he's not making his visitor uncomfortable. "When

I have something to say," he explains, "I like to write it down to make sure I'm saying what I intend."

The visitor blurts out some words about Jefferson. There is something reassuring about the entrance in the conversation of another leanfaced man of fastidious tastes, even if he has been dead for a hundred and thirty-six years. Dr. Oppenheimer gets up from the chair where he's been perching uneasily and walks into his outer office to find a quotation from a letter of Jefferson's which he used in a speech he recently delivered to some science students in Washington. He finds it immediately (his filing system must be perfect), and brings it back and sets it on the table. While the visitor reads he paces up and down the room. There's a peculiar weight to his flat rapid tread.

"It's that wonderful conviction," Dr. Oppenheimer says from across the table, when his visitor looks up, "the men of the Enlightenment held that there were no barriers to human knowledge." His voice is happier. "I still believe that. One realizes how imperfect and conditional the application of reason is"—he's speaking very firmly now—"but one doesn't despair of it for all that."

"I'm finding it hard," the visitor says, "to make Jefferson's terms ring true . . . in relation to today. Liberty, democracy did not need to be explained to the men of Jefferson's generation. The shape of society is so different now."

"Sometimes you do feel something spurious in the words," the physicist screws his face up, "even as you say them. For our time they lack the necessary exactness. To the men of Jefferson's generation they applied exactly to the facts they handled daily in a country of small and large self-sufficient estates, an agrarian society where trade and manufacturing was certainly important, but where it was the farm that moulded people's lives."

"Maybe," the visitor is stammering as he gropes for the thought, "if we could find ways . . . to apply the vocabulary of freedom . . . to our particular type of community."

The word "community" has struck an answering note in the physicist's mind. His eyes brighten.

"To live through the life of that community at Los Alamos," he says, suddenly seriously interested, "was an extraordinary experience. No one has really described it. We were physicians, chemists, mathematicians, engineers, none of us had the historian's or the novelist's equipment. There was a community of aim and effort that's very hard to explain. The work went on in an atmosphere of intellectual cordiality. People took pleasure in fitting their minds into other people's minds. That's what made it a community. Of course there was the wartime pressure, and perhaps the setting had something to do with it, the aloofness of the desert . . . If only it had turned out differently."

"How much is atomic energy going to change the shape of our society?"

His face has darkened. We sit in silence. From the outer office the light casual clicking of a typewriter comes reassuringly.

"You mean peacetime applications?" he cries out briskly as if the question had brought his thoughts back from painful channels to something innocent and friendly, a baby's prattle breaking incongruously into a conversation about death. "Of course there are possibilities for its use on ships and to generate power in places where coal and oil are lacking, atomic plants. . . I'm hoping we'll have some money so that we can get our feet wet in the problem. The trouble is that the atom for war so outweighs the atom for peace. That's what I was thinking of. The destructive possibilities of our technology had already outrun any humane control. It is a very worrisome thing. It is highly ironic that science should come up with atomic energy at a time when it was the last thing in the world we needed."

It's as if a cloud had blacked out the bright autumn afternoon outside the windows. "I don't see that being scorched by an atomic explosion," his visitor says, in an effort to be cheerful, "is any worse than being torn to pieces by old fashioned high explosives in a thousand plane raid."

"For the individual there isn't much difference. . . But now so much destruction can be tossed around in a small package. If it weren't for atomic weapons the war of ideologies between Russia and the United States could go on without doing too much damage, comparatively speaking. It would be just too hard for our countries to get at each other." He pauses again. "I still believe in the beauty of science." He breaks off suddenly and adds with a sort of disarming schoolboy frankness, "I wish you weren't going to write an article . . . I wish we were just talking."

"Ideas have to be communicated somehow." The visitor is still groping for words.

"Would you like some tea?" It is the host rather than the physicist speaking. "We usually have tea about this time."

When he comes back from asking his secretary to order the tea Dr. Oppenheimer drops into the chair behind his desk and sits for a moment looking at the floor. "There are things I would like to communicate but I always feel there is something not quite apt about the vulgarization of science. The thing itself is never transmitted. In the colleges young people are only taught the history of science, that is unless they are going to take it up as a career and then by the time they arrive at science, they are scientists. The others learn the chronology but they are never shown science as it really is."

He gets to his feet and walks up and down the room with that flat heavy tread. He seems to be searching for an answer in the green carpet.

"I admit that we seem further from a synthesis every day." The visitor asks an irrelevant question about the new generation. The physicist's face brightens: you can guess that he enjoys his students. He's a man who is at home with people, who wants to listen to what others have to say.

"The young people who are coming to me now are more specialized than they used to be, more hemmed in by their specialties. They have less interests outside of their own fields. A man like Jefferson took all knowledge for his province. Of course now knowledge is too complex. But these young people are careful. Their private lives are careful. You know their preoccupation with housekeeping, early marriages, small children." He's back in his chair smiling broadly. "Some of the young mathematicians are still a little wild."

"There are things I should like to communicate," he repeats in a serious tone. "Between science and the world outside there is a shut door. One has reason to be disturbed about it. It's a very worrisome thing. People know more about science than they ever did, but the beauty and the discipline of it doesn't reach them. Science is activity, a becoming rather than a body of doctrine. The scientific process demands qualities of optimism, tolerance, of selfless curiosity that society needs for the preservation of its future. Let me put it in ridiculously oversimplified terms: there's a point in anybody's train of reasoning when he looks back and says 'I didn't see this straight.' Men in other walks of life need the ability to say without shame, 'I was wrong about that.' Science is a method of having this happen all the time. You notice a conflict or some oddity about a number of things you've been thinking for a long time. It's the shock that may cause you to think another thought. That is the opposite of the worldly man's endless web of rationalization to vindicate an initial error. For the scientist the compensation is the marvelous revelation of a connection you had never suspected before and the perhaps only occasional reassurance, to use Jefferson's words, that there are no barriers to human knowledge."

Dr. Oppenheimer's pleasantfaced secretary is coming in solicitously with the teapot and cups and cookies on a tray. The tea does something to mitigate the constraint which the threat of publication has cast over the conversation.

The physicist turns out to be a man of very varied enthusiasms. It gives him pleasure to talk rapidly about music, about the transformation of the Soviet Union, and T. S. Eliot, and Whittaker Chambers. None of his random notions on any of these topics fall into the deadening stereotypes of the day.

Modern physics, I keep telling myself as I listen, is one of the really great peaks in the mountain range of human intelligence that stretches back into the past and forward, one can hope, into the future. To have reached that peak means a shaking off of the petty prejudices that stultify the minds of even many careful thinkers in other fields. But haven't some valuable convictions been lost in the process? Mountain peaks are solitary places, and perilous.

Dr. Oppenheimer is one of the really charming talkers. Much too soon the afternoon is over. It's time to go. The visitor leaves him on the terrace back of his comfortable professor's house, playing with his children in the glowing fall gloaming. His wife sits beside him. They are all smiling.

The heavyset young man who drives me to the station along a road that follows a stagnant old green canal under trees dark with spent summer foliage, is another plainclothesman from Washington. The physicist's peak is besieged. The secret of his peak is under guard.

American Modern

On the twentysecond floor of the United Nations Secretariat Building you find a broad tall ruddy man with closeclipped gray hair sprawled on two chairs in an office with somebody else's name on the door.

"Is this Mr. Harrison?"

He admits it. "I haven't got an office, never had one over here," he mumbles apologetically as he gets to his feet. Immediately you are up against the New Englander's knack for the deprecating statement. Wallace Harrison is a reluctant talker, particularly about himself. He lets his remarks drop like cigarette butts: it's up to the listener to pick them up.

It's not for nothing he was born in Worcester, Massachusetts. He's been around a great deal, but with the oldfashioned New Englander's home-bred assurance he has preferred not to take on the cosmopolitan lustre. He encourages a story that he never got his high school diploma, went to work in a carpentershop instead. Anyway he got himself in some capacity, as officeboy he implies, into the architectural offices of McKim Mead and White before the first world war. Purely by accident, he says.

New York Herald Tribune (1952).

When the fighting began after Pearl Harbor it turned out that he'd been studying navigation along with his other night courses at Columbia, so he found himself a navy lieutenant commanding a subchaser in the Mediterranean. We can surmise that in the course of his travels he took in a good deal of the architecture he found round the shores of that ancient sea. On his accumulated navy pay he studied for a year at the Beaux Arts in Paris. By the time the World's Fair on Flushing Meadows opened he had taught architecture at Columbia and had acquired a reputation as a designer of public schools and an architectural firm of his own which furnished the trylon and perisphere for the World's Fair theme center.

Already interested in South America (he built a hotel in Caracas) he was put in charge of cultural relations on Nelson Rockefeller's committee towards the end of World War Two. He had worked with the group of architects who invented Radio City, so when the Rockefellers gave to the United Nations the eighteen acres of downtown New York needed for a projected world capital, he was the logical man to head up the drafting of plans for the buildings. At the age of fifty-seven, when the Assembly Hall opens to receive the delegates in October 1952, he will be completing the most important work of his career.

You won't learn much by asking him about it. He's not a man who likes to talk about his own achievements. Already anticipating questions he's introducing Jim Dawson, another bigboned New Englander, who is his coordinator of construction, and little Mike Harris, the assistant who had the harassing job of maintaining contact between the international committee of architects for the United Nations and the gang of draftsmen (from the offices of Harrison and Abramowitz, Wallace Harrison's firm) who sat up nights to draw out the projects on paper as fast as the consulting architects dreamed them up.

"How did you ever do it? How did you ever get a co-ordinated plan out of a room full of geniuses?"

We are walking down a cool gray corridor in the Secretariat which from the inside seems merely the typical new American office building. Through open doors we look past men and women at desks into a great blue and gray sky of voluted autumnal clouds over the gray tumult of the Brooklyn waterfront where unrelated shapes are piled discordantly as on a city dump.

We stop to wait for the elevator.

"I had always insisted that when the consultants were hopelessly split I should have the final decision," says Harrison quietly. You feel the full authority of his quiet voice. You feel the man who is accustomed to pushing through difficult projects. You feel the power behind the New Englander's knack for the deprecating statement.

"I had to use that power only once, on the question of the location of the conference rooms in relation to the Assembly Chamber. I don't know that I was right—what the hell? —but somebody had to decide."

The lounge in the Conference Building which lies flat beside the tiptoe Secretariat is brimmed with gray northern light pouring in through a huge tipped window. The Mercator world map on the end wall gives a feeling of space. Entertainingly constructed screenwork gives privacy to the scattered tables.

As we settle at a table near the bar, Wallace Harrison is saying: "The problem itself imposed one type of thinking on a variety of plans. Architecture is determined by human beings. It is shaped by what people need to do. Just so many people had to get in and out of the offices. There would be so many delegates sitting in the conference rooms. You count the steps to the elevators. A conference room, an assembly hall, it's a question of finding places for so many rear ends. This building's built like a layer cake, the delegates and the public move through alternate floors; that way they won't interfere with each other. How about lunch?"

The restaurant, with its outlook on the restless river—barges, tugs, an excursion boat passing—has a chic transatlantic air. "Doesn't matter what you eat," whispers Harrison while you study the menu. "It's none of it good."

"There was Le Corbusier; there were the Communists. How did you ever get them to work together?"

"Of course we had the experience of Rockefeller Center. We learned a good deal there about getting architects to work together."

The first problem was that Le Corbusier, one of the world's great inventors in architecture, was a man for whom other people's ideas did not exist. A ferocious puritan. There's still a lot of Calvin in the Swiss. With his pupils backing him up he tended to form a flying wedge. Nothing worse for a committee than a flying wedge.

Then there was an Australian, a Belgian, George Niemeyer, Le Corbusier's brilliant pupil from Brazil—("He turned out mighty cooperative in the end," put in Harrison) —there was a Canadian, a Chinese archaeologist who wanted all the buildings to run east and west because that was the way they had always set buildings in China, a Soviet engineer—("Bassov was good," says Harrison, "he was really interested in how many steps a man would have to take to get to the elevator")—an Englishman, and Julio Vilamajo from Uruguay, a talented stylist specially versed in modern Italian methods of construction. And the whole thing had to be strained through a corps of American draftsmen and specialists and adapted to the methods of steel construction in New York.

"Towards the end of it I was about ready to crack up," Harrison breaks in. "There were fifty-three plans suggested, many of them with several variants . . ." He pulls a deep breath. "We had modelers in the room who threw them into three dimensions right while we were discussing them. That was a help . . . Suppose we walk around."

We walk through the fine airy corridors that link the Secretariat to the three Council Chambers. Three different solutions of the same problem. The first, presented by the Norwegians, was given a rather archaistic treatment.

"There had to be some variety," Wallace Harrison is explaining soothingly. "This place represents a number of conflicting points of view, to put it mildly."

Right away you understand how it was that he was able to pull a masterplan out of that conflict of tastes, talents, ideologies, dogmatisms.

Next comes the trusteeship council, the gift of the Danes, a great cheerful room full of light unexpected shapes and colors.

The Swedes gave the Economic and Social Council, the work of Markelius, their representative on the Board of Design. It's a brilliant piece of virtuosity in the modern style. Waterpipes and airconditioning ducts, artfully painted, are used for decoration instead of a ceiling. There are battens made of a beautiful light wood fencing in the working space.

The lighting glows in a pale canopy over the horseshoe table.

The entire end wall is a window. From the dimness of the public gallery you look out on the East River, an endlessly moving mural. The steel uprights of the windowframe give composition to the industrial chaos of the buildings opposite, accented by tall chimneys, with the red Pepsi-Cola sign scrawled across like a signature under the everchanging seabeach clouds that hang over Long Island. A steamship crosses the foreground. You could sit there for hours looking. . .

"Now," Mike Harris whispers, "we are coming to his great job. The Assembly is Harrison's."

"When the consultants left," Wallace Harrison adds musingly, "all we had was a Music Hall."

We duck under a steel shutter to slip through a set of unwashed glass doors into a broad corridor full of men in white overalls laying down the big black and white squares of a terrazzo floor.

"You mustn't forget the men who do the work," Harrison is saying in his low unemphatic voice. "You can plan what you like but they are the fellows that execute it. A great building like this . . . Men get killed. The men who do the riveting . . . No I don't trust welding . . . No way of checking on it. The stresses and strains on a building like this . . . The architect is in for some surprises sometimes. But if you have a hundred and fifty rivets you have a hundred and fifty places to look if something goes wrong . . . It's the spirit of these men. I tried to walk across one of those beams once myself. I froze when I got to the end and couldn't get back. A horrible exhibition! . . . There's something particular about this job. There's something particular about the feeling among the men. I tried to walk across one of those beams once myself. over backwards to let us do things they wouldn't usually let you do. Marble cut by foreign labor. Imported panelling. That sort of thing. Appliances installed in unorthodox ways. Since we are on United Nations soil we were able to take some liberties with the building code. In an ordinary building they'd make you rip 'em out . . . And individuals keep coming around with suggestions to save the United Nations money. Who was that Swede who arranged to have the dumptrucks bring us dirt for free fill instead of carrying it across the river?"

"He was a Lett," says Jim Dawson grinning.

"Anyway they seem to take a personal interest in doing something for the United Nations."

We are standing in the tall strangely shaped north lobby of the assembly building, looking out through huge glass doors, across a stretch of rubble that's going to be a landscaped park, towards the East Side drives with their morning traffic and the river and the island full of hospitals and the ugliness of the Fifty-ninth Street Bridge. "The landscaped area," somebody says, "is exactly the size of the Place de la Concorde. Doesn't look it."

Nothing could be further from the Place de la Concorde, from the elegant dogmatism of the European Modern, with its obsessing memories of the permanence of the ancient styles, you think, as you look up through the grim cold light at the ramps and girderwork contrived to lead the steps of walking people by the easiest possible slope into the hall beyond. This is improvisation. This is American Modern.

You remember looking up at the gleaming blue glass flank of the Secretariat before you walked in and seeing the western sky and the incongruous buildings of midtown Manhattan mirrored in it. At the same time, looking east through the glass doors of the lobby, you could see two tugs and a carferry churning up the river against the rapid tide.

The original impulse for the Secretariat must have been Le Corbusier's, but what it reflects is New York.

Henry Stern Churchill called the building an upended filing case for human beings, but to me it seemed more extemporized, even less monumental than a filing case—a temporary glass shelter stretched on steel girders.

Here in the Assembly Building we have gone far beyond the millionaire complacency that mars Rockefeller Center. Here's an architecture which mirrors America's greatest strength, America's ability to change. Steel frameworks sheathed with glass are as removable as the tents of the bedouin. They are elaborate mechanical bubbles. If they don't work we can take them down.

This is experimental shelter for a society which hasn't yet found its shape. The techniques can pull them down faster than they put them up.

If the United Nations doesn't work we can take it apart and put it together again. Each experiment adds to the know-how. Next time we'll know better.

We are walking up one of the ramps in the lobby of the Assembly Building. "Here," Mike Harris is saying as he pats a circular expanse of concrete, "we are planning to install a Faucault Pendulum . . . you know a kind of perpetual motion contraption that shows the movement of the earth, like Galileo's lamp."

The striking thing about this architecture, you are thinking, is how the sights and shapes of the city outside, girderwork, flues, ventilators, are echoed in the decoration. All sorts of cumbersome, unexplained and erratic mechanical forms have been drawn into the interior and worked into a certain order.

It's not the accomplished order of the Parthenon, or even of the University of Virginia; perhaps it has not succeeded yet in being an order at all; but it's working towards an order. When we reach that order we'll have beauty again.

You think of a Roman theatre, not frosted with marble as they were in Roman times, but raw and massive with all the functional plan exposed, as the ruins are now.

Harrison must be thinking of the same thing.

"I had to have one theatrical moment," he says as we dip down into a narrow entrance passage. We come up with breathtaking suddenness in the middle of the floor of the auditorium.

The hall above us is immense, very nearly as large as Radio City Music Hall, but it doesn't look it. Men installing seats on the podium look almost their natural size. In Radio City everybody's a midget.

"How did you do it?"

"It has something to do with the slant of the walls," says Harrison in his offhand way. Gilded wooden battens, that are there for their acoustic properties, slant in, at about the angle of the walls of an Indian tepee, towards an odd little dome overhead with an eye in it like the Pantheon used to have. The dome tips a little forward with a reminiscence of the domes the great telescopes are housed in. You think of a planetarium. Above the speaker's stand, masking the loudspeakers, a United Nations emblem is about to be installed between rows of round gilt buttons that will sport the shields of the various nations.

"I'd hoped to put something ornate there like a Mexican

retablo," says Harrison regretfully, "but we didn't have money enough."

The chairs at the delegates' desks will be white. The rest of the seats are pale blue, matching the colors of one of Fernand Léger's big designs that squirm vigorously on each of the side walls. Léger sent two designs from Paris and a pupil blew them up to the required size and painted them on. It's hard to see how decoration other than Léger's summary rhythms in black and white and red and blue and buff could accord with the uncompromising outlines of lighting fixtures, with the pipes and ducts of the mechanism of the building exposed upon the walls. Sitting in one new blue seat your eye glances along the strips of curved glass enclosing two tiers of cubicles round the apse-like wall over the podium. The walls behind are an opaque blue, so that the curved glass reflects the seats of the auditorium below, and workmen bending over their jobs, and chance staring visitors, in a sort of moving frieze.

"Here in the hall," Harrison is saying, "we'll just have the local audience. . . These cubicles for radio, television, the press, they are the eyes and ears of the great audience."

"What you've done here," says the visitor, "is to create a machine for making and recording speeches, a machine for listening comfortably in a crowd, a machine for broadcasting."

"We've tried to serve the needs of the people who are going to use the building," says Harrison gravely. "Anyway," he adds in his self-deprecating tone, "when the assembly meets, it will be ready."

We Give You... The Next President of the United States

President Eisenhower has invited some Russian observers to follow the presidential campaign of 1956. It is amusing to try to imagine what they'll make of it. Of course what they will report is already settled: the "new Soviet man" has no choice. He has to view the proceedings as an exhibition of the final contradictions of capitalist degradation.

But what will they really think, probably, to themselves? Suppose one of them is fuller of Tolstoy and Dostoyevski than he is of Marx and Lenin: what will he see? Perhaps he will go back to Moscow thoroughly confused. Confusion is as active a force in the world as conviction. Perhaps his confusion will be catching.

The trouble with airtight convictions is that they are so easily punctured. That's why the Communist dogmatists fear free thought the way the devil fears holy water. Take care Comrade X. The ceremony you are about to behold is full of dangerous confusions. Even after you have class angled it all away there will be something left you'll have trouble in explaining. That trouble in explaining you may carry home to your friends. Its contagion may prove as disastrous to the Mus-

National Review (1956).

covites as chicken pox to the Esquimeaux. The least danger you have to look forward to, Comrade X, is a ruined career.

I have to admit myself that although I've been exposed since childhood to the confusions of presidential campaigns every four years I still can't understand them. The results for one thing are so very paradoxical.

The first campaign in which I was heavily involved emotionally was Wilson's against Hughes in 1916. I was mad for Wilson the peacemaker. "He kept us out of war" was the slogan of the Wilson soapboxers. Needless to say Woodrow Wilson had hardly been sworn in on the Capitol steps before he was declaring war on Germany.

Now suppose Comrade X had been with me at the Liberal Party Convention on West 34th Street in New York one delightful summer evening early in the present campaign, what would he have seen?

The first glimpse of the street would have given him pleasure indeed. The street outside the hall was full of police on foot and horseback; naturally, cossacks to grind down the workers. But before our new Soviet man could have settled down to the pleasures of certainty—capitalist democracy is a fraud—he would have noticed that there were two kinds of workers being restrained on the sidewalk opposite to the entrance to the hall. One group of welldressed and wellfed young men and women were waving Stevenson placards while another group of equally welldressed and wellfed young men were angrily brandishing the initials "A.T.U." which formed the emblem of a dissident group of employees of the New York subways.

These young men were annoyed about something. They were booing and shouting and chanting derisive slogans. The Stevenson supporters were expostulating with them. "Can't you keep quiet? They are coming to speak on national and international issues."

"We're here to bull Wagner," the others would reply. It was not the ex-governor of Illinois who was about to arrive to receive the nomination of the Liberal Party they were mad at. Presumably it was not the Liberal Party. It was Mayor Wagner who had refused to recognize their union.

Now Mayor Wagner, as Comrade X would surely have known, was nourished from the cradle on his father's Wagner Act; by definition and inheritance he was the Friend of Labor. How confusing to a proper Marxist! This dissident group of the employees of the New York subways had managed to lash themselves up into such a frenzy that when the candidates of the great Democratic Party, their mouths full of national and international issues, arrived at the hall in a pair of funereal towncars behind an escort of roaring motorcycles, they booed them lustily.

Since Mayor Wagner was nowhere to be seen they even booed the busy little redfaced man with a large nose who stood beaming down on them from a platform outside the hall. Between the booing and chanting of the employees of the New York subways and the roaring of the police motorcycles it was impossible to hear a word Adlai Stevenson said. It was only when the tall mournful figure of Senator Kefauver appeared, staring down at the crowd through his plastic-rimmed glasses with the eyes of a lost dog, that there was comparative silence. He blurted out his customary assurance that he was for everything and everybody with some effect.

The booing of their candidates aroused the ire of the Stevenson and Kefauver supporters.

"Imagine how this will look in the papers," lamented one young man.

"They are all in the same pot," retorted a subway worker.

The first young man started spinning his right arm as if about to pitch a baseball. "Come on, let's walk over 'em."

At that point New York's finest tactfully intervened. With a good deal of skill and a minimum of jostling they introduced a wedge of wooden barricades between the picketers and their opponents.

Meanwhile inside the hall the elderly labor leaders and the social workers and the college professors and the pundits on the platform are settling back with a self-satisfied listening expression on their faces. After the confusion of the heckling and the ovation that greeted the arrival of their candidates, after the uproar and the handclapping and the acrobatics of the photographers and the teetering of the floodlights and the snaky uncoiling of the cables of the television cameras, they are settling back contentedly to play their part in the main business of the evening. Only the chairman shows a hangover from the first confusion by muffing the ritual cadence of his nominations. In fact he finds himself inexplicably nominating Estes Kefauver for United States Senator.

"That was unintentional," he apologetically groans.

Of course the audience sympathetically laughs off these little Freudian errors. They are all such nice people. Nice people on the platform. Nice people in the gallery. The audience is made up of just about the nicest people in New York, kind good plump jowly people, well-heeled but not rich, people who in their day have made sacrifices for worthy causes. Looking them over, by the way, it doesn't look as if they had suffered great losses by their liberalism. The good cause has triumphed. Many of them are incrusted in the bureaucracy of labor unions, colleges, foundations. Many of them have built up lucrative practices in the law, in publicity, in labor relauons. Even so some of them can remember the old days when the cops were beating them on the head with their nightsticks. It's a reminiscent audience; they first banded together as liberals a couple of decades ago to support the idealistic aspects of Franklin Roosevelt's New Deal. It has all come to pass. They have grown gray in the liberal faith. Here is a man who expresses for them its fulfillment. At the sight of Adlai Stevenson smiling from behind the microphone the whole audience purrs like a gigantic cat.

Adlai Stevenson is a nice man himself. He too is beaming with good intentions. When the former Governor of Illinois starts to speak he makes it up to them all for the confusions and heartburnings of the evening. Those rude picketers. He makes them laugh. This is the sort of audience he is really at home with. He treats them to a series of witticisms at the expense of the Republican administration. He couldn't be more amusing.

His delivery is crisp and unassuming. Instead of the greasy pomp of the run of the mill politician, he has humor, the self-deprecatory manner of the accomplished after-dinner speaker. The man is agreeably shy; he doesn't take himself too seriously. Through it all there emerges the serious intent. Under the sparkle of the after-dinner speech he has serious things to say he does not intend to leave unsaid. What he has to say is exactly what the members of the Liberal Party want to hear. It is just what they've been thinking all along. It's just what they have been thinking for the last twenty-five or thirty years. They listen to him enthralled.

Comrade X from Moscow, had he been present at the Liberal Party Convention, would have had a thoroughly enjoyable evening. If at the sight of America's industrial might doubts

167

had risen in his mind as to the inevitability of the worldwide dictatorship of his Communist Party they would have been quickly stilled. This was the way they talked in Russia before the Bolsheviks took power. He would have seen these nice people before in Budapest and in Poland and in Prague. He would have seen them pop like puffballs at the sight of an automatic pistol. But perhaps, in spite of his Marxist certainty that the professional liberals, detaching themselves from the capitalist class must inevitably pave the way for the coming of the Communist conquerors, he would still have had a question to ask. Why? Especially in America, why?

We most of us grew up with the idea that if the better element could only be induced to take an interest in politics the safety of the republic would be assured. No man has ever more adequately filled the specifications of that prayer than Adlai Ewing Stevenson.

He comes from a family that have represented the better element in middlewestern politics for three generations. The Stevensons filled somewhat the same sort of role in Bloomington, Illinois that the Taft family filled in Cincinnati. Young Adlai was brought up in a household crammed with the historic traditions of American statesmanship. The good traditions. During the absorbtive years of his childhood, the grandfather he was named for was still living, a stately blue-eyed old man, hearty enough to run for governor of Illinois at 73 and almost make it. Young Adlai and his sister regularly ate Sunday dinner with these grandparents. In the book Mrs. Ives compiled to help her brother in his presidential campaign of '52 she told of the long Presbyterian grace which preceded the meal and the long political yarns that followed it. The first Adlai Stevenson was a storyteller of the grand old school.

Enough of the flavor of these yarns remains in the political reminiscences he published towards the end of his life to make the book still readable. The long Sunday dinners were torture to the children, but in spite of the tightness of the Eton collar and the misery of sitting still, it is likely that the small boy stretched his ears wider than he knew.

The first Adlai Stevenson, a small planter's son, was born in Kentucky but moved to the black soil belt of Illinois before the Civil War. There he studied law and married the daughter of a college president and grew up with the booming countryside in the tradition of cornfed oratory and homespun storytelling of Abe Lincoln and Stephen A. Douglas and Robert Ingersoll. To the end of his life he loved to describe the Lincoln-Douglas debates on the Nebraska bill. One of his favorite stories was how when Bob Ingersoll went to Europe and saw the tapestries at Windsor Castle he likened them to the stained tablecloths in the dreadful old inn called the Traveller's Home where the young lawyers gathered during the terms of court at Metamora.

The first Adlai Stevenson never quite shook off his Kentucky background. He remained a Democrat. He campaigned for Douglas against Lincoln. With the ebbing of the Republican tide in 1874 he was elected to Congress, and became a leader of the low tariff soft-money party in Illinois. So much so that Grover Cleveland during his first term appointed him assistant postmaster general.

Adlai Stevenson I had made himself such a reputation for tact and genial manners that it was thought he could accomplish the ousting of the Republican postmasters with a minimum of recrimination. The Republicans dubbed him "the Headsman" for his pains and retaliated by blocking his appointment in the Senate, when Grover Cleveland tried to make him chief justice of the District of Columbia Supreme Court. Still, his labors earned him the esteem of deserving Democrats.

He headed the Illinois delegation to the Democratic Convention in 1892 and was himself nominated for the Vice-Presidency. Cleveland was a hardmoney man. It was inevitable that the second place on his ticket should go to a greenbacker. Vice-President Stevenson made himself so many friends among both parties in Washington while presiding over the Senate that when the Democrats were defeated in the next election, McKinley appointed him to a commission he sent to Europe to discuss the international adoption of a combined gold and silver standard with the finance ministers of the various European governments. In 1900 Adlai Stevenson I was nominated for the Vice-Presidency again and campaigned with William Jennings Bryan in his unsuccessful crusade against imperialism and the gold standard.

Grandmother Stevenson was a personage in her own right, one of America's first clubwomen. She helped found the Daughters of the American Revolution, which was intended by its founders to bring together women of gentle birth from the North and South with the aim of healing the rift left by Reconstruction. She also was busy in the formation of an organization of mothers to interest themselves in public schools which was the ancestor of the Parent-Teacher Associations.

The present Adlai's father, Lewis Green Stevenson, inherited the family's Democratic affiliations. He seems to have been an exuberant erratic sort of a man, a great faddist for health foods and dumbbells and fresh air and orange juice. He was a business man of very varied occupations. He managed a group of Illinois farms and an important mining property for old Mrs. Hearst. In 1900 he became assistant manager of William Randolph Hearst's *Los Angeles Examiner.* This was why his son was born in California instead of in the family mansion at Bloomington.

Young Adlai's mother was the granddaughter of Lincoln's great friend Jesse Fell. She too was very much of a personality, an intense slender woman with gray eyes and glossy black hair. There was an elegance about the way she carried herself that people never forgot. There was a strong Quaker streak in her upbringing. She shared her husband's health fads. She was terribly afraid of germs. She hated smoking. She coddled and dominated her children. Some felt she dominated them too exclusively. They were all Republicans on her side of the family. It was through her that Adlai inherited his financial interest in a Republican newspaper, *The Bloomington Pantograph.*

Adlai and his sister grew up in the center of a large welltodo, welleducated and affectionate family, surrounded by grandparents and greataunts and aunts and uncles and cousins in the twin Illinois towns of Bloomington and Normal. They all took it for granted that they were people of prominence in the world.

It was a delightful childhood. Always plenty of cousins to play with. The children went off on winter vacations with their Davis grandparents in Florida. July and August they spent in Charlevoix in northern Michigan where both sets of grandparents had summer places. Charlevoix in those days was one of those old fashioned resorts, frequented by the rich and fashionable to be sure, where a frontier simplicity was still the rule. Even the rich and fashionable had to keep up the pretense that they were just camping out in the north woods. Mrs. Stevenson was a nature lover. It was the heyday of Ernest Thompson Seton. All the children had to recite passages from *Hiawatha*.

When young Adlai was twelve he was a party to an unhappy accident. With a group of cousins he was practicing the manual at arms with a twentytwo rifle supposed to be unloaded. It happened to be in his hands when the gun went off killing one of the girl cousins instantly. It was only through the sympathetic solidarity of all the members of the bereaved family that the tragedy was kept from bearing down too hard on the boy. When a newspaper man asked him about it far along in his political career he was able to say quite truthfully that he had not thought about it in forty years.

In spite of the luxury and wealth of his upbringing Adlai Stevenson was never a man who found life very easy. His schooling was scrappy. His courses at the Normal High School were broken up by trips to Florida, by a trip abroad with his mother, by a move to Springfield when his father was appointed to fill an uncompleted term as the Illinois Secretary of State. He failed his college board exams and was sent to boarding school in Connecticut for two extra years. His studies were again interrupted by the first world war. At eighteen he enlisted in a naval training unit but he took his training at Princeton where he was planning to go to college anyway.

He was a pleasant young fellow, a slow worker but painstaking. He was generally liked. At Choate he managed the school paper. At Princeton he made the *Daily Princetonian*. His mother rented a house there one winter to make a home for her son. She played the college town hostess so agreeably that even that did not hurt him in the opinion of his classmates.

The family was so well off he did not have much stimulus to plunge into a career. He played with the idea of journalism, but went off to the Harvard Law School to please his father. He found the work there hard. He dropped out before finishing to take a job on the family newspaper. Then he went to Northwestern to take his degree. He was finding it harder to finish things than to begin them. Outings on the ranch out west, trips abroad interrupted his studies. When he finally did pass his law exam there was no question but that a young man of his prominence must be admitted to the most respectable law firm in Chicago.

Before knuckling down to the legal grind he rushed off for one last trip abroad. He had a notion it would be amusing to interview Chicherin. His father got him credentials from the Hearst papers and he made his way to Moscow. The foxy old Bolshevik foreign minister had no time for middlewestern journalists, no matter how prominent their families were in Illinois. After cooling his heels for a month in the Moscow Hotel, Stevenson drifted back to his lawfirm in Chicago. A couple of years later he married Helen Borden, a wealthy young lady of artistic tastes who was considered the catch of the season. From then on his home was in suburban Chicago.

The depression was taking the glamor off the business of moneymaking for a whole generation, particularly for those who had plenty of money to begin with. The solid old middlewestern fortunes of such families as the Stevensons and the Bordens were rooted too deeply to be much damaged by the stockmarket crash. A young man with all the money he could spend could see no sense in making more.

Newly married young Stevenson had hardly settled down to the routine of a law office when Franklin Roosevelt's election all at once made Washington the lodestar. For a Democrat and the son and grandson of a Democrat the attractions of New Deal Washington were irresistible. Roosevelt's fireside talks were filling young men, particularly wellheeled young men who felt they could afford it, with a desire for public service.

Everything had to be reorganized from Washington. The farmer was on his beam ends. Now Stevenson had been brought up amid his father's explanations of the management of farms. It was easy for a young lawyer who had stemmed originally from rural Illinois to think of himself as indispensable to the American farmer. In '33, during the famous hundred days, he found a job with George Peek who was administering the A.A.A. Rewriting the rules for American life was bloodheating work. It was all for the benefit of the common man. Hardly a man who underwent the first heady experience of telling the common man from Washington how to run his affairs (for his own good of course) ever got over the feeling that he was indispensable to the public business.

When Stevenson went back to Chicago he turned his attention to foreign affairs. Chicago was full of crackpots trying to tell the American people that the less they messed in foreign affairs the better. To combat the mistaken isolationists Adlai Stevenson began to make speeches. He became prominent in the Chicago Council for Foreign Relations. It was the style in those days to rail against isolationists. In their sacred horror of Hitler, the liberals were learning to tar with dirty names that stuck anyone who disagreed with them. Stevenson joined William Allen White's Committee to Win the War by Aid to the Allies. The liberals were bound they would stamp the isolationists out of the Middle West. There was no room for dissent in a country on the edge of war. When Roosevelt started building his twoparty cabinet where Dr. Win-the-War was to take precedence over Dr. New Deal he offered a post to a newspaperowner of liberal views who had been the Republican nominee for Vice-President in '36. When Frank Knox left *The Chicago Daily News* for the Navy Department in 1941 he took Adlai Stevenson along with him as his personal assistant.

Franklin Roosevelt had gone Woodrow Wilson one better. Having been re-elected for his third term in 1940 on a keep the peace platform, he so arranged things that the crazy Japanese attacked Pearl Harbor and pushed the nation into war willy nilly.

Washington hummed. The men who gathered in the nooks and crannies of the enormous war bureaucracy had the overwhelming imperative of a nation at war behind their conviction that it was their business to tell the common man what was best for him. The New Deal in its sprightly salad days had established a certain *esprit de corps* among the administrators. Roosevelt's war administration established a ruling mentality so profoundly selfrighteous that any critic became an untouchable.

The pleasant young man from Illinois held all the fashionable views. He made himself useful wherever he could. He played the airborne V.I.P. on a number of errands for the Navy Department. He was in on the portentous London conference that laid the framework for the United Nations. Hardly a man came out of wartime Washington whose ways of thinking were not profoundly influenced by that environment. The liberal tenets had become a dogma that a man questioned at his peril.

With the coming of peace there had returned to Chicago another man whose ways of thinking had been profoundly influenced by his war experience. Jacob M. Arvey did not belong to the better element. He had spent his life among men who fought their way to the top out of poolrooms and corner saloons, out of the slugging and gangwars and the crass buying and selling of precinct politics. These men had no inheritance of altruism and ease. They made their living the rough way. They had managed to make the public business their business and a very good business they had made of it. When Jacob Arvey came back from the theatres of war a colonel, he astonished his associates, so the story went round Chicago, by telling them that things had to change. Clean politics was good politics from now on.

Maybe he had been touched by the sight of the common man dying for his country. Maybe the blind patriotism of the Marines had gotten under his skin. Maybe he felt the common man deserved a better deal than he had been getting from the politicians.

Illinois politics stank. Colonel Arvey had to admit Cook County was a sink. He began to look around for representatives of the better element he could back in a general housecleaning. He found a University of Chicago professor who wanted to run for governor and the grandson of a Vice-President who was willing to be convinced he might do well in the Senate. The upshot was, so they say round the court house in Chicago, that Colonel Arvey ran Paul Douglas for the Senate and Adlai E. Stevenson for governor.

In spite of being father and mother of three fine boys Adlai Stevenson and his wife were not getting on. It seems hard for the very rich to stay married. Mrs. Stevenson had her own ideas of a career. Her husband's politics bored her. She liked poets and painters. She felt it was important for a woman in her position to patronize the arts. And besides she had become a convinced Republican.

When Stevenson decided to go back to Bloomington to start his campaign from the grass roots he had to call on his sister to open up the old family mansion for him. Bloomington, with a little prodding from devoted friends, greeted the candidate with a torchlight parade. People marched in old-time costumes. The ladies of the League of Women Voters pulled their grandmothers' dresses out of their attics. There were oxcarts and Model T Fords. They decorated a float with blownup photographs. "Three Generations of Stevensons." Such a crowd turned out to greet Bloomington's most distinguished citizen that Democratic leaders from all over the state were impressed. The colonel hadn't been crazy after all. Contributions began to come in for the campaign.

Wherever he spoke Adlai Stevenson played the newcomer in politics, the reluctant candidate, the earnest amateur. His speeches were said to be over the common man's head. To everybody's amazement he was elected by the largest plurality in the history of state elections.

There's still a certain amount of discussion in Illinois as to how good a governor Adlai Stevenson made. The state administration was an Augean stable. He seems to have done pretty well in cleaning up the welfare department which employed one third of all state employees and which had become an endowment fund for successful precinct captains. In other departments he seems to have had trouble in curbing the strongarm boys. There was the cigarette tax scandal; some ingenious officials were found to be printing counterfeit tax stamps which enabled them to sell standard brands of cigarettes startlingly cheap.

There was the horsemeat scandal: inspectors of the health department were conniving, for a price, with some enterprising butchers who had made the lucrative discovery that the common man couldn't tell whether he was eating horsemeat or cowmeat in his hamburgers. There was the case of Stevenson's labor director who was found to be involved in an insurance racket which was one of the Syndicate's sidelines on the West Side of Chicago.

There was the mysterious explosion in a "Model" mine at West Frankfort that killed a hundred and nineteen miners and made it painfully evident that somebody somewhere was failing to enforce the safety regulations. And on top of all that there was the public breakup of Stevenson's marriage.

In spite of his easy circumstances Adlai Stevenson had not led an easy life. He was a lonely man. If it were not for the public service he would be hard put to know what to do with himself. While he was in the Governor's Mansion at Springfield a reporter tried to interview him about his private life: he answered truthfully, "I haven't any."

He went ahead doggedly with his decision to run for another term as governor of Illinois. A conscientious man, he knew that it was his duty to finish the cleanup he had tried to begin. All his life he had been finding it hard to finish things once he began them. Now everybody he saw began telling him that the Democratic Party needed him as its candidate for the Presidency. To run for governor or to run for President. The decision was a tough one. In the end he let himself be talked into running against General Eisenhower for the Presidency.

When he arrived at the Governor's Mansion in Springfield after his nomination he was greeted by twentyfive thousand cheering people. His friends tell the story that late the same night, to escape the buzz and hum of politicians clustering around him, he slipped out of the back door of the Governor's Mansion and ducked through the hedge out onto the side street to Abraham Lincoln's old house. The astonished caretaker let him in and he sat for a while in the dark amid the old furniture of the front parlor. It was the only place he could find a little quiet. If the Railsplitter had any advice to give his words have not been reported.

In the 1952 campaign Adlai Stevenson was very much the candidate of the better element. He tried to avoid the rubber stamps of political controversy. He argued rationally and well for a great many things that a great many people already believed in. No more than his opponent did he betray any basic understanding of the conflicts and powers that had come to dominate the world in the racketty mid-twentieth century.

The liberals loved his speeches. Not to try to understand was first imperative of their dogma. The college professors supported him. Their students supported him, and the reporters and columnists and radio and television performers, and the laborleaders who know what's good for the working man, and the socialworkers and the foundation bureaucrats who know what's good for all of us, and such of the old time big cities where Democratic bosses could still dragoon the electorate. If you check on the popular vote, you'll see that Dwight Eisenhower didn't win by such a large marjority after all.

Towards the end of his campaign, when he was speaking in Pittsburgh, Stevenson received a painful reminder that he was still governor of Illinois. A riot broke out in the state prison at Chester. The rioters seized nine guards as hostages. He flew back from Pittsburgh in the middle of the night and helped his lieutenant governor draw up an ultimatum to be read to the rioters. After a few shots over their heads from the state police they capitulated without further violence. Governor Stevenson flew back to New York in time to address a rally at the Academy of Music in Brooklyn.

The men and women who saw him concede defeat at the Leland Hotel in Springfield came away full of admiration for his spirit. He remained the same smiling selfdeprecating political amateur. The nomination had been forced upon him. He had no regrets. He told Lincoln's story of the small boy who stubbed his toe and said it hurt too much to laugh, but that he was too old to cry. His sister Mrs. Ives, who wrote tenderly and well of him in the book she helped get up for his 1956 campaign, reported that the only time during the period she saw him near a breakdown was when he made his last address to the Illinois legislature. He seemed on the verge of tears. Could it be that he knew in his heart that he should have stuck to his post as governor?

Waiting, one beautiful October morning in 1956, for the Democratic candidate's plane to arrive at Newark Airport I began to wonder again what President Eisenhower's invited observers from Moscow would be saying among themselves about the campaign. Eisenhower would not be confusing to them: the Russians understand patriotic generals; they have several of their own. But, in spite of their huge literature of Communist polemics against socialists and liberals, Adlai Stevenson's position might confuse them for a while, until maybe one of them would suddenly remember his Marx.

"Meester Steevenson's case is classic." He would wave the didactic finger. "Marx himself predicted it. Certain members of the capitalist class abandon their class affiliations and identify themselves with the victorious proletariat."

"But tell me, Comrade X," I might have answered, "when you say "proletariat" in America, who do you mean? Do you mean all the rich and prosperous people who agree with Stevenson and the A.D.A.? Do you mean all the people who talk the liberal line? Three-quarters of the Democrats campaigning for office and at least two-thirds of the Republicans are running on the same stock of ideas."

Comrade X's answer would undoubtedly have been in Russian.

The plane is coming in for a landing slenderly shimmering under the low haze in the rosetinted early light. All planes are beautiful on a beautiful blue morning in early October; planes, gastanks, hangers, firetrucks, perambulators, even the cars embellished with political slogans waiting in line for the motorcade are beautiful in the mellow light. If I'd had Comrade X beside me I would probably have whispered in his ear: "You may be beating the pants off us in world affairs but you Muscovites never have October weather like this. Maybe that's why you are so anxious to get out of your own country and to take over the rest of the world."

At the sight of the plane coming in the welcoming delegations begin to chant "We want Adlai." It is certainly not a large crowd but it is a thoroughly mixed one. Local businessmen, realtors, a group of union officials, small town lawyers, clubwomen, a couple of serious looking Negroes of the professional class, pretty girls in blue top hats, an ample beaming Negro lady with an enormous bunch of orchids pinned to her coat. If there is a "proletarian" note it is struck by some hur-

riedly lettered placards: ENJOY YOUR DAY ADLAI . . .
JOE SMITH WANTS ADLAI. Quite a lot of small children
have tagged along and have been furnished with blue balloons.

When the gangway is pushed up to the open door of the
turboprop "Viscount" the photographers take over. After a
flock of unnewsworthy faces has been allowed to hurry down
the steps, the newsworthy profile of New Jersey's handsome
Democratic governor is seen mounting them. Beside his beaming tanned countenance with its mouthful of white teeth—
Governor Meyner is a handsome man with a knack for showing
his profile to the crowd—there appears the ruddy face and
large irregular beak of Adlai Stevenson. The erstwhile governor of Illinois is not a handsome man but something about
his looks attracts forbearance and sympathy; the girls all want
to mother him.

"He doesn't look too tired," one of the pretty girls in the
blue top hats whispers to another. "I wonder if he still has a
hole in his shoe. . . How can he stand it?" she sighs.

Well may she ask. The man's been campaigning since
August. Only two days ago he flew into Washington from
Minnesota.

The photographers can't get enough of the scene on the
aluminum steps. The candidate shakes hands with the governor.
The governor shakes hands with the candidate. Both of them
of course grin insistently from ear to ear. (If any American
politician ever stopped grinning all the TV sets would short-
circuit, the blended tones on all the two-tone cars would begin
to clash, everybody's shaving cream would turn to sand.)
Patiently and conscientiously as a pair of performing seals
Governors Stevenson and Meyner repeat their handshaking
act again and again in response to the barked orders of their
trainers. "Smile . . . Shake hands . . . Wave . . . Look this way.

No that way." The photographers shout as they scramble about the tops of the cars.

"What a hell of a way to make a livin'," one of them remarks out of the corner of his mouth to nobody in particular.

The motorcade is on the road. Led by a police car with a flashing red light, the cars decorated with blue and white slogans file off through the Jersey suburbs. To save their throats while we move through the hinterlands the governors huddle in a closed machine. Only the candidates for local office, and the wardheelers and committee members sit staring forlornly out of open convertibles at billboards, gas stations, lumberyards, nursing homes, pet hospitals, miles and miles of mowed lawns, shade trees, hydrangea bushes, moderate sized indentically comfortable dwelling houses. No cheering crowds on these green roadsides.

In the middle of the parade three chartered buses trundle along full of newspapermen in their eternal raincoats. Some of them have portable typewriters on their knees. Long strings of words on yellow flimsey continually trickle out of their bus and are duly disposed of at each stop by a plainclothes Western Union man identified by a yellow card he holds up on a stick over his head. Among the newspapermen on the press buses you can pick out the knitted brows of campaign assistants, speech writers, idea men; some of them are busy thinking up spontaneous witticisms in case the candidate's imagination should flag. The press and staff have been together for weeks now. They have come to share a sympathetic protective interest towards their candidate. Together they wince when he muffs a phrase, or forgets the name of a local politico, or leaves out the crucial sentence of a speech, or pulls his mouth too far away from the mike.

There are whistle stops in front of supermarkets, in empty parking lots, at intersections in small towns. The candidate has switched to a convertible. He blinks through the warm sunlight into the faces of the haphazard crowds which have been collected by the neighborhood wardheelers. Wherever he speaks he always seems to have the sun in his eyes. He praises his listeners for their youth—the Democrats are the party of youth—for the good weather—the implications are that the Democrats are responsible for that too. Certainly the midwestern drought is to be blamed on the Republicans. He makes his little speech in favor of the local Democratic candidates for the legislature, for sheriff, for freeholder.

Adlai Stevenson used to eschew rubber stamps but in this campaign he's using all the rubber stamps his advisers have furnished him with. He can't get himself to bear down on them very hard. He still winces at a platitude. He's a conscientious man. This is a chore he has set himself to perform as conscientiously as he can, speaking day after day, week after week, month after month. Today he keeps bringing out one crack that seems to amuse him. Speaking of his fine ruddy tan he tells his audience he didn't get it playing golf. He got it campaigning out in the open on the public platform.

Under the great trees of the public square in Morristown there's a more important stop. A platform has been erected right in front of Republican headquarters. About half this crowd is made up of high school kids, most of them with Ike buttons or posters. Either the teenagers really like Ike, or else someone has carried on a very fruitful campaign to make them think they do. To even things up there are handsome young women with Democratic parasols, a little girl in an Indian headdress leading a Democratic donkey, Democratic matrons marshalling a horde of small blonde children.

It's all very pleasant. Stevenson gets a cheerful hand when he points out that he's the first Democratic candidate to come to Morristown within the memory of man. The Republicans didn't need to and the Democrats didn't dare. He loses a little time explaining that he wishes he could stay longer but that he's behind schedule already and can only speak for five minutes. He tends to overdo the explaining.

In his five minutes he finds time to spread out his wares. The Republicans have fallen short on federal aid for schools. They have favored business against labor. The Republicans have fallen short on slum clearance and housing. The Republicans have fallen short on health insurance, social security for the aged. They have shortchanged the farmer. The Democrats will cure all these ills by pouring out more federal funds; not a word about whose pocket the money will come out of. They have fallen short on foreign policy. They have not worked effectively for peace. . . There he gets a hand.

(If Comrade X had been there he would have applauded too: nobody talks more about peace than the Communists.)

Then the candidate launches into a complaint. His manner becomes scolding and schoolteachery. You expect to see him wagging his finger. President Eisenhower in Cleveland has just referred to his criticism of administration policies as "wicked nonsense". . . Now Stevenson would be the first to admit that everybody talked a lot of nonsense in a presidential campaign —he gets a real laugh on that one—but calling it wicked is a blow below the belt. He'll have more to say about that later. Honest disagreement is freedom's red corpuscles.

The five minutes are up. With illconcealed relief the candidate settles back into his car. The motorcade moves on. The reporters scan their schedules for the name of the next whistle-stop.

Maybe it was wishful thinking on my part—"wishful thinking" has become the prime rubberstamp of this whole campaign; no speechwriter writes out a speech without accusing the opposition of "wishful thinking"—but it did seem to me that the common man after he had taken the trouble to turn out to listen to the speaking on that fine October day, deserved better than he got. Looking in people's faces it was hard to imagine that they all were so dumb as he candidate's advisers seemed to think they were.

Wouldn't they maybe have responded to something a little more to the point than all this shadowboxing? I know it's a presidential campaign. Anything but doubletalk is against the rules. Maybe it is because no candidate has the nerve to bring up any issue that a man can put his teeth into that they find themselves falling back so lamentably on petty recriminations. "Teacher, that big bully over there called me a dirty name."

Comrade X, had he been there, would have ribbed me unmercifully about our boasted two-party system. He could easily have pointed out that both the Republican and Democratic parties were so firmly entrenched in their common past errors—or in their common past successes for that matter—that there were no real differences between them to argue about. "You haven't any more got a two-party system than we have."

The motorcade's next stop is in front of the town hall at Paterson. There, with the sun still in his eyes, the candidate speaks from a platform jammed with local politicians. He remembers all their names and the offices they are running for. There is the biggest crowd yet. The streets of the industrial town are full of noontime bustle. Perhaps the historian among his advisors has reminded him that Alexander Hamilton had something to do with founding this city. Alexander Hamilton gets honorable mention. Certainly Stevenson's advisers have been prodding him to take issue with President Eisenhower's remark about "wicked nonsense." Talk back to the big bully. To call honest criticism "wicked nonsense" is an effort to stifle discussion. The President is taking the low road instead of the high road. He is as bad as his Vice-President who used such dirty words in the last campaign. Honest discussion is the life-blood of democracy.

Paterson has a large immigrant population; so the Mc-Carran Act comes in for a beating. The Democrats will see to it that their kinsmen overseas will be able to join them in the land of opportunity. There are union officials on the platform: the Taft-Hartley Act is denounced. The candidate ends up his address with a slogan which hardly sounds as if it came from his pen: "We'll take the government away from General Motors and give it back to Joe Smith."

A scant hour off for lunch and the motorcade is on the road again. More whistlestops, more intersections, more public squares. The campaign is an endurance test. How does the man stand it?

In mid-afternoon there is a formal thirty minute speech on the campus of one of those new G.I. Bill of Rights colleges, Fairleigh-Dickinson University on the Hackensack River. The candidate speaks from the portico of the gymnasium. At least he can speak without having the sun in his eyes. The boys and girls have stretched ropes on the lawn so that the campaigners can come and go without having to elbow their way through the throng. Tables and comfortable chairs have been set out for the press. This spot has been chosen for the launching of the day's balloon. The president of the institution wears a broad smile. The faculty and students are all very happy about it. A philanthropic businessman has endowed the university with a course in armaments control. Everybody's delighted that this is to be the context for the launching of Governor Stevenson's great balloon.

The candidate looks more at ease. He is happier addressing students than trying to talk down to the common man. After the Governor of New Jersey has sounded the academic note by some remarks about Plato's *Republic,* which some of us find it a little hard to follow, Governor Stevenson delivers himself of a speech which on the face of it sounds pretty reasonable. He is suggesting that it might be a good idea to call the Russian bluff on peace by offering to agree to postpone further hydrogen bomb tests. Our scientists would immediately know from their instruments if the Russians failed to fulfill their part of the agreement. Naturally this went over big with the students. Had I had a real Comrade X beside me I might have learned how it would go over with the Russians. The candidate has spent a happy half hour but he has neglected to explain how this pretty plan would restore the dislocated balance of power to the world.

And so it goes. The campaign is a Marathon. Nine speeches a day, five days a week. For a few minutes of sensible talk such as you might expect a man of some intellect to address to people who—however low the professionals of politics rate their IQ—can't all be halfwits; for a few sensible minutes we have hours of shadowboxing, of the painstaking demolishment of straw men, the ritual beating of dead dogs; in endless repetition the appeal to unenlightened self-interest. "He's got a firmer grip this time" the professionals in the press bus proudly tell you. "He has grown in stature."

The Democratic candidate is a conscientious man. He is dogged with determination to play his part well in this endurance contest. On the turnpike back to Newark he stops the motorcade on the side of the road for twenty minutes while he wrestles with a new paragraph he's writing into the speech he will deliver that night in Jersey City. Adlai Stevenson is one of the few politicians who writes even half of his speeches. Now he's planning to lambast President Eisenhower for his charge of "wicked nonsense." He wants to make it stick. The newspaper men have to file the new paragraph in time for the morning editions.

And so it will go on to the end. Speeches, addresses, remarks, wherever two or three are gathered together. Today it was New Jersey. Tomorrow it will be the hardcoal district of Pennsylvania, and the steel and iron belt, and then West Virginia, and then back to New York for a visit to Harlem and then New Haven and Providence, Rhode Island, and Springfield, Massachusetts, and out to the Coast. And Washington and the Mountain States on the way and Oregon and San Diego, California. If he is elected will there be anything left of him to inaugurate on January 20?

To try to let all the people see their candidates for President face to face is a noble aim, but doesn't it perhaps defeat itself? Perhaps the country has become too densely settled for the human endurance of the candidates. In the old days, before communications were perfected, a presidential candidate could go around repeating a few well-worn addresses the way a minister does his sermons, but no man has a large enough stock of ideas, even of the old stale shopworn ideas of the Liberal ritual, to furnish nine addresses a day. And the hundreds of thousands of hands to shake, the babies to coo at, the tots to pat on the head, the officeseekers to congratulate. It's too much for one poor candidate.

Perhaps we are wrong to complain that Adlai Stevenson is neglecting the real issues. Isn't this a presidential campaign?

Perhaps the real issues are too urgent and too frightening to be sifted down to their lowest common denominator by a busful of lowdowners trundling along in a motorcade. Campaign issues are only paper issues anyway. That's where Mr. Eisenhower's Russian observers may come a cropper. In spite of their conviction that the issues are all made in Wall Street they'll have to write them up in laborious dossiers to be filed away in Moscow. Nothing is ever forgotten that's filed away in Moscow. Maybe the Communist policymakers will rely on them. Meanwhile back home in the United States the campaign issues, Republican and Democrats, will be forgotten the morning after election. They lie in the same wastebasket with the tornup ticket stubs from this fall's World Series games.

Pundit

It's at the Metropolitan Club, back of Stephen Decatur's old brick mansion, just a block from Lafayette Square where Andrew Jackson, prancing above the flowerbeds on his bronze horse, perpetually takes off his hat to the White House, that official Washington likes to be seen eating lunch. At the Metropolitan Club, every day when he's in town, there arrives promptly at one a tall spare neatly dressed individual with dark hair and eyes and the restrained impatience of manner of a man whose every moment is very very valuable.

In his sixty-third year Walter Lippmann still looks the precocious young deep thinker of the days of the old *New York World* and the new *New Republic,* when, in the century's dawn the reading public of the United States, infatuated with the word "young" and the word "new," had come to believe that, if only the dull old vested interests would let them, all the problems of the universe could be solved by a bright young man with a fresh approach and a logical mind. Sufficiently to describe the brightness of Walter Lippmann, who was certainly the brightest, the best intentioned and the most self-righteous of these bright young men, the word PUNDIT had to be brought into the language.

Time (1952).

Today, in the dingy mid years of the century, he still arrives for lunch looking fresh and trim, ready to appraise in the light of reason and superior information today's problem which he will pick out of the maunderings of his luncheon guest, or from a chance remark dropped by a person of importance over a quick drink at the bar, or out of the confidence-laden air which insiders breathe.

Yesterday's problems have already been laid away. As soon as he awoke at the Englishstyle house across from the Episcopal Cathedral on Woodley Road, where he lives amid green lawns and shrubberies and the songs of well-fed urban birds in the admiration of a highly intelligent wife, two secretaries, a young lady researcher and a pair of French poodles, he propped himself up in bed to digest the daily papers. Then, at his desk, in bathrobe and slippers, he polished off the morning's chore of writing, deploying today's opinions in his neatly tailored style, balanced and punctuated according to the principles of unity, coherence and emphasis, that the instructors used to din into the boys' heads in English A at Harvard College in the days when they still believed in syntax and grammar.

With the help of the research young lady who has an office on the third floor, he has checked and rechecked his facts. If it is the day for the column to go to the press he has recited the finely polished sentences, with every comma, semicolon and period, into a dictaphone, and his secretary is already typing them; and soon they will be teletyped by Western Union into the offices of *The Herald Tribune* on 41st Street in New York. Thence, after an editor has read them with reverent care, a messenger boy will carry a carbon copy to the syndicate which will syphon the column by airmail and telegraph into the most prominent papers in Bombay or Des Moines or Dallas or Detroit or Copenhagen or Halifax or Nashville, Tennessee. If a comma is misplaced or a paragraph mangled the editor will hear from Mr. Lippmann. In a hundred newspapers readers seeking the balm of certainty will find in Walter Lippmann's column the roughage of daily events reduced to marketable opinions easily assimilated and stamped with the stamp of authority.

It's not from these dim millions, dropping their nickels on newsstands, fishing the morning paper out from behind the milk bottles on the doorstep, craning at the folded page in subways and buses, that the columnist gets his response. There's fan mail of course, but it's not often of much interest: the public is not in a position to know. It's at the Metropolitan Club, from the retired administrator stepping out of a cab, or the head of a government agency pulling off his coat in the lobby, or the senator on his way up in the elevator to the bar that the columnist learns whether his words have hit a mark.

"Walter a crackerjack editorial" "One of your better columns, boy." "Very much to the point," or silence or a shaking head: "Not quite up to the old standard." "Smooth reasoning but I disagree."

A Washington column is part of the record of a conversation among very important personages. The eventual reader is a dim small figure far away.

It's at lunch that the very important personages of the second string are most easily seen. The top flighters eat off a tray in their offices. In the bare old dining room on the third floor of the Metropolitan Club, with its memories of Mark Hanna and the gold Democrats and grizzled moustaches and madeira wine and terrapin Maryland style, the unleisurely men of today take a few minutes' leisure to give each others' characters a light dusting off over a hurried meal of rye krisp and iceberg lettuce.

There are prominent faces at every table. A man speeds up the conversation with his luncheon partner to get a chance to exchange a word with someone more important who's just shoving past his chair. A columnist, of course has to hurry. A word from a very important person may net him a column.

Walter Lippmann has spent his life among very important people. He was fortunate in his beginnings. His parents belonged to that highly literate wave of immigration that brought a hundred years ago the civilization of the Rhineland to America, Beethoven and Brahms, a respect for learning and a tenderness towards the unfortunate. In the reformed congregations such as Temple Emmanuel much of the asperity of ancient Jewish life had been refined away.

These people managed to keep a little of the best of both worlds, the sense of freedom and the excitement of money to be made in brownstone New York, and the summer trips abroad to the bricabrac and band concerts and the nostalgic scenery of the tourists' Europe of before the wars.

The Lippmanns were in easy circumstances. Walter was an only son. A studious argumentative handsome boy of seventeen, he took up his abode at Weld Hall in the Harvard Yard and proceeded to make a name for himself. Being of Jewish origin cut him off from a few debutante dances and from a great deal of unnecessary drinking at Gold Coast clubs but from very little else. Certainly it gave him more time to explore the world of thought and of aspiration for the improvement of mankind that centered around Cambridge, where the do-good tradition of the Unitarian churches had not yet quite crumbled into sterile aestheticism.

It was Harvard College's most vivid moment. Eliot was president. William James was still teaching. Fellow students of the famous class of 1910 became in later life the poet T. S.

Eliot, the emotional journalist Heywood Broun, the romantic revolutionist Jack Reed, the inventive scene designer Robert Edmund Jones. Right and wrong were very clear to these young men. The crusading spirit of Bull Moose was abroad in the land. They were all going to make their mark in the world by casting down evil from its lofty seat. A friend introduced young Lippmann to a reforming club as the future President of the United States.

His career was brilliant. Scholarships. Phi Beta Kappa. He hurried through college in three years and returned for a fourth as assistant in Santayana's fashionable philosophy course. Lincoln Steffens sought him out to help him muckrake the politicians in *Everybody's Magazine*. After a turn as a socialist reformer in Schenectady he retired to the Maine woods to write *Preface to Politics*. T. R. wrote an admiring review.

When Herbert Croly founded the *New Republic* it was inevitable that Walter Lippmann should be invited to become an editor. When Woodrow Wilson swung the New Freedom to the defense of the British Empire he was one of the first of so many swarms of bright young men to swarm round the White House. He worked on the Fourteen Points, he was an aide to Colonel House, an officer in Army Intelligence.

Disillusioned with the Peace Treaty he resigned from government service and went back to the plain living and high thinking of liberal journalism. During the great days of *The New York World* he handled the editorial page. When the Pulitzers sold the paper Walter Lippmann carried his crusader's banner over to *The Herald Tribune*.

With the Roosevelt Revolution Washington D.C. became the capital of the United States in fact as it was in name. A columnist who forms opinions must keep in touch with the circle of very important persons whose gyrations produce events. Only in the capital can he find the stamp of authority. Lippmann moved to Woodley Road.

From Woodley Road he sets out daily to the intelligent lunch, the enlightening interview at the Carleton, or the ancient Willard; only rarely he visits the Hill. Sometimes he garners a few words heavy with meaning over late afternoon drinks and canapés in a Georgetown back parlor. But mostly his contacts come to him.

Very important persons are pleased to be invited to dinner (black tie) with the Lippmanns on Woodley Road. When the guests step out of their cars the cathedral rises behind them hazy above the streetlights. A white-haired parlormaid of the type that would be found tending the canon in the green quiet of an English cathedral close opens the door.

In the long drawing room they find drinks, a very important person seated beside the fire, respectful black poodles tethered under the piano. It's a house full of discretion. At dinner it is on Mr. Lippmann's right that the very important person sits and the charming intellectual lady (with political connotations) who had just arrived from England on his left.

After dinner, according to the protocol of the Supreme Court justices, there has to be some legstretching. The ladies flow into the drawing room, the men find themselves in a small parlor with brandy in their hands in glass balloons. The less important guests, a frizzly-haired man from a government department, a muscular public relations expert, a random author, listen with discreet appreciation. The pundit gravely nods, occasionally emits in a word or two the voice of reason.

During the evening a change has come over the pundit's face. His eyebrows have bristled to little points at the corners, bags have appeared under the eyes, there's a touch of an actor playing Satan in evening dress or of the croupier at the roulette table at Monte Carlo: *faites vos jeux, messieurs, mesdames.* The ball starts rolling.

Everything is delightfully off the record. Among friends who are in a position to know and in whose discretion he can confide the very important person outlines succinctly a few things he would like the public to be informed of without having to broadcast them himself. He goes on to urge Mr. Lippmann to urge another very important person to take a certain course of action. It can't come from him. Spontaneously, you understand.

It's the diagram of the Washington social evening. A urges B to urge C to take the step that honor and patriotism demand. Of course it can't come from A directly.

The columnist's eyebrows bristle with portent. The very important person has finished his brandy. A round of Scotch fizzed up with a few general remarks and the wife of the very important person rises to her feet. It's time to go.

Once the very important person has gone there is nothing left to say. As if the house had caught fire the less important people are handed their wraps and breathlessly herded towards the door.

III. That Something
More than Common

The Changing Shape
of Institutions

Men have always found it hard to keep up with the changes in the shape of society which their own inventions bring about. In times of drastic technological change like our own, institutions evolve so rapidly that all the old frames of reference go by the board. New situations arise faster than the mental processes can keep up with them. To a certain extent we lose the power to tell good from evil.

Men who have lost the certainty of what is good and what is bad find themselves without any sextant to check their position by. When they set out to explore the society they live in they have no way of finding out whether the terrain from which they are making their observation has remained firm and stationary. The old illustration of the man driving his dogteam northward all day over a drifting icefloe only to find himself further south that night than when he started out in the morning becomes very much to the point.

The very words we need to describe what we see change their meanings. Slogans and phrases that yesterday pointed steadily toward the lodestar of good today spin waveringly

From *The Theme is Freedom,* by Dos Passos (New York: Dodd, Mead & Co., 1956).

round the compass and tomorrow may have taken on meanings opposite from the meaning they started with. A moral judg-ment will turn inside out on you overnight.

The mind cannot support moral chaos for long. Men are under as strong a compulsion to invent an ethical setting for their behavior as spiders are to weave themselves webs. New cosmogonies are continually being rebuilt out of the ruins of past systems. Somehow, like the degenerate last Romans, who had forgotten the art of turning columns and had to use the débris of old temples to build Christian basilicas with, we have to improvise at least enough of an edifice out of the fallen dogmas of the past to furnish a platform from which to re-build the society we live in.

The creation of a world view is the work of a generation rather than of an individual, but each of us, for better or for worse, must add his brick to the edifice. A generation can't go much further than the average of the achievements of the men who comprise it, but every outstanding effort affects that aver-age. Every one of us has to go as far forward as he can. The first step is to try to form for ourselves an accurate picture of the society we live in.

Start from your street or from the apartment house where you live; you'll find that most of the men and women you know make their living by working for some sort of a corporate organization. Whether these concerns lend money or sell bread or manufacture automobiles or publish newspapers or peddle humanitarian ideas their schemes of behavior are remarkably similar. The corporation with its board of directors, its chain of command, its hierarchy of power is such a routine feature of our daily lives that it hardly ever occurs to us that its pattern has become only very recently the dominant social pattern of the life of a large part of the human race. Up to a hundred years ago the family was still the social unit.

The corporation is the top part of the pyramid. The working people in the factory or office or store do their work under its orders. Wherever you find it the pattern is uniform. In the United States we call it capitalism. If you go over to England you'll find people behaving in much the same way but calling it socialism. In the Soviet Union and its satellite states you'll find a remarkably similar social structure going under the name of "dictatorship of the proletariat," or by the oddest reversal of the meaning of terms, "people's democracy." Other factors account for the greater wellbeing that results from the pattern in some countries than in others. The same plant will yield differently in different soils. You can be sure that if an eighteenth-century libertarian like Tom Paine were resurrected today he would find more similarities than differences in the three systems.

People have been pointing out for years that the government of the Soviet Union, leaving aside the police power—the power to kill is a very different thing from the power to fire—resembles more than anything else the government of a great American corporation. When you change from capitalism to socialism the corporations which administer industry or banks or railroads or chain laundries retain their structure. What happens is that under socialism the men who reach places of power tend to do so through their political rather than their financial influence. Both systems suffer from bureaucratic intrigue and internal politics. Only occasionally does a man find himself in a job through plain ability.

To a dispassionate observer the fascinating thing about the structure of life in the Soviet Union is that in their efforts to produce socialism the Communist dictators have produced a brutal approximation of monopoly capitalism. Their system has all the disadvantages of our own, without any of the alleviations which come to us through competition and through the division between economic and political power which has so far made it possible for the humane traditions of the western world to continue.

If you want to find out what is happening to a society the thing to study is the behavior of the people in it and not what they say about their behavior. But most of the writing and arguing about social systems is about ideologies and not about behavior. The processes of thought are constantly being confused by a basic lag in the recognition of events. Groups of words which were once fairly descriptive of a given situation will survive for generations, becoming more and more charged with righteous emotion as they become less and less descriptive of the situation involved.

Suppose that, having tried to forget political slogans and ideological camouflage, you spend an afternoon talking with the men who work in one of the great stratified industrial enterprises either in this country or in England. You'll notice two things. First you'll discover that the antithesis between capitalism and socialism is beside the point, that it doesn't affect the way in which the people who work the machines and sit at the directors' tables and run the teletypes and sweep out the offices actually behave. Secondly, you will be struck in either case, by the centralization of power and the isolation of the individual in his routine at an office desk, or in his job on the assembly line, or even at the more varied work of turret or lathe.

We mustn't forget that changing the name of an industrial system doesn't change the fact that the kind of man who has only learned to drive a tractor will go on driving a tractor and the kind of man who has only learned to sit at a desk and organize other men's work will go on doing it and the man who gets his pleasure from power to boss his fellow man will continue to find a way to boss his fellow man.

The knot which our society must untie is the problem of controlling the power over men's lives of these stratified corporations which, whether their top management calls itself capitalist or socialist, are so admirably adapted by the pull of centralization to despotic rule. Machinery must be invented to control the power of the administrators not only in the public interest but in the interest of each private individual man. In this country some of that machinery already exists.

An inseparable part of this problem is the problem of communication between the isolated units which are the cogs in our society. An isolated man is an ignorant man. He has no frame of reference by which to test the selfserving propaganda which is daily pumped into his ears by the political climbers who use corporations, labor unions, stratified organizations of any kind, as ladders to positions from which they may ride to glory on the backs of their fellows.

Even a hundred years ago most of the operations of agriculture and industry were within the reach of the average man's radius of information. A Connecticut farmer living outside of Stamford, say, knew how you kept store. He understood the business of buying and selling from personal experience on the marketplace. He knew how a bank worked: the banker kept a stack of goldpieces in a safe and lent them out to you at interest under proper security. A clipper ship was a complicated machine but he'd sailed a small sloop enough as a boy to understand what made it go through the water. Commerce was a matter of ships and buying and selling. The world outside was not too different from its microcosm in the farming community where he lived. Most of the events which occurred in it were comprehensible to a man of average intelligence. When the farmer went to town to listen to a politician tell him how to vote he could test the reliability of the orator's words against his own experience of practical life, against his fairly wide acquaintanceship with various types of men, farmers, mechanics, millers, merchants, the local judge and the doctor and the lawyer. For final arbiter he had his Bible, and the inner voice of traditional ethics.

Look at this man's grandson living in the same house. Like as not he works in an office and commutes into New York. He knows his family and his wife's family and a few neighbors and the men in the office of similar rank in the concern. When he was in school he used to know something about sports but now he watches sports on T.V. He understands his car and his lawnmower but he can't mend the washing machine when it gets out of order. Ask him what the place of money is in our economy or how powerful the executive is in our government. He can't tell you and you can't tell him. All you can do is treat each other to the views of some favorite columnist.

His friends are in the same boat. He hobnobs with a few other men of similar experience and outlook in some club or lodge, but apart from their observations, all he knows about the world is what he reads in the papers, hears over the radio or sees on T.V.

These agencies of selfserving propaganda from one group or another tease and inflame his mind with a succession of unrelated stimuli. These stimuli are rarely sustained enough to evoke the response of careful study and understanding, and the resulting satisfaction which is implicit in the word "understanding"; so in the end they leave the man frustrated. The mind of a frustrated man becomes a sink of fear, ignorance and hatred; his main response to the problems of community and national life, which demand cogitation and decision, is a stubborn apathy.

Apathy is one of the characteristic responses of any living organism when it is subjected to stimuli too intense or too complicated to cope with. The cure for apathy is comprehension. What happens when a problem has been made comprehensible is that it has been reduced to understandable component parts so that unfamiliar elements can be measured off by analogy against familiar elements which have already become usable terms in a man's own experience. The same man who stubbornly refuses to think out the problems of a presidential election will use his brains lucidly at a meeting of a union local or a parent-teacher association. The continuance of self-governing institutions will depend upon the invention of methods of communication by which the operations of the great macrocosms that rule our lives can be reduced to terms which each averagely intelligent man can understand, truly understand the way a good mechanic understands the working of an internal combustion engine.

Selfgovernment demands real and not parroted information. If we are to govern ourselves we have to know how the machinery of our society works. We have to learn to measure the drift of change. As a society changes the men change who are its component parts. There has been too little exploration of industrial society in the terms of human behavior. One reason is that obsession with socialist-capitalist antithesis (with socialism equals good, capitalism equals bad or vice versa) has kept investigators from seeing clearly the prospects that were opening out under their noses.

A sectarian approach to a study of society means a search for a bogeyman. You don't need to understand why people behave as they do if you've already made up your mind who is to blame. If you are going to study an ant's nest you have to start out with a mind blank of preconceptions about the behavior of social insects. Difficult as it is to be unprejudiced about ants it's a whole lot more difficult to be unprejudiced about people. The fact that it is difficult doesn't mean it is not possible.

The intellectual tools with which to examine societies in the spirit of the search for knowledge rather than for party purposes are already in the language. In the parts of the world where free inquiry is still allowed by the police the investigation is easier to undertake than it was twenty-five years ago. In America at least the study of behavior, in the good old empirical tradition, has not run its course nor reached its highest fruition. We've just begun to take up the problem. An entire science lies ahead. In that science we may find the tools with which to build out of our runaway institutions a society which will offer participation to each individual man.

The principles of representative government by checks and balances based on law and not on administrative whim are as sound as they ever were. What has happened is that the political structure no longer conforms to the economic and social structure. Paralleling the political setup we have a host of new forms of government set up by the needs of industrial management and labor, and of all the various regiments of men that make up our society. Pressure groups are organs that have appeared because they were really needed, as links and channels between the corporate organizations which make up the community and the national and state and municipal governments. Some of these new organs are socially good and some of them are bad. We must start weeding out the bad and saving the good. The nation should be like a battleship stripping for action. We can no longer keep on board any apparatus that doesn't contribute directly to our safety.

If we are to save the republic we must continually be aware of the aims of the republic. Our safety lies in the fulfillment of these aims. Lincoln said that the United States differed from other nations in that it was "dedicated to a proposition." That proposition has remained basically unchanged through our history, though the means of putting it into effect change as the shape of society changes. That proposition implies that the cohesive force which holds our nation together is not a religious creed or a common ancestry but the daily effort to give to every man as much opportunity as is possible to fulfill himself in his own way, protected by law from the arbitrary measures of those in authority. The men who founded this nation tried the unheard-of experiment of founding a state which would be the servant instead of the master of its citizens.

Our safety in each crisis in our history has been measured by how near we came to achieving that aim. Our crimes and failures as a nation, and there have been plenty of them, have always occurred in situations that found the electorate and its leaders forgetful of the basic reason for the existence of the United States. In the old days our isolation gave us a vast margin for error. The margin for error has narrowed with breathtaking rapidity. The time is coming when every citizen will have to ask himself at every hour of the day: is what I am doing helping to save the republic or is it not?

We need to harness our technical knowledge directly to the task of increasing liberty and opportunity day by day. Instead of asking is this measure or that turn of affairs tending to benefit this or that class of citizens we must ask: is it tending to increase personal liberty for all? Testing organizations by that standard we will find that some services can be performed most efficiently by the federal government, some by the states and cities, some by licensed monopolies, or by cooperatives, or by private enterprise. The United States form an immensely complicated edifice built on a series of constantly changing adjustments brought about by the stresses and strains of the struggle for survival among the multitude of organizations which make up our national life. The only gauge we have of its worth as a method of organizing society is how it affects each separate individual citizen.

Every society has to be born again from time to time. Even in our short history as a nation we have had a series of rebirths; the various openings of the West, the inception of the railroad age, the invention of assembly line production, the renewed search for community planning and improvement and the renewal of the sense of responsibility of one for all and all for one which accompanied the first enthusiasms of the New Deal, have all been national rebirths. Since the aims of the New Deal were forgotten and degraded in lowest-common-denominator politics, the sort of inventiveness that makes for statebuilding has been stalled in the doldrums. The time has come for a fresh surge of invention.

We have to remember, before it is too late, that this nation was founded not to furnish glamorous offices for politicians, or to produce goods and services, or handouts of easy money, but to produce free men.

The prospect before us is one of mighty effort against great odds but it is not all black. You can't travel back and forth across the continent without seeing the occasional beginnings of a better balanced society. Our economic problems are the problems of surplus; it's hard to get used to that when so much economic thinking is still based on notions of scarcity. There is now no visible limit to the productivity of agriculture or of manufacturing. In spite of Marx's prophecy our society has not solidified into rigid classes. Not even the struggle between the management of industry and the leadership of labor has produced a proletariat. We are still a mass of vague and rambling individuals who have barely begun to build ourselves a civilization. We lack standards, we lack ethics, we lack art, we lack that instinctive sense of direction that is the sign of an achieved civilization. But some of our faults may turn out to be virtues. Somehow we have managed to escape being rammed into the mold of a stratified society.

There are only rare moments in history when a community of men finds itself in the position to choose alternatives. We may still be in that position. For a few short years we may be able to make the choice between a stratified autocratic society more or less on the Russian model and the selfgoverning republic which is our heritage. The republic must find its origins in the shop, in the union local, in the management conference room, in the school district meeting, in the county seat and the small town and the city ward. The republic can only be attained by intelligence and courage and the selfsacrifice of the individuals who must dedicate their lives to leavening and informing the mass. They must find the brains and the will. If enough of us want a selfgoverning society, in which every man can participate to the fullest of his ability, we can attain it.

A Letter to an Editor

Key West, Florida
March 15, 1947

The Editor,
The New York Times Book Review Section,
New York, N. Y.

Dear Sir,

There appeared in your paper on March 9 a review by Mr. Lawrence Lee of Mr. Godfrey Blunden's *A Room on the Route* which dealt with that novel in such misleading terms that I can't help calling your attention to it. I had read the book already or assuredly I should never have read it at all, so well-calculated was the review to dampen the interest of even a fairly close student of the Soviet Union.

I imagine that you are not unaware of the fact that there has existed in the New York press for a number of years now an invisible censorship of all books dealing frankly and seriously with Russian life and especially of books which do not fit into the pattern of thinking which our enthusiasts for the

New York Times (1947).

Kremlin regime have learned from the subtle and diligent propaganda fostered by the Communist Party in this country. I don't mean to imply that you personally share the enthusiasm of these people for each and every aspect of Soviet life or that you don't feel your responsibility as the editor of one of the important literature organs in the country, but I do feel that the time has come to make a particular effort to impress upon every American in a position of authority the need for an open mind and for continually fresh evaluations in relation to every topic that deals with the Soviet Union. For quite long enough now the country has been flooded with propaganda from the dominant party in Russia. It is time we heard from the underdog. And by underdog I don't mean the political dissidents, I mean the great tortured majority of the Russian people.

In my opinion, *A Room on the Route,* quite apart from its subject matter, is one of the most important novels to appear in English in years. It marks the first appearance of a brilliant new talent. Perhaps you won't agree with me, but I think I have a right to ask you to read the book yourself. I don't think you will regret the experience. Then if you feel as I do that injustice has been done perhaps you will be willing, in a spirit of fair play, to help right that wrong by giving the novel a fresh review by someone who can be trusted to deliver an unbiased judgment.

In the second column of his review you will find Mr. Lee writing:

Mr. Blunden was in Russia during the fighting around Stalingrad. His novel in no way indicates that he is aware of the ideas, energies or moralities which must have been in conflict everywhere then.

Anyone who has read the book will agree that this is a falsification. I find it impossible to reconcile this statement with the fact that *A Room on the Route* contains descriptions of the fighting in the defense of Moscow which I consider almost worthy of being set beside Tolstoy's great battlepieces in *War and Peace*. Can it be that your reviewer was so carried away by the illusions that have been implanted in his mind that he did not dare let himself read a true account of those events that have so stirred his emotions?

The novel furnishes the only picture we have from the pen of an Englishspeaking writer of the basic realities of life under the Russian despotism. It has that truth that you only get from firstrate literature. It happens that I picked up a certain amount of knowledge about the Russian people during a stay in Moscow a number of years ago. I found in *A Room on the Route* characters and situations I had known in happier times when the pressure of the Terror was much less intense than it is today. I felt that Mr. Blunden was telling about people I knew. There has been no such writing about Russians in English since Hugh Walpole's *The Dark Forest.* Mr. Blunden has penetrated deeply where that novel only skimmed the surface. As a picture of the underside of the Communist dictatorship only Koestler's *Darkness at Noon* compares with it. Koestler only exposed the torture of spirit of the isolated Communist idealist, but Mr. Blunden has painted for us the agony of the Russian people.

Obviously I would not be taking up your time and mine with this letter if I did not consider this issue of Russophile censorship one of paramount importance. It is impossible to read reviews of this sort, and there have been many of them, without getting the impression that they are part of an organized campaign to smother free discussion of the realities of Soviet life. At this moment above all others the people of this country need to know the truth about the people of the

Soviet Union. To most Americans Russia is beginning to look more like an enemy than an ally. There is no better way to serve the cause of peace than to tear down the barriers which the enemies of liberty have thrown up against free discussion. It's only by understanding the realties that we can tell the true friends of the Russian people from the propagandists for their government. In this sympathetic and touching story of their heroisms and miseries Mr. Blunden, besides proving himself a novelist has proved himself their true friend. Their enemies, who happen to be those of the American people too, are those fanatics for Communist dictatorship whose efforts are going to bring about the ultimate tragedy of World War III. There are those who are trying to hide the truth about Russian life from Americans at the same time as they distort the facts of American life for readers in the Soviet Union.

Sincerely yours,

England under a Labor Government: 1947

An eighteenth century Sunday. At London Airport we walk off the plane into the middle of an endless warm midsummer afternoon. After the motors' long vibration the dense air is startlingly quiet. In the distance the shadows are soft under the softgreen trees. A few rooks fly lazily, far away. Everything has a faraway holiday air. Outside the terminal building the welltilled flowerbeds are on fire with snapdragons sprouting great spikes of red and lemonyellow and garnet and maroon so much taller and finer than we could grow them at home. They smell of honey. "Yes they are fine sir," admits the uniformed man at the gate with a pleased and deprecatory smile. "It's the fine summer weather."

We drive sleepily into London along broad thoroughfares where to eyes fresh from New York the traffic seems sparse and Sundaylike. On the greensward of Hyde Park under great trees that seem to bulge with the weight of their watery green, men and women sprawl barearmed. As far as you can see motionless groups of recumbent figures spread over the glaucous grass.

From *The Prospect Before Us* (Boston: Houghton Mifflin Company, 1950).

The great houses on Park Lane where the wealthy and fashionable flourished in Edwardian days stare out with blank windows. Their owners have moved away for longer than the holidays. At first glance the Dorchester Hotel has the old look of quiet ostentation and expense, but except for a sprinkling of anxiousfaced sleek East Indians and their childlike women in silk tanagra costumes, the people in the lobby look shabby and frayed. Gone are the uniforms and the swagger of wartime. Gone are the wellheeled gentry with their look of having just come from the huntingfield or the paddock with the assurance in the very knot of their Ascot ties that their sight drafts will be honored by the banker. Gone are the horsefaced gentlewomen in tiaras. Instead you see officials with shallow countenances blank from sitting out too many conferences, or the shark and remora shapes of flybynight financial operators who skim a rich living off calamity, the buzzard features of the scavengers of sick currencies.

Out in the streets again we look down from a bus on grey uncrowded streets of tidied ruin. London is no longer the mart and nerve center of the luxuries and miseries of an empire, no longer the tense magnificent fortress where every airraid warden stood like Horatius at the bridge. The glint of power has gone off the windows of Bond Street. Through the unwashed panes of Piccadilly clubs here and there the moustached face of an elderly Indian colonel stares out at emptiness. The theatres round Leicester Square have taken on a dim provincial air. In the bookshops there's nothing to be had. "England's dead, quite dead, quite," the young man in the bookshop on Charing Cross Road whispers in my ear in fluty Oxonian tones. We're the lost island of the Atlantic, sunk in everlasting ennui, the Scandinavian ennui."

Down in the City, past Victoria smug on Temple Bar, and

the gutted Temple and the roofless churches of the Strand, there's a smell of burning left in the air from the great fire. Giant fireweed grows out of the heaps of the broken stone among the bared foundations of the ancient hilltown round miraculously intact St. Paul's. Fireweed is new in Britain. In America we are used to its magenta stalks sprouting up out of the charred loam wherever a forest fire has passed. In Wales they say it now grows round the abandoned mines and people call it Miners' Blood. In midsummer London the air is thick with the small silky seeds of fireweed drifting through disfigured streets.

In Westminster the red steel framework of the new House of Commons is almost complete. From the moment you step into the lobby you can feel the rigid structure of the Labor Party machine firmly in control of the stationary engines of bureaucratic government. The Labor election was a revolution but a very partial one. A few representatives of business and of the ancient castes and privileges were pushed off one end of the bench of the national coalition and a few trade union officials and agitating intellectuals climbed on the other end, and the workingman was in the saddle. By proxy. The government benches are full of people who know better what's good for the workingman than the workingman himself.

The Commons still meet in the Lords' Chamber. In spite of a certain amount of argument in the accustomed style of the great debating club, as measure after measure comes up to curtail the already frail liberties of the individual Briton, the machine moves smoothly. After one of Bevin's canny four-square statements in rebuttal has dug the ground out from under the gentle remonstrances of the Opposition, the guillotine falls and the bell rings for a division, calling the members from their whale steak and their Pym's Number One in their pleasant diningroom by the Thames; and Labor representatives of all groups troop obediently through the proper door. When the tellers come up the aisle bowing in unison to the Speaker three times, like the frog footmen, the vote is always Labor by a hundred and fifty voices or more.

At the corner of Hyde Park beside the Marble Arch under the immense lavender twilight of eleven o'clock on an English summer's night the popular debating academy, which has somewhat the relation to Parliament that the curb market in New York used to have to the Stock Exchange, still fills the heavy London air with oratory. There the Commies and the dissident Socialists have their pulpits. A skinny evangelist leads his group in singing:

> Abide with me, fast falls the eventide,
> The darkness deepens . . .

"Question time hasn't arrived yet," barks a Socialist shaking off the Communist hecklers. At a reading desk marked *Poetry* an illfed youngish student with a soft hat pulled down over his tortoiseshell glasses is reciting *The Hound of Heaven* and reciting it damned well. A tired little fat man climbs on a stool to defend private enterprise. The adherents of private enterprise have already joined the forlorn minorities. Patiently he explains to a hostile crowd that socialism is leading them to starvation, slavery and ruin.

"Not so farst, it's our government," roars a barebreasted navvy.

"The best government England's ever 'ad," echoes a hollow-cheeked man in a peaked cap.

"I'm better off than I've ever been in my life," says a stocky fellow with a mat of blond hair like shredded wheat.

Beside me a young man in a frayed jacket shiny with grime starts to blow his top. " 'Ave a 'art," he shouts. "Ah've seen the starvin' kiddies run barefoot down the streets to beg a bit of bread. Ah've seen too much of that, Ah 'ave. That's 'ow I grew up. Now there's the school lunch and five bob a week for every child." He turns to me and grins confidently. "Under a Labor government it's a delight to get married."

One day we find ourselves walking round Golden Square looking for the house where Thomas Jefferson had his lodgings during his stay in London in the spring of 1786. Number 14 had disappeared but number 11 has a beautiful Adam doorway that must have been standing freshpainted and fashionable at the time. While we are looking at the delicately carved mouldings under the scaling green paint of the door a comfortablelooking middleaged woman opens it and obligingly invites us in to see the oval drawingroom which she explains is now a lawoffice. "A bomb fell in the back of the house but it didn't explode," she says briskly. "It makes you appreciate lovely things all the more, doesn't it, to know they are so fragile?"

At the corner as we turn away we catch sight of a pushcart full of Italian peaches moving along swiftly propelled by a sweating young man in a torn shirt. As the pushcart proceeds another man weighs out the peaches and sells them to people tagging along after, elbowing their way through the noontide crowd that packs the narrow pavement. Both men keep looking nervously over their shoulders as they go.

"Why won't they stop?" you ask.

"They're barrow boys, they carn't stop."

Then you notice that a tall cop in a tall blue helmet is sauntering along after them.

"But what's illegal about selling peaches?"

"Barrow boys 'aven't no license to set up a stall but there's no law against trundlin' a barrow through the streets," your informant considerately explains. "It's a cyse of regulytions," he adds in a tone of finality.

When Jefferson lived on Golden Square, most likely in a similar house as fastidiously decorated in the fashionable Pompeian style as the house we had just seen, he was Minister to France. He had crossed the Channel to talk over matters with his dear friend John Adams, who was our Minister to England. After months of tedious and fruitless conversations with the Portuguese ambassador, about a scheme they had to get the European nations to unite against the Barbary pirates, and a thorough snubbing at the Court of St. James, the two American diplomats agreed to take a little restful jaunt round the country; so, early on the morning of the second of April Jefferson drove around to Grosvenor Square to pick up Adams and they set out amid the jingle of harness and the cracking of the postillion's whip.

They drove over the cobbled streets of new elegant Mayfair and out through the rutted roads of Hyde Park and the rural lanes of Kensington and Hammersmith. Their first stop was to be at Chiswick where the showplace was the Earl of Burlington's famous reproduction of a Palladian villa. It was the passion for architecture and landscape gardening which Jefferson shared with the ruling gentry of England that impelled him to the trip. He carried Whately's recently printed *Modern Gardening* in his hand as a guide and undoubtedly read passages from it out loud to John Adams, who was going

along more for the ride and for a sight of spring after the
mud and soot of a city winter and for the pleasure of political
and philosophical discussion with his Virginia friend. As they
jounced along in their rattling hired chaise, they tried with
keen transatlantic eyes to penetrate every detail of the green
countryside which was like home to them and yet not like
home.

On a fine summer Sunday a hundred and sixtyone years
later we are following on their trail in a minute English automobile.

When Jefferson and Adams took their tour England was
reaching the peak of empire as a seafaring and mercantile
nation. The manufactories which were to dominate the next
century were just beginning. The loss of the Thirteen Colonies
was being made up for amply and fast by the wealth pumped
out of the East India trade and profits on Jamaican sugar and
rum and on the exchange of goods on the Board of Trade's
own terms between England and the American ports. Although the merchants and bankers were growing more powerful year by year, the great landed families of the Whig aristocracy still controlled preferment and place sufficiently to
siphon a stream of guineas out of government into their own
strongboxes.

They spent it on their mansions and their parks and gardens.
Brought up from boyhood on the literature of Imperial Rome
and Periclean Greece the ruling English moved in a pomp of
personal power and dignity that seems unbelievably Olympian
to any massmoulded man of today. In every corner of England,
in the great parks and hunting forests and farming estates they
inherited from the feudal lords of the past, they were building

themselves palaces in the imperial style they learned from Palladio's version of the work of the Roman architect Vitruvius; and these palaces they were surrounding with parks landscaped by the square mile according to the taste for the natural, pioneered on the Continent by Claude Lorrain, Poussin and the painters of the late Renaissance.

Their heads full of the Augustan verse their teachers at Eton and Charterhouse had made them learn by heart, and of Cicero's reconstruction in stately rhetoric of the senatorial republic, they governed the rustics and burghers of England by the right of birth and wealth; and imagined a background for themselves of Roman colonnades overlooking royal vistas where, between mighty oaks the red deer ran shaking their clumsy antlered heads; and of grand lawns sweeping to the sedgy edges of lakes, where the gleam of a white swan or the reflection of a stucco temple accented the blurred sap greens of the island countryside. For all their treading down of the men and women whose humble work helped to produce their glory, their aristocratic pride in power was helping stamp on the mind of the English-speaking peoples a conviction of the potential majesty of man.

In those days the noble lords were so proud of the estates they had put so much thought and planning and money into that they were more than willing to have them shown to the less privileged traveller. Jefferson and Adams carried no letters of introduction. As upstart Americans they were barely recognized as gentlemen by English society.

At Chiswick it cost them four and six paid out to the Duke of Devonshire's servants to see the park. A century and a half later we saw what was left of it free. It is a public park now. The iron gates and palings that were such a feature of the

English countryside were all broken up for scrap during the war, so landowners couldn't keep out trespassers if they wanted to.

After the racket of the crowding green busses and the lorries and the tall elephantlike trams of the thoroughfares out of London, Chiswick village looks quiet and yellowed and faded as an etching in the window of a secondhand store. Behind dooryards full of great fragrant roses a row of eighteenth century houses sinks into greenery and forgetfulness on low alluvial ground facing the puttycolored Thames.

In a loop of the river a couple of barges, built of dark varnished wood, lie stranded on gleaming mud banks fringed with loosestrife and reeds. At the far end of the mall an old stone church sleeps in the green graveyard where Hogarth and Whistler were buried. Searching for Hogarth's summer cottage we find a tottering frame shell within the highly dilapidated confines of an abandoned brewery.

"If you're looking for the pictures," says a busconductor who's waiting at the corner, speaking without any inflection of reproach in his voice, "they've been sent to America. Nothing left 'ere."

A grove of magnificent evergreens still shelters Chiswick House. The original design was distorted by additions soon after Jefferson saw the place and caught from it part of the notion that finally developed into his second plan for Monticello, but the pedimented core of the building, cracked and battered and boarded up as it is, still has beautiful balance and proportion. Temporary wooden fences cut at random across alleyways of yew and box, down which you can still catch a glimpse of a carefully composed view of a balustraded bridge reflected in a green stream.

There's a litter of broken campchairs on the trampled lawn.

A considerate child has rouged the cheeks of one of the Frenchified Regency sphinxes that guard the approach to the house. In the basement there's a squalidlooking municipal lunchroom marked "Refreshments" and the stench of public toilets. When we ask the caretaker to let us visit the house, he says without looking up, "It's agynst the regulytions."

"Gave servants at Twickenham, Pope's garden 2/-," Jefferson next entered in his accountbook.

Today an elderly nun with steelrimmed glasses shows us around gladly and gratis. She explains that the place is a Catholic school. She loves to show the garden and the grotto, she says and she seems to mean it. She shows the shells and the lumps of lava embedded in the plaster wall. "He was a great poet and people sent him things," she says.

In the grotto one statue was of St. James. "The pilgrim shell, that meant something to him." The other, some people said, was Dante's friend Beatrice but the sister thinks it was his sadness. She is Irish.

"Now don't be frightened now," she titters as she runs ahead through the tunnel under the road. We come up blinking in the garden. "Two sisters and an old gardener that's all we have to do the work," she says breathlessly indicating cabbages and sprouts and kale and lettuce and potatoes in flower with a wave of her hand. Beyond are berrybushes and appletrees. "During the war and now in the austerity we have to rely on our vegetables. We wouldn't eat without the garden," she says.

The lower walls of the house, which was rebuilt in Victorian days in a sort of Swiss chalet style, are still as they were in Pope's time. There are still traces of the sloping paved landing you see in the old engravings of the place. The green river in the sunny morning is full of shells and punts. A fat cheerful looking excursion boat packed with excursionists passes headed upstream.

When we drive into Hampton Court the river is even more crowded. The excursion boat is just pulling in. The green bank opposite is strewn with swimmers. In the gardens people walk quietly. In the long rectangular pond that opens out from Wren's garlanded façade a man in shorts stands up to his knees in water, fishing. Children play quietly along the edge and point out the fluffy gray cygnets. Tonguetied courting couples sit on the benches and stare down the long avenues.

The English have few pleasures now. With quiet passion they enjoy their countryside and the parks and gardens out of the royal and aristocratic past, the flowers so abundantly blooming, the meadows bounded by the soft trees of the island landscape, the play of the sun on their lean and sallow carcasses.

After Hampton Court we strike out into the country. We pass cyclists in shoals, whole families out for the day with babies and pet dogs strapped into the baskets on the handlebars. Men and women sit out in the sun on benches and doorsteps in front of the pubs drinking their thin ale with expressionless faces. In this rich Thames valley the trees are magnificent. You could stop for an hour to study the spread of the small-leaved English oaks, the majesty of the beeches.

At Esher Place where Whately had admired a grove of trees Jefferson paid out six shillings. We find the park turned into a modern residential development in the American style. The windows of the gray seventeenth century hall are full of the peaked faces of little girls. While we are admiring the balance of a doorway in the wing a flustered woman comes out to ask us what we want. She looks at us with a cold suspicious eye.

Have we permission to visit the orphan asylum? No thanks; already we are on our way.

At Payn's Hill which Whately mentions as an example of a magnificent park, the servants got seven shillings out of Jefferson and Adams. We find the estate still intact but there are signs on the gateposts: *Auction sale this day of antique furniture and furnishings.* The glass is broken in the greenhouses. The fountains are dry. The gardens are overgrown with weeds. Nobody has cut the dead limbs out of the great trees or filled up the slit trenches an antiaircraft battery left there during the war, but from the terrace of the vacant Regency house you can trace the design according to which the trees were planted to emphasize the steepness of hills, or to outline a little valley, here screening, there opening a vista through to the reflection in a mahogany pool of the old stone arches where the road crosses the stream.

At Wotton-under-Wood, which John Adams described as great and elegant though neglected, we ask a man living in a wing of the great house whether he can let us walk in the park. He passes the buck by sending us to find the postmaster. The postmaster, a Mr. Phipps, is even more careful not to commit himself. "If you meet the bailiff," he says, "maybe he'll take you up for trespassing but I don't imagine he will. You may tell him you've seen me and that I couldn't give you any authority but that I didn't think you'd be doing any harm."

We have a feeling that nobody has walked in that park in a hundred years. Wild ducks fly up from Wotton water. Loud-voiced doves coo in the elms of the avenue. Frogs croak in the little temples that frame the clearing up the hill towards the shuttered mansion. Magpies squawk indignantly. Clouds of black squashy flies whine about our heads. "Great and elegant though neglected."

We followed Jefferson and Adams through lanes that wind between hawthorn hedges, among hillsides misted with palest green blue of ripening oats. Occasionally after passing a sign *danger* we drive for a mile or two through ranks of corrugated huts full of ammunition which hasn't been moved since the last German plane was shot down over Britain.

We turn into the main road at a village built of small squared stones. We pass airstrips and great dumps of war machinery under camouflaged canvas covers. We pass fire stations with red buckets and longhandled paddles to beat out the flames from incendiary bombs, a used-car lot, and an old lady speeding along in a motorized wheel chair, imperturbable as Britannia in a streaming veil, and allatonce we are in Oxford. Jefferson and Adams visited the colleges there but had nothing to report about them.

"Edgehill and Worcester," wrote John Adams, "were curious and interesting to us as scenes where freemen had fought for their rights. The people in the neighborhood appeared so ignorant and careless at Worcester that I was provoked and asked, 'And do Englishmen so soon forget the ground where liberty was fought for? Tell your neighbors and your children that this is holy ground.' ". . . Through sheets of rain we look out over the battlefield of Edgehill from the small castle on top of the sharp steep wooded rise that gives the place its name. On the sloping meadows where Cromwell's psalmsinging footsoldiers beat back the Royalist charge are scattered the boxlike buildings of a munitions factory left over from the latest war. In the cottage garden below us a gangling boy is tying up the climbing nasturtiums which the rain is beating down. It is raining too hard to try to talk to him.

Further on at Worcester, to be sure, the beadle in the cathedral seems to remember that battle. "It was outside those walls. The cathedral towered above it," he says in tones of ecclesiastical pomp.

Looking after the cars in the parkinglot outside the cathedral we find a tall broadshouldered bony man with a west country accent. As soon as he notices that we are Americans he starts off as if in answer to John Adams' question. Liberty is lost in England, he says. Here he is out of the army after fortyfive years' service . . . Gib, Malta, the Punjab, Singapore, he's seen them all, every blarsted place on earth; and now that he is out with a bit of a pension and a bit of money saved up, he and the old woman had hoped to start a bit of a business and spend an agreeable old age, but it was no go. What did they get? Regulations. There was no liberty in a land ruined with regulations. Rights? What rights did an Englishman have if he couldn't start up a bit of a business to better himself by? He and his old woman didn't even have a roof over their heads they could call their own. "It's a ruined country I've come 'ome to. . . Their regulations'll 'ave us all in our graves before our time."

Driving back to town through the long evening we talk with the young man who is driving the car about Robin Hood and about the Howard Pyle world of our childhood, the yeomanry and the beef-fed men-at-arms of Chaucer's day with their longbows and their crossbows; and of the knights and their ladies we'd seen lying in their stone robes on the early tombs in Worcester Cathedral; and of the muttoneating eighteenth century England of haughty rich and sodden poor, both jostled by the rising middle class; and of the suburban

England of Victoria's reign when all traditions and snobberies seemed embalmed in an endless imperial afternoon; and of Wells and the socialist aspiration towards a better world for all, which had grown out of the nonconformist conscience and the Commonwealth and the glorious Revolution.

Suddenly the young man changes the subject hard: "It's not the austerity," he says. "We could put up with anything if we felt we were getting anywhere. But they (he meant the government, everybody speaks of the government as "they") can't seem to start anything. A young fellow gets out of the services. He's sick of being ordered around. He wants to do something on his own. Now you can't even get married because you can't get a flat or a house. The small businesses that pulled through the war are having a hard time making a go of it. There are plenty of jobs but there's no future to them. The expense and the regulations make it impossible to start anything new on your own, unless you're a spiv and toady around and keep your notes in your pocket. There's no opportunity for a young man. If you try to go to the colonies you're blocked. Every passage to South Africa is taken for eighteen months. If all you want to do is loaf it doesn't matter, but if you want to make your way in the world a little, every direction you turn it's a blank wall. . . I used to be so proud of being British, but now I don't know."

We've passed Windsor. The castle's gray battlements still hover above the trees behind us. We are driving slowly, stopping and starting in a double rank of cars, in the Sunday afternoon traffic jam, gradually making our way across a green meadow littered with resting cyclists and parties sitting on the grass eating picnic suppers on the sunny side of parked cars. The Thames is dense with punts and canoes. Bathers are still stretching out pale arms in the last ruddy sunlight. What is this place? I ask the driver. He thinks for a moment and answers: "Runnymede."

Reflections on the failures of Marxism. The soldier coming home from the wars has always had a tough time. The fact of killing carries a rough sort of catharsis with it. The fighting man's mind isn't distorted by aimless hatred as the stay-at-home civilian's is. He usually comes home with a commonsense outlook on what he's been through. Though in the first war the nearest I got to combat was driving an ambulance, I can remember very clearly how hard the returned doughboy found it to talk to civilians. We found people back home hopped up with German atrocities and "brave little Belgium." Their thinking was frozen in the mold of the interallied propaganda. They were mad for atrocities. We were sick to death of atrocities. We knew that atrocities were universal in war. We tried to explain how the fighting man felt. It got so that to keep out of arguments we only talked freely among ourselves. In that case a reaction set in. In two or three years the wartime psychology melted away and the returned soldier, against loud opposition we mustn't forget, was allowed to have his say.

Like the people I talked to in England, I again found myself at cross purposes with the stay at homes after World War II. Those of us who protested against the abdication of the American will to victory were talked down whenever we raised our voices. The wartime obsessions, though they never reached the depth of hysteria of the wartime obsessions of the first war, lingered on in the public mind year after year.

The language of protest of the oldtime Greenwich Village radicals had become the language of an entrenched political party. Many an old radical found himself hoist by his own petard.

We had run mad for government ownership of this and that, and for labor unions, and for a minimum wage, and unemployment relief because we thought those things would increase the happiness and dignity of the majority of men. A great many of the things we argued for came to pass under the New Deal in the United States and under the Labor government in England. In America they became honeycombed with ingenious rackets.

They became established institutions defended by all the vested interests that got their living off them. When some of us, applying the standards we had learned in trying to defend Sacco and Vanzetti and the Harlan miners, the Spanish Republicans and a hundred other less publicized victims of oppression of one sort or another, started looking with a critical but not necessarily unfriendly eye at the new institutions, we got a good shellacking from the paladins of the established order for our pains. The businessman, who used to be defended with such fury, was now fair game, but you criticized a socialized institution at your own risk.

If some of us, who had seen the Abominable Snowmen, pointed out that the Communist Party was a greater danger to individual liberty than all the bankers and industrialists from hell to breakfast, we were promptly written down in the bad books as reactionaries.

One day I found myself talking to a pleasant and well informed woman reporter in a newspaper office in a prosperous city in the middlewestern corn belt. Although the region is usually chalked up as "black Republican" in politics, the paper she worked for wore a "liberal" complexion. I was trying to explain to her that socialism as I had seen it working in Great

Britain was not necessarily a force for progress. "But I thought you were a liberal," she kept saying almost tearfully, "and now you have turned reactionary."

"The Socialists are the conservatives now," I told her, "and the Communists are the real reactionaries."

She remained unconvinced. The reason our conversation was so fruitless was that she had made up her mind that certain words like "liberal," "labor" and "rationing" had a virtuous connotation. There was no way of getting her to look directly at the events that lay behind the words.

It was just this sort of wall of incomprehension we used to meet years ago when we argued the right of working people to form unions and to strike for improved working conditions, or tried to explain that Americans ought to show a sympathetic interest in the social experiments that were going on in the Soviet Union. Then it was the capitalist slogans that were holding the fort; but during the past twenty years a new set of words has gradually become charged with a virtuous aura in the public mind.

Now *public ownership, planned economy, controls* and *socialized* have become words heavy with virtue, while *profits, free enterprise, investment* and even *dividends* have taken on an evil context that needs to be explained away.

Partly this comes from a reasoned change of attitude brought about by the success of some of the socialistic measures of Franklin Roosevelt's New Deal, but mostly it comes from the unthinking acceptance of the vocabulary of "liberal" propaganda that spread out in ripples from New Deal Washington, becoming vaguer and more confused and more destructive of clear thinking as the ideas that engendered it lost their vitality at the source. It is in this confused region of the popular mind that the Communists have been able to carry on their most successful propaganda operations. Thus it comes to pass that the "liberals" who think a man is defeated in argument when they call him a "reactionary" show very little curiosity about the actual functioning of any of the socialistic going concerns.

Actually the world is becoming a museum of socialist failures. It seems likely, from what we hear faintly through the screen of lies that hems in the Soviet Union, that even there the illusions are losing their power in the face of the regime's failure to produce the rudiments of decent living for its subjects.

Even Americans opposed to the Communists talk as if it were an excess of progressiveness and idealism that caused Russian socialism to fail. We find Frenchmen and Americans and Canadians, in all other respects apparently capable of sane and normal thinking, who are willing to turn their backs on the traditions they were brought up in and to give their allegiance to the Kremlin. The success of the aggressions of the Soviet state in the last few years depends almost entirely on the Kremlin's command over adherents and sympathizers in the outside world. Because the western world has not understood it the Russian socialized state has been allowed to develop into a vast military force of pillage and conquest. Still the faith of many of our "liberals" in the Kremlin's idealistic aims has not faltered.

Those of us who believed in socialism in the radical twenties hoped that some new system of production would promote selfgovernment, expand individual liberty and make for wider distribution of life's goods. The Soviet Union is surely not the place to look for these things. Not even the American Communists really claim any of these achievements; what they say among themselves is that present miseries will be atoned for by the regime of justice and bliss that will be established once Communism has completed its conquest of the globe.

The Russians are barbarians, the western Socialists used to tell us; in England it will all be different.

How different *is* it? If you go around Great Britain asking questions of as many different kinds of people as possible, you sense that in its ultimate implications British socialism is turning out to be not so very different from the Russian brand. Of course there's not the public terror of Stalin nor the Hitlerian pomp and parade through which the Kremlin daily expresses its power over the bodies and minds of men. There's not the proselytizing enthusiasm of a quasi-religious dogma which accompanies the agents and the armies of expanding Russia. There's not the daily and visible and universal servitude; but neither has socialism brought any broadening of personal liberty. On the contrary: personal liberty in Great Britain has been contracted.

The humane and wellintentioned people who are running the Labor government are the first to deplore the losses of liberty you bring to their attention. They reassure you with pious hopes that the "direction of labor" measure, which limits the individual's right to work where or when he likes, will be only a passing phase. Listening to these pious hopes, I couldn't help remembering similar reassurances from equally humane and wellintentioned Russian Communists who used to tell me in the Caucasus in 1921, that military communism was a passing phase which would disappear as soon as the reactionary opposition was crushed.

Thirty years went by, and military communism marches on to fresh massacres. A man has a right to ask the British Labor Party whether thirty years from now direction of labor won't be the cornerstone of a new system of exploitation of the productive workers by a new ruling class.

If there is one thing that mankind should have learned from

the agonies of the last half century it is that it's never safe to do evil that good may come of it. The good gets lost and the evil goes on.

Of course we must admit that the present situation of the people of Great Britain would be difficult enough in any case. The island's economy was built up as the processing and financing center of an empire which has irrevocably gone. The class which ruled that economy through control of the government, ownership of the land and domination of centralized finance and industry had become overwhelmingly rich and powerful. In their wealth and selfsatisfaction the owners of Britain neglected to keep their industries tooled up to date or to protect the standard of living of their working people or to conserve their natural resources. When the Labor government came in after the war it inherited a concern which was very nearly bankrupt.

Government control of virtually the entire economy had been instituted during the war. About all the Labor government did was to amplify the wartime apparatus of bureaucratic management. The living standards of the working people, who were Labor's chief constituents, had improved during the war. The labor government continued that improvement, particularly for the lowest-paid third. Because there wasn't enough to go around anyway, this was done at the expense of the middle class, traditionally the nursery of British brains and initiative. Virtually everybody was reduced by high taxes and high prices to the same level of subsistence. Incentive for effort and innovation tended to disappear. A man was better off if he soldiered along in the shop and spent his Saturdays betting on the races than if he worked his head off trying to rise in the world. The more his income rose the more taxation would take his earnings away from him and the more he would feel the dead weight of the bureaucratic tangle hampering his every move.

Bernard Baruch's remark, that socialism might not succeed in distributing wealth but would certainly distribute poverty, has never been better exemplified. Socialism in Great Britain accomplished little more than to freeze the capitalist economy at its point of least efficiency.

Man does not live by bread alone, the Socialists will be the first to tell you. Very true. Stronger than the urge to eat is the urge to exercise power over other men. British institutions have done a pretty good job in the past in curbing this deadliest of instincts; but, in spite of political democracy, British capitalism too often gave too much power to people whose only social gift was the knack of accumulating money. With the advent of a Labor government, British socialism began to give too much power to people whose only knack was getting themselves elected to offices in trade unions.

England found a new ruling class. Added to such remnants of the old ruling class as remained in office through administrative jobs there was an infusion of new blood from the trade-union leadership, leavened by an occasional intellectual who talked or wrote his way into office. Trade-union officials were trained from youth to try to hamstring production for the purpose of wringing concessions from the owners for the workers. Neither idealistic intellectuals nor civil service employees had any training in industry.

The result was that at the very moment when the British people needed to discover new ways of producing food and clothing and housing and export goods, they found themselves in the hands of managers who were hampered by tradition and training from doing anything effective. Britain's new ruling class was so blinded by the utopian glamour of the word "socialism" that it could not really envisage the problems contingent on the production of coal and steel and consumers' goods.

If the government can't help them, why can't they help themselves? The British people represent western civilized man at a high point in development. In the middle and upper classes you find a much higher level of education than we have reached in America. The level of individual skill and craftsmanship in most trades is higher than ours. In the professionally trained part of the population, though there may be some flagging of creative spirit, there's a great reservoir of brains. Their scientists are still firstrate. The British people proved themselves to be a great people by the dignity and discipline with which they fought off the German air attacks during the war. This great highly trained, highly disciplined and civilized nation is in danger of dying of inanition because in the elaborate structure of the welfare state there is so little room left where individual initiative can take hold.

One symptom of the loss of concern for individual liberty which seems inevitable to follow the socialization of enterprise appeared in the postwar period in the toleration of new forms of slavery. We were used to the stories of the vast slave camps in the Soviet Union and its satellite countries, but it came somewhat as a shock to find the humane British tolerating the use of gangs of German prisoners to do agricultural labor.

In all my conversations with farmers in England in the summer of 1947 I found only one man who disapproved of the practice. The farmers paid the prisoners' wages to the government and the government allowed them a few pennies for cigarette money. The farmers found that they got more work out of the prisoners if they fed them a hot meal in the middle of the day, but they didn't seem to feel that the working of prisoners of war in this way constituted a backsliding of civilization; most of them regretted that the industrious Jerries would soon be sent home.

Agricultural wages improved during the war and the Socialists took justifiable pride in this achievement. The question they didn't ask themselves, when they tolerated the enslavement of the German prisoners, was how long a highly paid plowman or tractor operator would be able to compete with slave labor.

This brought us squarely up against the prime historical fact of our time. Under the cover of the dazzle of socialist illusions, just at the moment when technology is opening up the certainty of really widespread wellbeing in material things, the masses of mankind, under the rule of Communist dictatorships, are being plunged back into a regime of servitude such as has not existed in the West since the days of serfdom.

Marxism has not only failed to promote human freedom. It has failed to produce food. It has stirred up wars instead of promoting peace. Socialism is not the answer to the too great concentration of power which was the curse of capitalism. We've got to do better.

But has Marxism really failed? In a way it has succeeded. Both in England and America the Marxist creed has retained a curious negative hold on the mind of the educated classes that makes it hard to induce them to examine any very divergent ideas. Our college population isn't exactly socialist, but its hackles rise if you try to clear any of the socialist preoccupations out of the way in order to discuss industrial society from some different point of view.

Traveling across the continent to deliver some lectures in the fall of 1954, I had occasion to stick my nose into a number of schools and colleges. It was the first time I'd had any real contact with our institutions of learning since I had emerged out of the dim light of the academic halls some thirtyeight years before.

In those days Business was the great vested interest. Even the more broadminded teachers, in whose minds the humane or scholarly moods predominated, were pained when a pert youth questioned any of the preconceptions of the businessman. "Profit" was a sacred word. The professors took a dim view of criticisms of *laissez faire.* The educated people the colleges were turning out identified their own interests and prestige with the interests and prestige of the business class. Labor unions were anathema.

In 1927 President Lowell of Harvard, a kindly man of unblemished private life, put his name to the report that sent Sacco and Vanzetti to their death. To his way of thinking an anarchist or Communist—he never managed to get the difference between them through his head—was an agitator capable of any crime. He certainly would have been horrified if you had told him that, in performing what he considered a painful civic duty, he was merely acting in defense of capitalist vested interests. He was applauded for his courage by most of the college presidents of his day.

Today you find that the vested interest is government. Where in my day we used to wisecrack that the colleges were geared to turn out football players and bond salesmen, today you could say that they turn out football players and bureaucrats. The college man is educated to identify himself with government. I mean with institutional authority. Government, we must remember, has many phases. There is the United

States government; and then there are a host of other governments in fact if not in name, the office forces of the corporations that govern production and the office forces of the labor unions that govern the workingman. The man who values the good opinion of his fellows today flinches at any questioning of the right of the men who sit in the offices to run the lives of the rest of us.

Institutions of learning eternally form the sacred ark through which the ruling dogmas of any particular era are protected from the criticisms of the profane. Remember the Sorbonne in the great days of the canon law. A historian today could make out a very good case for sampling the opinions of college presidents as a way of uncovering the mentality of whatever ruling class is emerging. Since the business of a college president is to raise money, he has to be the type of man who will appeal to those who control the available funds. Forty years ago he had to be congenial with the individual capitalists of the day. Now the money, even when it has the names of individual fortunes still attached to it, is in the hands of institutions. So the college presidents of our day have to have the institutional mentality. How can they help feeling tender toward socialized institutions, whatever form these may take?

The institutional mind drifts naturally into concepts of socialism, which, after all, only means a society run from one central office. The odd tenderness toward communism and Communist causes, which seems to be felt by so many men in the foundations and colleges, may be explained along the same lines. Communism is the most vigorous form of control from a central office which exists in the world today.

If the office workers who man these institutions were even neutral in the battle to dislodge the Communists from strategic positions, so many of them wouldn't vent their ire upon the anti-Communists instead of on the Communists, now would they?

Isn't it possible that the same sort of new ruling class that reached power by violent means in the Soviet Union has reached power by peaceful means in this country and England?

The New Deal revolution took the management of the economy out of the hands of the bankers. The faucets that control the flow of credit are all in Washington today. We are more and more governed, instead of by the oldfashioned politicians, by people who are adept at institutional manipulation. We haven't quite found the terms that describe them exactly. When we like our new rulers we call them public servants. When we are mad at them we call them bureaucrats, but it is the business of selfgovernment to see that they remain servants of the public instead of becoming its masters.

A Book Review

Maybe it isn't St. Augustine or Rousseau or Cellini; maybe it lacks the passionate zest for life in all its diverse and varied forms of the very great autobiographies. But still I think this book will stand high among the testimonials of the suffering spirit of man. I would place it somewhere between Dostoyevski's *The Possessed* and such narratives of the adventures of the light within as *Pilgrim's Progress* or George Fox's *Journal* which abounded in seventeenth century England. Amid all the soggy hysterics that have characterized American writing during the last few years this is the only book I have seen that really penetrates into those depths where every man, in the agony of solitude, has at last to make his decision. No wonder Chambers keeps quoting the last line of Dante's Inferno. It is the story of a descent into hell.

That there is something uplifting in the prospect of the immensity of pain which the human soul can contain is one of the great paradoxes which make life supportable. The appalling part of the book to me was the landscape that formed itself in my mind as a background to the gnawing agonies of

Saturday Review (1952).

the narrative; a landscape with figures, the living picture of a society dedicated to its own destruction.

How can it be that in a few short years we have sunk so low? A society or a nation has some aspects of a living organism. We all know that a living organism that fails to react to danger is sick or dying.

The questions raised in the mind by the moral lynching of Whittaker Chambers by the right-thinking people of this country are so grave and urgent that a man breaks out in a cold sweat to think of them. Can it be that the "liberals" who control communications in the press and the radio and the schools and the colleges in this country have already crawled under the yoke of the Communist Party? I mean in spirit. We know they are not dues paying members. Or has an immensely clever propaganda machine been able to make them dupes of a world wide hoax?

Anyone who has heard the rumors circulated in journalistic circles to the discredit of Robert Vogeler, the American business man arrested and framed by the Hungarian Communists, will be struck by their similarity to the rumors circulated about Whittaker Chambers. It is likely that both smear campaigns have the same origin.

There is nothing appalling in the fact that Communist Party members should continually try to discredit people who have turned against them or who have escaped from their dungeons. If they can't be eliminated physically slander is the most convenient weapon. But what shall we say of the right-thinkers, of the men and women of position and education who repeat these slanders without investigating their origins and who refuse, in the light of all the evidence, to recognize the existence of a conspiracy of assassins who are bent on the destruction of these same right-thinking liberals, as much as on the destruction of the rest of us.

The day when this mystery becomes clear, the day when this delusion is swept out of the public mind, as was the deportations delirium that arose in another "liberal" regime, that day we will be able to go to bed secure in the thought that if these United States are doomed, by forces of history too great for us to overcome, to destruction, at least we will go down fighting.

Anonymously Yours

. . ."I'm sorry I can't sign my name as it may mean my life or my livelihood. We may as well admit we are living under a labor autocracy—graft, rackets, intimidation, goons, etc. For fear of being bumped off, ostracized, or deprived of making a living I'm afraid to sign my name. There are many others like me". . .

Is this the translation of a letter some unfortunate has smuggled out from beyond the Iron Curtain? Not a bit of it. These sentences are copied out of a letter from an American working man received a few weeks ago by a committe of the United States Senate. The Select Committee on Improper Activities in the Labor and Management Fields, popularly known as the McClellan Committee, has hundreds like it in its files. These letters have furnished Senator John L. McClellan of Arkansas and his chief counsel, Robert F. Kennedy, many valuable leads in their investigation of racketeering, violence and extortion in the labor movement. Their investigation has thrown a ray of startling light into the dark places of American life. It has revealed conditions of exploitation and servi-

Printed in condensed form by *The Reader's Digest* (September, 1958). Since this article was written the Landrum-Griffin Act has been passed. It has proved a palliative, a feeble palliative. J.D.P.

tude that few of us dreamed existed. The words "improper activities" in the committee's official title would seem one of the understatements of the year.

Letters of this kind have been piling up on the desks of the McClellan Committee's investigators ever since hearings started. Congressional committees are accustomed to handling an enormous bulk of mail, but this correspondence bids fair to set a record. Three months ago it was estimated that a hundred thousand letters had been filed away in the steel cabinets in the committee's crowded offices in the basement of the Senate office building. Hundreds more pour in every week.

The men and women who write these letters are taking a chance to write at all. Reprisals, they tell the Senator, will immediately follow if their identity becomes known. Most of them rely enough on the committee's discretion to sign their names, but it is the exception when they don't ask that their names be kept secret.

The senator and his chief counsel are in dead earnest about protecting their correspondents. They guard their letters jealously. The rare journalist who is allowed to read some samples of them must promise on his honor not to reveal the names of the writers or to describe any circumstance in such a way as to identify them.

Perhaps a quarter of the letters are anonymous. In some cases people have even tried to disguise their handwriting. "Anonymously yours" is a common signature.

How strange that a hundred thousand American citizens don't dare write openly to their representatives in Congress. Why won't they come out in the open? you ask. "Read a few of the letters," the investigators answer. "You'll see why they are afraid to sign their names."

Fear, it is fear that strikes you when you open some folder at random and pick out a letter. Letter after letter is written in fear. Can it be that a hundred thousand Americans are living in fear? How many hundreds of thousands more do these letters represent? Through every sentence runs the fear of the loss of jobs and livelihood.

The writers of these letters are trying to tell Senator Mc-Clellan that they are helpless in the face of reprisals from the union leadership. The wellintentioned legislation of past years has delivered union members bound hand and foot to the union bosses. The man who doesn't like the way his union is being run and who raises his voice in protest does so at his own risk.

"I regret that I am unable to sign my name," writes one man. "This omission should help to point out the rotten conditions existing, for I know that my job and my future would be in extreme jeopardy if my identity were known." The union bosses can say whether a man shall work or not. In many trades the working man holds his job at the business agent's pleasure. "The denial of employment is a whip over everybody's back." "The unions really punish people unmercifully, really to the point of starvation," writes a bricklayer. "I'd never have another job on the waterfront if they knew I'd written this letter," writes a stevedore.

A number of men have typed out a petition asking the committee to investigate the strong arm methods used by their business agent to control their union local. When it comes to signing they lose their nerve. "Can't sign names," they have scrawled at the bottom of the sheet. "We'd be blacklisted."

They all tell Senator McClellan that they are afraid for their jobs but that's not all. Many of them are afraid they will be beaten up and killed. "I shall be very thankful if you withhold my name," writes a construction worker. "If they find out I've written you, they'll send gangsters after me." He adds that he's a man in his sixties and can't put up the fight he could have in his younger days. "They would kill me," he adds simply. "I am not giving my full name and address," writes another, "because I fear reprisals in the form of acid in my eyes, being waylaid and pushed in front of a truck." Some of them put it jokingly: "I'd sign my name but I don't like my undertaker." "I don't want a brick to fall accidentally on my head." They have seen what has happened to other men who got in wrong: "If I signed I might wake up at the bottom of the canal."

These letters are written in anguish. "Save us while there is still time." They are desperately urgent. "Please, Senator Mc-Clellan, please, please help us . . . We all pray that you will come to this city. I would like to sign my name, but I fear for my family and myself."

Many of them state that the writers would be willing to risk their own lives by testifying before the committee, but they fear for the lives of their wives and their children. "If this letter gets into the wrong hands I shall be finished and so will my wife and children." Many of them have been actually threatened. Snarling voices frighten their wives at night. They remember that their children play on the street. A passing truck can run over a child and no one be any the wiser. There is no police protection in labor disputes. The writers of these letters have nowhere to turn. The Senate committee is their last hope in the world.

Some are pervaded by a sullen despair. "My hands are completely tied, just as every other poor man's are." "The working man has to eat and support his family; that's why he sits quiet and takes this kick in the teeth."

Not all of the writers have let themselves be terrorized.

Many of them are ready to fight. "You are our last hope," writes a union member to the senator, "I don't like to testify before your committee unless there is a dire necessity that I should do so. I don't like to live in fear for the rest of my life but if I am asked to testify I shall." Here's a housepainter that's full of beans: "The goons got nine tenths of the rank and file scared. That's the reason they don't come to meetings, afraid of the goons. I'll face any of 'em for you Senator. I've lived 63 years now, how much longer can I live?—but for God's sake give these young men a chance to raise their families like I did."

The young men, when they write, write angrily. What has happened to the country they were brought up to believe in? they ask. "Is this the United States of America or where are we?—when a man has to lose his job and see his family in want all because he didn't approve of what the union officials were doing and had nerve enough to say so." A veteran writes: "Is this what I fought for in World War II, is this the world my children are growing up into?" Another, a truckdriver this time: "Is this the America I went out to fight for and then come back to find run by a bunch of criminals." "How can you call this a free country when a working man has to pay for the privilege of working to a bunch of gangsters. A free America . . . Ha Ha. Life Liberty and the pursuit of the working man so that the union big shots can live in clover."

The high living of the labor bosses is a favorite theme. Why are they always in Miami when the working men are freezing at home? "It used to be the capitalist got fat off the working man's blood. Now it's the labor leader."

"In the old days we banded together to protect ourselves against these big companies," writes a steamfitter. "Now we are slaves to the union business agents. We can't even talk about it on the job as the steward will have you fired and the business agent will see to it you don't get another job. Please give us a law to protect our free speech and our union treasury!"

A Texan is already reaching for his gun. "Either Congress must deal with these racketeers without gloves and do it quickly or else the day is coming when the people must arise to do the job by direct action."

"Is it freedom when a man can't work at a job without paying the union for the benefit of doing so?" asks another man. "Is it freedom when a man cannot work because the union boss says 'strike'? Is it freedom when our streets are blocked, cars overturned, windows broken, buildings and houses blown up by gangs of hoodlums who call themselves pickets? Is the right to vote any more sacred than the right to work?" A railroad worker sums up the grievances of the rank and file: "The larger the union's income, the less the worker gets. We don't have a secret ballot. We don't vote on anything, so I've quit going to business meetings as we aren't allowed to say anything. I suggest we send the Statue of Liberty back to France and quit calling America a free country. If we don't do something we will go like Russia . . ." For all his indignation he insists on remaining one of the nameless ones: "I'm afraid to put my name on this or I may be liquidated."

These are not cranks and professional malcontents who are writing Senator McClellan. Of course there are inevitably some nut letters: a woman wants the Senate to investigate the fact that her enemies are torturing her by radar, or a crackpot offers a thirty day cure for inflation; but the lunatic fringe accounts for a very small proportion. There's some airing of personal grievances but very little. The more carefully you sample the correspondence the more you become convinced that the great bulk of the letters are written by public-spirited men and women, appalled by the situation they find themselves in, who are racking their brains to find a remedy.

They are worried about the future of our country. "What kind of world are our children growing up in?" they keep asking. Most of them still express faith in the American way of doing things. They believe in Senator McClellan and Robert Kennedy and in the honesty and sincerity of the committee as a whole. "God bless you," writes a woman garment worker. "I know that some day there will be laws to protect us from all this."

The impression you get is that the great bulk of the people writing in to the McClellan Committee never finished high school, but as you read their letters, you can't help feeling pride in your fellow citizens. The letters are well expressed, level-headed, reasonable. The suggestions they offer are practical and carefully thought out. Robert Kennedy, who has had experience with the correspondence of other committees, estimates that at least thirty percent of the suggestions for legislation offered deserve consideration in the drafting of new labor laws. He rates this percentage as unusually high. Ten percent of usable suggestions, he says, is about average. Maybe our public school education hasn't been quite as bad as we feared.

None of these letterwriters is opposed to unions as such. Not a single one wants to abolish labor unions. Many of them are from men who have devoted their lives to the labor movement. They all proclaim that labor must have mass organization to cope with the mass organization of industry, but they want laborleaders to be subject to the law of the land like everybody else. Again and again they draw the distinction between the labor leaders and the rank and file. They insist that Labor with a capital L has ceased to represent the little man. "Our representatives have only one side of the story, that of the men who make their living from the unions."

They feel that proper legislation, before it's too late, can save the labor movement. "All labor will profit more than they will ever know by these investigations," writes one man enthusiastically. "Your investigation has been rough on unions but all unions will be the better for it." "Clean up this mess," another man begs the senator. "Make it so a man has a right to work and not have to bow down to them damn Hitlers."

The letters come from every state of the union. They are written by men and women working in every conceivable trade and occupation. They come from hodcarriers and seamstresses, from the operators of draglines and cigarette-making machines and the makers of delicate dental equipment. They come from steelworkers and ditchdiggers and salesmen and miners and musicians and machinists. With one voice they complain of the denial of democracy, the misuse of funds, the abuse of authority. Though the conditions they describe are much worse in the unions frankly exploited by jailbirds and musclemen that control road transportation and construction than in the blueribbon C.I.O. unions, their complaints cover the entire field of labor organization. "We welcome your efforts to restore ethics back to our unions so that we can be proud of them again," they tell Senator McClellan. "We cannot help ourselves because our servants have become our masters."

They emphasize the working man's helplessness. "Bondage" is a word they often use. "Compulsory unionism through legislation is nothing short of putting a man in bondage to a labor leader." The word "slavery" appears often. "As the unions are now operated the rank and file membership has no more freedom of action than the slaves did during slavery days."

A surprising number of letters deplore the closed shop. "The closed shop means Force." They want union membership to be voluntary. "In order to keep your job at one time we only had to please the employers, but now we have to appease and please our union heads and of the two I'm more fearful of the union than of the employer." "If our union is so sick we must have forced membership," writes another, "there is something wrong with our union."

They ask the Senate committee to find some way of restoring selfgovernment. "Please pass a law to protect our free speech, free elections and our union treasuries." Most of the unions have constitutions which are supposed to assure democratic processes. The leaders have taken care of that. Where they haven't changed the constitution to legalize autocratic rule they see to it that the members vote as they want them to. "We ordinary rank and file," writes a member of a railroad brotherhood, "have little or nothing to say about administration or electing our officers. There is no such thing as democracy even attempted. The general idea is you close your mouth and go along if you want to keep out of trouble."

From every sector of industry comes the tale of individual helplessness in the face of strong-arm organization. No man who doesn't belong to the ruling oligarchy dares raise his voice. "Economic fear of reprisals are the main reasons why the good honest members of the union do not seek election or speak up at meetings." "The business agent has never no opposition," writes a bulldozer operator, "nobody wants to get killed."

A sailor at sea out in the Pacific has scribbled a letter which he explains he'll let nobody see till he gets it into Uncle Sam's

254

mailbox: "When we voice opposition at the union meeting we are dumped and sent to the hospital or we have our union book taken away so that we can't ship." Here's a round robin from a group of electrical workers, only without any signatures. "If we signed this we surely would have reprisals against us. Please but please, we beg you do not pass us up. An investigation is the only thing that will stop this little bit of Russia right in the USA. Please come and restore our union rights and privileges and our right to choose who we want to vote for and to spend our money for in national politics."

A little bit of Russia. They harp on that theme: "If anyone enquires about where the union money goes he's turned in to the company and fired. . . . I really think the people of Russia must be treated a lot better. The workers in this plant have fought in the army for this so-called precious thing called democracy and where is it." "We have nowhere to turn for help," writes a man organized by a subsidiary of the Teamsters. "The Communists in Russia hold no firmer hand over the unfortunates in Asia and Europe than the czars of our local hold over our heads." "Where is our democracy," another man asks; "What about the Bill of Rights? We have to belong to this union in order to hold a job. We have what I call a Russian election. It is one candidate and a hired bunch of goons to work for him."

These men don't have to read books to understand that the essence of the Communist system is the exploitation of the working man by a ruling oligarchy. They see a similar system taking over in America: "They have taken the liberty away from the American worker. When I've got to get permission from union bosses to go to work, it's time our government did something about it or we'll have to get another name for the Land of Liberty."

The story they tell is that wholesale unionization has placed millions of working people in the hands of organizers they don't even know: "We have no meeting hall, no right to vote, nothing to say about a contract or anything," writes a mechanic who finds himself a member of some boilermakers' outfit he has to join to hold his job. He calls it a mailorder union. "We must shell out $5.00 a month and 6 cents an hour for every hour we work. We don't know how many members there are or how much money is in the treasury. We just don't know anything. A business agent comes around and if a man's not paid up he has him off the job."

These letters make nightmarish reading. You come away with the feeling that in the United States today almost any gang of thugs looking for an easy living can call itself a union, force its services on a group of working people as a bargaining unit and levy tribute thenceforward on wageearner and employer alike.

Hundreds of letters elaborate on the theme that the laboring man, in many unions, gets nothing in return for his loss of liberty, and the dues he has to pay. "We have no protection from graft," writes a clothing worker from the Middle West. "We have no vote on who we get for officers. If we don't like one shop we can't quit and go to another. The union won't let us." "I have paid dues etc. every month since April 1931," writes a West Coast truck driver; "I have derived no benefit whatsoever, as I have explained to meeting after meeting. I have paid by hardearned money and it has been stolen. . . . It's the same as if I'd thrown the money down the drain. Isn't there any provision in the law in favor of the individual?"

Why, if there is as much discontent within the unions as these letters seem to indicate, don't we hear more of clean-up campaigns and rank-and-file action? Senator McClellan himself asked that question in a speech during the investigation. Why, he asked, can't individual union members help themselves by banding together for reform inside of their organizations?

This speech stirred up a great deal of comment from among the committee's correspondents. "I did what the Senator suggested," wrote one man. "When I did get the floor they adjourned the meeting right under my feet." "Nobody could get nominated but the man with the strong arm bodyguard," another explains. "You state, Senator, that members can do a lot to clean up their unions by standing up for their rights," wrote a railroad worker. "We did just that and there are fifty men in this little mountain city walking the streets for a job."

There's a flavor to some of these letters in the McClellan Committee file that makes you want to meet the people who wrote them. This reporter took the train to Cumberland to meet the man who made this crack. Let's call him Jones, though actually he has nothing more to lose. His job is gone. His fight is in the open. His case is in the courts.

It is a rainy Sunday afternoon. Mr. Jones and his friends have called a meeting of most of the fifty men he spoke of as walking the streets for a job. The meeting is in the assembly room of their social club. People smoke and drink cokes and eat salami sandwiches as they talk. There are young men and old men, plenty of weathered outdoor faces. They are locomotive engineers, conductors, brakemen, switchmen, railway clerks. They are so eager to tell you about the raw deal they got from the Brotherhoods they keep interrupting each other. Mr. Jones steps up and calls them to order.

It comes as a shock to an outsider to find that so many railroad workers are discontented with the railroad Brotherhoods. The railroad Brotherhoods are among the oldest of American

unions. They command a respectful press. They have a powerful lobby in Washington. "What could be the trouble?" this
reporter asks.

"Don't have no respect for the rank and file." "All they care
about's your money." "They've been in there too long." "The
only thing they think about is making you buy insurance."
"Business unionism." "Some of them are making a bigger salary
than the President of the United States."

"If you don't like the leadership why can't you put them
out and elect somebody else?"

The whole room breaks into a loud horselaugh.

"Mister you don't understand," Jones cries out. "The only
way you can get your ballot counted is by voting the way the
Grand Lodge wants you to." "They had it their own way so
long they just think we are a bunch of suckers."

To prove this point an elderly locomotive engineer tells
the story of the loyalty certificates. A great many years ago
before the 1929 depression the management of the Locomotive
Engineers made some bad investments of the union's funds, in
banks that went broke, in Florida real estate, in various imprac-
tical schemes. When the crash came the union faced bank-
ruptcy. The management appealed to the members to bail
them out by buying bonds. Some men invested hundreds and
even thousands of dollars of their hardearned savings. Even so
the bonds didn't sell fast enough to suit the management, so
they made the investment compulsory. Everybody was assessed
twentyfive dollars over and above his dues for a bond.

These bonds were printed to look like real bonds. They were
supposed to carry four percent interest. They had a lot of small
print on the face of them. Nobody took the trouble to read the
small print. The small print read that the certificates would be
payable "when and if" the trustees "at their discretion" found

it advisable to repay. They never have found it advisable. They raised six million dollars from the rank and file. This in spite of many a suit in the courts from retiring locomotive engineers who had believed their bonds to be an investment for their old age. Of course they weren't really bonds at all. "When they sold them bonds," explained an angry old man, "they had larceny in their hearts."

It was this sort of deal, repeated in the form of other investment plans that never brought in any return which made the men in this room feel that the management of the Brotherhoods was more interested in high finance than in their membership's interests. When a new industrial union for all operating railroad crafts was formed these men decided to go along with it. They liked its constitution that called for direct election of officers, limitation of salaries, the referendum and recall, local selfgovernment and public accounting of funds. This union was known as U.R.O.C. As freeborn Americans, Mr. Jones explained, these men felt they had a right to join a union of their own choosing.

They had reckoned without the closed shop established by the railway labor acts. When they joined the new union they were cited by the Brotherhoods. The Brotherhoods claimed the new union was no union at all. The men put up a long fight but in the end the railroads were forced to fire them. The U.R.O.C. insurrection was suppressed.

Afterwards some men managed to get back to work as new employees without seniority, but the men who had been conspicuously active in the movement were implacably persecuted. "Did you ever go hungry, senator, for want of a job?" one of the men wrote Senator McClellan "for the fear of the wrath of the labor leaders?" Most of them lost everything that was due them in pensions and welfare funds. There were the usual musclemen to beat them up. The fight had gone on year after year. In the end the rank and file of the Brotherhood petitioned to have these men reinstated, but the leadership remained implacable. They had families to support. Their faces showed the strain.

"We've been under pressure for five years," one of them wrote the McClellan Committee. "You never knew which day would be the last you would work. You never knew which knock on the door would mean an act of violence, or which phone call would be a threat. Don't sound like we lived in America, now does it?"

A hundred thousand letters. A hundred thousand different stories each giving a flash of light into some dark corner of American life. The men who don't like their own unions can't get away from them, but also there seem to be cases of people who did like their old union and woke up one morning to find it taken away from them by what one of the letterwriters calls "this plague that is sweeping the country."

Here's a man tells a story of what happened to his small independent union. Let's call him Mr. Smith because the organization that took his union over is the Teamsters and the Teamsters play for keeps.

Mr. Smith is a middle aged man with steel gray hair who lives in a neat little house in a western city. He has a neat little wife who runs a small newsagency on the side. Their children are a couple of curly haired teenagers, a boy and girl who keep running in to snatch at the family telephone while he talks. Mr. Smith will almost do for a *Saturday Evening Post* cover of the typical American working man.

Mr. Smith had worked for a number of years in the plant of a foodprocessing company. He's a laborer. He makes an average of sixtyfive dollars a week. Not much pay but it's a pleasant place to work, he explains with a smile; at least it used to be. They had an independent union, no not a company union, but they got along all right with the company. They had a grievance committee that thrashed out any beefs every Friday. The dues were low, $1.75 quarterly. The officers were elected annually and were paid $25.00 a month for their trouble. They were all men who worked in the plant. There were monthly union meetings where everybody felt free to get up and say what they thought. "But now two men don't dare to be seen talking together. . . . 'Better split up,' we say in the plant, 'the Communists are watching us.' "

"Of course they are not real Communists, but in some way we older men can't understand our union got taken over by the Teamsters' local. What the Teamsters have got to do with food processing we don't understand. They seem to have made some deal with the management. We were caught in the middle, I guess. They got hold of some of our men who began to talk about how we had a lousy contract and all that and before we knew what happened the Teamster boss had had a secret meeting with the management and called an election. No the NLRB wasn't notified nor nothing. They told us it was just a trial election. The real election would come later. A lot of guys didn't even vote. Well the Teamsters said they had won the election and that was that. The old union was scrapped, the old contract was scrapped. At the next meeting they had tough guys standing in the back of the room to glare at any man who spoke out of order. Nobody dared run against the guy they ran for president. He came from the Teamsters, doesn't even work in the plant. We don't know how much salary he gets. We don't know how much the business agent gets. All we know is we get three dollars a month checked off our pay.

We had eight thousand dollars in the treasury of the old union. We never could find out what happened to that. None of your damn business we were told when we went to the B.A. to ask.

"A bunch of men went to the management and said they wanted a chance to vote in a properly supervised election. The business agent said he'd get them fired and threatened to pull the plant, so they shut up. I went myself to see the NLRB man in our state capital. The NLRB man said I'd wasted my money on the trip; too late to do anything. They got us hogtied. Only Congress can help us now."

Call it business unionism, call it racketeering, call it professionalism, the story these letters tell is that the men "who make their living from the unions" are taking over the labor movement. No place for the independents. No place for the idealist who gives his time to organizing for the benefit of his fellow workers. The letters are urgent. "Send your investigators now. . . . Tomorrow will be too late."

Here's the story a man tells who has just lost a battle for honest unionism inside one of the best internationals in the country. The professionals are getting into the fringes of even the Rubber Workers Union. This man says that if the Mc-Clellan committee had investigated the situation in time he might have won.

Let's call him Mr. Murphy because he's an Irishman. He's a husky bullnecked young fellow, wears a T shirt. He was a paratrooper in the European theatre during World War II. He's an energetic fellow, a member of the American Legion and the Veterans of Foreign Wars, a doorbell ringer in local and national political campaigns.

When he got out of the service he went to work in a rubber

plant. Heavy work demanding strength and skill. Five years later he found himself working in a plant that made insulated cable in an Eastern city. A great many foreign born workers were employed. They spoke little English. They were getting a raw deal. He said maybe it was the Irish in him that made him always stick up for the under dog. He felt the men he worked with were being exploited. They were hard workers. They seemed to take it for granted that they should be kicked about and abused by the bosses. It was hard dirty dangerous work. Safety regulations were often neglected. It wasn't only in the plant that the foremen exploited them. Often the foremen did a little moneylending on the side. Some held mortgages on the working men's homes. The foremen had a contemptuous way of speaking of the men as "donkeys."

Young Murphy found himself trying to stiffen their spines. He got up a class in English for them after work. The independent union in the plant seemed to him to be company dominated. He had friends working in a similar plant across the street organized by one of the great industrial unions of the C.I.O. Through them he got in an organizer from the union's headquarters and threw himself into organizing the plant. They lost one election, petitioned for another to the N.L.R.B. and won it.

Young Murphy felt he had really accomplished something for the men. He had a natural flair for leadership; the men believed in him. This rubber workers union had the reputation of being one of the best in the country. He was a member of the organizing committee. He was elected trustee and shop steward, and chairman of the safety committee. His local sent him as a delegate to union conventions. A career was opening up for him as a labor leader.

Still he wasn't satisfied with the way safety regulations were enforced at the plant. He felt some men were being unfairly discriminated against in the wage scale. He believed in equal pay for equal work. He began to feud with the president of his local, a foreign born man like most of the workers in the plant, whom he had helped elect. This man's brother was the industrial union's field representative.

These two men had become labor professionals. They were taking the easy way. The president of the local did no more work in the plant though he was paid full time. He never wore work clothes any more. He sat all day in his office smoking cigars and drinking whiskey. He traded favors with the management. He was building himself a thirty thousand dollar home and playing the stock market. Let's say his name was Joe Cermak.

Young Murphy was still sticking up for the rank and file. Whenever he had a discussion with Joe Cermak, Joe's brother, who as an industrial field representative, had the ear of headquarters backed up Joe. They intimated to young Murphy that if he'd only take it easy and go along with them a fine career would open up for him, president of the local maybe, money and soft living. Let the donkeys do the heavy work.

Murphy decided to go on sticking up for the rank and file. It was a hard decision to make. He had two small daughters. He wanted them to have a nice life. For a while his wife argued that he ought to take the easy way but at last he talked her around. They knew it was going to be tough. Already she was getting telephone calls telling her Murphy was going around with other women, hinting that her husband better keep his nose clean.

The men in the plant believed in him. He had to stick up for their rights. He had enough votes lined up to take the presidency of the local away from the professionals at the next election. For some time he'd been on really bad terms with Joe Cermak. Joe had taken to swaggering drunk around the plant and lording it over his underlings. He tried to bawl out Murphy and took a poke at him one time. Murphy who was a husky fellow gave him a severe beating. The management suspended them both for ten days for fighting in the plant.

Now when the Cermak brothers found that Murphy was really challenging their authority they had to get rid of him. The management didn't like his harping on safety regulations or talking up improved working conditions, either. They laid for him when he got into a dispute over safety regulations with his foreman. They brought charges against him for using abusive language and he was fired. . . Murphy hired a lawyer and took the case to the state labor arbitration board. The union and management put their heads together to pick the arbitrator. Their lawyers collaborated. The union dragged its feet when it came to defending Murphy. Against union and management together he was helpless. He lost his case for reinstatement. The representatives of management celebrated his defeat by taking the Cermak brothers out to dinner.

Murphy, fortunately for him, is a resourceful fellow. He took up a new career in a different type of work; but that was the end of one man's fight for the rights of his fellow workers.

But how can a thing like that happen when this particular industrial union has a central leadership reputed to be honest and intelligent?

"Bigness," answers Murphy. The large unions are directly supervised by the top leadership. The international president sits in on their contract negotiations. He just doesn't have time to keep an eye on the smaller locals. He trusts his field representatives. If a field representative keeps up his per capita on dues collected he's asked no questions. The rank and file are far away. Let them settle their beefs among the lower echelons. The field representatives can build little satrapies of their own. The men who are in the union for the money hate a trouble maker as much as management does. Murphy was a trouble maker so he had to go.

"They just don't have time to pay attention to little guys like me," adds Murphy. "That's why we've got to have the proper legislation, because the United States is made up of little guys like me and that's the only way you can get us a square deal."

Not all of these battles are lost. Sometimes a man of courage wins a round. Among Senator McClellan's correspondents is a carpenter in a southern city who tells with understandable pride of his twenty years' fight for the rights of his union local against one of the biggest A.F. of L. internationals. He was born in Sweden so let's call him Mr. Swanson. He came of an old trade union family. He served for a while in the Swedish army and came to this country right after the first war. To ply his trade he had to join the union.

The local of his craft union turned out to be run by a trustee from the international office. For seventeen years Mr. Swanson and his friends struggled to get back its autonomy. At last in 1943 they were granted a "partial election."

Mr. Swanson was elected president. Sympathizers filled the executive board. Immediately they started to try to put the local's house in order. The years of World War II were golden days for the construction trades. Thirty thousand carpenters poured into an area where there had only been 500 before Pearl Harbor. Dues came in so fast the business agents had to stack the money away in nail kegs. Representatives from the international swarmed about the union premises. When Mr.

Swanson took office he found that they had printed eightyfive thousand work permits. These became known as "dobies" in many parts of the country. The game was to charge a man from $23.50 to $55.00 and sometimes even more for the right to work. Then after thirty days the business agent would pull him off the job and he'd have to pay another fee to get hired again.

Mr. Swanson was trying to find out the state of his union local's funds. The financial records had been shipped off to the international office, to be audited, the business agent said. By threatening to have him arrested Mr. Swanson managed to get the local's secretary to disgorge what records were left. There were stubs of enormous checks made out to cash. He found $230,700 in initiation fee blanks for which there was no corresponding record at the bank. Safe deposit boxes in various agents' names were stuffed with money. The local's property was held by various business agents in their own names. After several months of investigation Mr. Swanson felt he had enough evidence to report his findings to a special meeting of the membership. They appointed him chairman of a committee to demand an accounting of the local's funds from the international.

Mr. Swanson and his committee besieged the international. Although it was hard to find lawyers to take their case owing to the international's political power, they finally found a nervy attorney who would do it. He filed suit in federal court. At that point the international president tried to buy Mr. Swanson. Nothing doing. The customary threats followed. "I only fear God in heaven," answered Mr. Swanson.

"If there's anything I hate it's a thief," he added, and swore out a warrant for the arrest of the chief international representative whom we'll call "Mr. Bock." Mr. Bock discreetly retired to Florida. The local D.A. kept forgetting to do anything about his extradition. By the time Mr. Swanson found a U.S. district attorney willing to press the case the statute of limitations had run out on Mr. Bock. Mr. Swanson reported the amount of Mr. Bock's plunder to the Internal Revenue Department but the taxcollectors were busy with other things.

The upshot of it was that the international refunded the quarter of a million dollars that could be proved in the courts to be missing. The international president lashed out with a libelous speech at Mr. Swanson at the next convention. Mr. Swanson was expelled from the union.

Misfortunes rained on Mr. Swanson's head. His wife died. He had to sell his home to finance a libel suit against the union president for conspiracy to keep him out of the union. An effort was made through one of the international president's lobbyists in Washington—a gentleman who is now serving time for extortion and income tax evasion—to deprive Mr. Swanson of his American citizenship.

Mr. Swanson is an old man now. They settled his libel suit out of court but for years he couldn't work as a carpenter. He never got back the presidency or even membership in the local for which he recovered the funds. Only recently a court ordered the union to restore his work card. He had to agree not to attend union meetings pending an appeal, but at least he can work at his craft. In his spare time he gets up recommendations for legislation. He has studied the Swedish labor laws, and wants something of the kind enacted in this country.

A hundred thousand letters. A hundred thousand different stories out of construction, the waterfront, manufacturing, small business, the service trades. Not all of these people are helplessly submissive. Some letters tell the story of men who are risking their lives right now every day to fight for what they consider their rights as Americans.

Here's a man who drives a taxi in a teeming industrial city. Let's call him Mr. Bronski. He's been a taxi driver for thirty years, likes the independent life. He's always been a union man. Years ago when a huge nationwide concern came into this city and gobbled up all the little cab companies, Bronski was one of the men who tried to organize the drivers. His union called a strike for improved working conditions. The big company hired a professional strikebreaking agency: scabs with tin hats, riot sticks, field kitchens. Strike breaking was a fine art in those days before the New Deal. The big company won. No contract was signed. Bronski was blacklisted and had to move to another city.

When he came home from several years in the armed services he went to work for a new small cab company. After the nationwide company broke the hackdrivers' strike they established a monopoly in this great industrial city. They were entrenched at City Hall. They raised rates and cut down on the service.

Now as far as unions are concerned they seem to have changed their policy. The shoe is on the other foot, Mr. Bronski will tell you with a roar of laughter. Now the nationwide company is hand in glove with the Teamsters Union. Drivers organized one hundred percent. Unions, Mr. Bronski points out, tapping the side of his nose with a thick forefinger, are put to strange uses these days.

Let's call the small company Mr. Bronski works for the "Blue Cabs," and the big company the "Red Cabs." Mr. Bronski says he likes the Blue Cabs because the management is progressive. The drivers get a square deal and an unusually high percentage of the fare. Blue Cabs is owned by an aggressive young fellow who is trying to break the monopoly. He gives his men better terms and the public better service. He refuses to discriminate against qualified Negro drivers.

It's public knowledge that Red Cabs is fighting to put Blue Cabs out of business. Their union moves in to organize the Blue Cab drivers. Although he was a member years ago, Mr. Bronski says he doesn't like the deal. He already has a better contract than the Red Cab drivers have, and he doesn't like the looks of a certain Mr. Grosso who runs their local. This Grosso is a professional. He has a finger in half the unions in the city. He's in and out of City Hall.

So Mr. Bronski and some of his friends invite an organizer from another big union, an out of town union, to form a local for the Blue Cab drivers. They are only a hundred and fifty men. They don't need to be protected from the management but they've got to have a powerful organization behind them to protect them from Mr. Grosso. Right from the first Mr. Bronski has suspected that this Mr. Grosso is being paid by the Red Cab Company to drive the Blue Cabs off the street.

The fight is on. Mr. Grosso's Red Cab union calls a strike of the Blue Cab drivers. A few of the Blue Cab drivers go out but most of the men decide to cross the picket lines. They are content with working conditions. If they must have a union, they want one of their own. The usual pattern of violence develops. Drivers are slugged, cabs are burned, bricks are thrown into windows. Passengers are intimidated, gasoline supplies siphoned off, tires slashed. While the union is fighting Blue Cabs on the street the nationwide company is harassing their management through the state public utilities commission and the state labor board.

Needless to say there's no police protection for the Blue Cab drivers. When an out of town wholesaler is induced to send two tank-trucks of gas to keep up their gasoline supply, under escort in the middle of the night, a cop is seen copying down the license numbers and turning them over to the Red Cab union's pickets.

Meanwhile Mr. Grosso is letting it be known that the man who runs the Blue Cabs had better look out for lead poisoning.

At the height of the battle the Blue Cab drivers hold an election. Negro drivers and white line up to fight it out side by side. They manage to keep Mr. Grosso and his hundred and fifty musclemen, all equipped with red armbands so that they won't slug each other, at bay at one gate of the compound where the cars are parked, while their men sneak out one by one through a small door in back to the voting machines. The vote is ten to one in favor of the Blue Cabs' own local.

Mr. Grosso announces that picketing will continue. Acts of violence keep up day after day after the election, until the Blue Cab drivers decide one night that they are tired of going about their business in fear of their lives. A mysterious fire destroys a couple of taxis belonging to the Red Cab Company. After that everything is suddenly quiet. No more bricks are thrown. The pickets seem to feel a strange new respect for Blue Cab Company's property. No more drivers are beaten up. Mr. Grosso is even heard to announce that their manager needn't be afraid to walk out on the street.

This young man never did let them scare him: that's the moral to the tale. The drivers all tell you that none of this would have come to pass without his courage and coolheadedness. He is a war veteran. He says he came from another city and bought into this company as an investment without knowing he was buying into a hornet's nest. Well, once he was in he was in. He decided to stick it out. Now saving the Blue Cab Company has become a crusade with him. He knows he's risking his life, as well as his money, but he feels he's risking his life for American principles just as much as when he fought in the war. His wife agrees with him.

They live in a hotel. Their children stay with their grandparents and go to school in a city three hundred miles away. Every weekend they fly back to see them. The doors leading to this man's office have good stout locks. He never stirs without a gun. He's tense but smiling and cheerful like a man in the front lines. His wife is his business partner. She works in the office with him. She is a courageous young woman, but she can't help a quick glance up and down the street when they step out of the hotel lobby to get into their car. "Mustn't let 'em worry us," he pats her soothingly on the arm; "I'll never look behind me."

There are plenty of brave men in American business. There are plenty of honest men in the labor movement who put the interests of the rank and file before the interests of their own pocketbooks; but they get tired. When they find themselves fighting unscrupulous management united with corrupt labor leaders who in turn are united with corrupt politicians they begin to feel that the odds against them are too great.

Mr. Sanford is a big rangy fellow from the Texas Panhandle, sandyhaired, blueeyed. He runs a cigarette making machine in the plant of one of the larger tobacco companies. He's been a union man since he went to work in the coal mines when he was fourteen. When he helped unionize his plant years ago he wanted it organized under the C.I.O. but the C.I.O. men were too busy and a socalled independent union got in instead.

This union is subsidiary to a whole group of unions controlled by a professional, a big operator, the kind that is in it for the easy money. He's a convicted embezzler, in cahoots with every successful criminal in the region. He's always indicted but never goes to jail. There are a lot of women working in the plants, says Mr. Sanford, Negroes and hillbillies who can't write too good. This man pulls the wool over their eyes. He's clubby with management. "Sometimes it looks like they'd rather give their money to a hoodlum than pay it to their employees."

When the racketeering union's contract was about to expire Mr. Sanford worked for months getting up a petition to the N.L.R.B. asking for an election. He wanted to switch to an honest union. Everybody was for the petition but nobody dared circulate it. Anybody seen with that paper was sure to be fired. Mr. Sanford was afraid, not for his own life, but that harm might come to his wife and his children.

Out of four hundred men and women only two men would take the paper around. It all had to be on the q.t. A few of the girls passed the word along. He could trust some of the Negroes not to turn him in. Although as a committeeman he had a certain standing it was only after heartbreaking effort that he got a hundred and thirty names on his paper. When he took it to the N.L.R.B. he was told the petition was in the wrong form. The names should have been on cards.

He went back to the plant with the proper cards, but by that time a new contract had been all signed, sealed and delivered to run for two years. The racketeering union was there to stay. No chance of an election now, said the N.L.R.B.

That was the sort of thing took the heart out of you. "There's no defense for a man that stands up," Mr. Sanford says. "So far as freedom of speech we're in a worse state than Russia. . . . Give me a little defense and I'll come right out in the open and fight. I want to be proud of my country."

There's one point on which the writers of these hundred thousand letters all agree: they are solid behind the investigation. "Senator McClellan," they say, "pay no attention to this cry that your committee is out to break up unions. The rank and file know better. . . . You are doing a great service to the union cause and the good old USA." "You have brought encouragement and hope to millions of union men who despise the tactics of their leaders." "Don't let our leaders fool you that you will lose the labor vote. We don't vote the way they would like to have us."

They want action. They want legislation. They want protection. They want democracy.

"We pray to God that we will some day find a man in our government who will help us working people rid ourselves of these dictators so that we can govern ourselves."

Faulkner

Faulkner's storytelling appeals to me so much, I suppose, because it is the kind of storytelling I remember as a child down in the North Neck of Virginia. Sitting in a row of men on some rickety porch after the dishes had been cleared off the supper table on a hot August night when the dryflies shrilled, rocking and smoking or chewing tobacco a man would start talking. Usually he didn't explain who the people were he was telling about. You were supposed to know that. It would be "he" or "she" or sometimes "what's his name" did this or that. Gradually out of a web of seemingly disconnected incidents a story would evolve. Characters in situations scary or mirthful would take shape. A scene would light up as if you were there watching. Listeners would draw in their breath or laugh and slap their knees. I'd be sitting on the porch steps keeping out of sight for fear somebody would notice me and send me off to bed, never minding the mosquito bites, listening till my ears burst.

Reading Faulkner brings that lost world back to me. It's so often an elevenyearold boy who is the listener through whose ears the outlandish scrambled tales pour into the reader's blood.

National Review (1963).

Faulkner's writing has a way of pouring direct into the bloodstream like a transfusion. It was his oldtime rural storyteller's gift that enabled him somehow to keep his steaming turgid inventions—blood and thunder mixed with often false psychological subtleties out of the psychiatrist's clinic—within the margins of the tall story tellingly told. You are carried away whether you believe it or not.

At his best Faulkner's gothic caricatures of men and women, for all the claptrap of the plots, come to life as Dicken's did. Always the emotions ring true.

Storytelling is the creation of myths. A good acting myth doesn't have to be plausible but it has to impose its own reality on mankind. I defy anybody who has been reading Faulkner to look at a map of the state of Mississippi without expecting to find Yoknapatawpha County there.

Faulkner's characters impose their nightmare reality upon you because they are built out of truths, the truths of the stirrings of the flesh and blood and passion of real men observed tenderly and amusedly and frightenedly, just as Homer made his goddesses and heroes real because he built them out of traits he knew in men and women. In Faulkner what I like best is the detail, the marvelously accurate observations he built his narrative out of, the raw material of his inventions. Has there ever been a bear more real than Old Ben in The "Big Wood"? His unendingly cordial study of the struggle between the bloods of various races under one man's hide is truthtelling of the highest order. So are his descriptions of the happy symbiosis that builds up under certain conditions between men of discordant races and disparate backgrounds. The Chickasaw Indians who bought the steamboat, the hound dogs, the hunting dogs, the little fyce dogs, the horses, the mules, the trees, the streams and the swamps; and the kitchen clock (I think it was in *Soldiers' Pay*) that ticked out: life, death; life, death.

And now the great storyteller is dead. I don't imagine death came too hard to him. He had met death before many times in his storytelling. His stories are full of the knowledge of death. He did not meet death as a stranger.

Cogitations in a
Roman Theatre

It was exciting to speak in Rome, where I read the original version of this paper in a tiny theatre a stone's throw from the column of the Antonines. Exciting but also sobering. In Rome, more than any other city in the world, one feels the weight of history. Crushing and exhilarating, history stands manifest at every streetcorner.

Man in society can, I think, be most aptly described as an institutionbuilding animal. He builds institutions the way the ants build hills. At least during the few thousand years that we know anything very definite about his activities the building of institutions seems to have been his chief concern.

Rome has been the pivot and hub of some of the most awesome and majestic institutions men have ever constructed. The very name connotes empire.

These connotations are particularly sobering to an American. We Americans were brought up to believe that history didn't exist. For a number of generations we thought the Declaration of Independence had repealed history. During the last fifty years the American people have gone through a painful and costly education in the realities of history. As a nation perhaps

Modern Age (1964).

we haven't made as much progress as we might have in our education, but as individuals, here and there, a few of us seem to be learning.

One of the teachings of history is that whole nations and tribes of men can be crushed under the imperial weight of institutions of their own devising. History further teaches that, through all sorts of terrors and despotisms, a divine something in the human spirit has managed to keep alive and to leaven and permeate the institutions that channel men's destinies.

The working of that divine leaven is what I mean by civilization. Civilization in the abstract remains one of man's eternal aims; but civilizations, in the concrete, are subject to growth and decay, like living organisms. We are here today, I said, to exchange ideas about what can be done to defend our own peculiar type of western Christian civilization against its own decay, and against the inroads of the brutal and arbitrary institutions which grew out of the national and ideological wars that have devastated the century we live in.

It would seem a staggering assignment if it weren't one of the laws of human behavior, well expressed in Toynbee's useful catchword, that it takes challenge to provoke response.

It is my belief that at last western civilization is beginning to show response to the challenge of the monolithic Communist state that allows no liberties at all, and of its corollary, the bureaucratic socialist state, where a few loopholes of freedom still survive. We can call one type the illfare state and the other the welfare state. Young people throughout the western world and even under the Communist regimes are beginning to question the socialist slogans. Our problem today is to ask what can a few scattered men of letters do to cherish and stimulate that response.

Before we go any further I think we need to examine our own

capabilities somewhat searchingly. How well are we equipped to cope with this titanic assignment?

Somewhere in the middle twenties a Frenchman named Julien Benda wrote a book called *La Trahison des Clercs* that made a great impression on me. As I look back on it, it was a somewhat superficial work, but its title summed up for me my disillusion with most of the men of letters I had considered great figures in my youth. This was during the period of the war of 1914-18. I was studying at Harvard up to the spring of 1916 and followed with growing astonishment the process by which the professors, most of them rational New Englanders brought up in the broadminded pragmatism of William James or in the lyric idealism of Ralph Waldo Emerson, allowed their mental processes to be so transformed by their conviction of the rightness of the Allied cause and the wickedness of the German enemy, that many of them remained narrow bigots for the rest of their lives. In joining in the wardance the American intellectuals were merely following in the footsteps of their European colleagues. Their almost joyful throwing off of the trammels of reason and ethics is now generally admitted to have been a real transgression against the cause of civilization. I can still remember the sense of relief I felt in taking refuge from the obsessions of the propagandists of hate in the realities of war as it really was. The feeling was almost universal among the men of my generation who saw service in the field.

Benda analyzed this state of mind with pain and amazement. For two thousand years he saw the people we now tend to describe as intellectuals, whom he described as *les clercs,* as having been on the side of reason and truth. As he put it, although helpless to keep the rest of mankind from making history hideous with hatreds and massacres, they did manage to keep men from making a religion of evil. "L' humanité faissit le mal mais honorait le bien." Surveying the racial hatreds, the national hatreds, the class hatreds that rose from the wreck of civilization in that most crucial of the worldwide wars, he concluded "On peut dire que l'Europe moderne fait le mal et honore le mal."

Western civilization is only just now beginning to recover from the carnival of unreason that went along with the military massacres of the first world war. The hideously implemented creeds of the Marxists and the Nazis and the Fascists of various hues were rooted in this denial of humane and Christian values. The task before us is somehow to restore these values to primacy in men's minds and hearts.

It has been my experience through a pretty long life that the plain men and women who do the work of the world and cope with the realities of life respond almost automatically to these values. It is largely when you reach a certain intellectual sophistication that you find minds that have lost the ability to distinguish beween right and wrong.

To be of use in the world the man of letters has continually to be on his guard against the professional deformations of his calling. The man who lives behind a desk or on the lecture platform has to seek daily confrontations with reality to keep his mind clear of the delusions and obsessions of the current verbiage.

In other words, he has to find every day some new way of telling the truth.

Language from its very beginnings has served two purposes: one purpose is to deceive and the other is to convey truth. One has to reach a fairly ripe age before one comes to a full understanding of how hard this is to do. Lies come easier.

The truth is hard to come by and when you do manage, by hook or crook, to come up with some fragment of it you are likely to find it as dangerous as strontium 90.

Socrates liked to call the search for truth "the examined life," and we all know what happened to Socrates. Perhaps we can take some comfort from the fact that the Athenians let Socrates live till he was seventy years old before they handed him the hemlock.

Ever since man began, the pursuit of truth has been an activity beset by many occupational hazards. The institutions through which, in almost any society, the bosstype men impose their will on the workers and the producers and the builders are invariably founded on lies. Even a tiny fragment of truth tends to produce an infringement of public order. The automatic reaction of the bossmen who hold the police power is to stamp it out. The tremor runs through the whole hierarchy of timeservers and lickspittles whose lives and careers depend upon the bossmen. In any human society that you care to study you'll find that the bossmen's hangers-on have equipped themselves with the most delicate sensibilities to enable them to feel the pain in their own corns when somebody steps on the bossman's foot. Truth is by its very nature painful to authority.

History is full of examples of the danger of truth telling, but it was not until we reached the epoch of masseducation and masscommunication that we came to the full understanding of the difficulty of discovering the truth in order to tell it.

Your uneducated and illiterate man in the old days would hardly have been likely, if you showed him a pig, to have called it a goat. Today, with our minds continually indoctrinated with whatever fallacies the authorities in charge of radio and television feel it to their interest to promulgate, you can't be too sure. Your college educated intellectual is likely to explain to you that it may be on account of your own psychological disabilities that the creature in the pen looks to you like a pig. He won't go so far—everything is relative you know—as to claim that the creature is a goat; but he may well point out that treatises have been written to the effect that epistemologically speaking, the creature may be described as having goatlike characteristics.

The man of letters finds it particularly hard—as the old saying went—to tell the truth and shame the devil, because he is, by the nature of his calling, an intellectual. The intellectual's mind deals in concepts rather than in things. That's what they teach you to do in college. Of course abstract concepts are useful in the processes of thought, just as poker chips are useful when you play poker, but you have to remember that it is what they represent that counts. In the painful search for the words needed truthfully to describe an event, every word has to represent some real thing. In spite of his larger vocabulary the intellectual is sometimes more at a loss when it comes to that than the ignorant wayfaring man.

The intellectual is always taking the poker chips for real money. This flaw in his way of thinking usually combined with an arrogant disinterest in the thought processes of the average man, shuts him into a conceptual universe divorced from life as it is really lived.

Truth is always a discovery. The discoverers are people who

see the thing before they name it. For the intellectuals everything is already named.

In modern bureaucratic societies intellectuals are becoming a dominant class through their furnishing the bossmen with the slogans and delusions by which they control the general public. The twentieth century may possibly end by being known as the century of the intellectual. As they become giddy with power the usefulness of the intellectuals as a class to the cause of civilization becomes more and more doubtful.

I have been a good deal in South America during the last few years. There, as I suppose in most Latin countries, you find a much greater cleavage between the man who does the work and the man who sits behind the desk than you would find in Englishspeaking America, in Canada or the United States. The educated and the uneducated live in different worlds. The universities are full of halfeducated young men who, out of sheer ignorance of plain workaday human behavior, snap up all the slogans fed to them by Marxist agitators. Since little in their schooling fits them for engineering or dentistry or veterinary work, and they have been taught to scorn buying and selling over the counter, and would rather die than work with their hands, they have no career open to them except politics. The Communist Party offers to these young men who have no intention of soiling their hands a magnificent prospect of bossing their fellows and attaining, through revolution, the use of the automobiles, airplanes, hotels and restaurants which in their countries are reserved for the very wealthy. The success of the Communists in those countries stems from their appeal to the disoriented intellectual.

Of course their careerism is veiled in idealistic verbiage. Benda's *Trahison des Clercs* in modern form. It's all for the good of the workers and peasants. This is the basis of what you might call the Fidel Castro mentality.

In our own universities you find a parallel mentality, except that outside of a few indoctrinated Marxists, the aims are less drastic. Young men who dread the risks of the competitive world of business look forward to more placid careers "in government" as it is called.

Willy nilly, the world over, the man of letters belongs to the class that staffs the bureaucracies. Before he can perform his duty to tell the truth about the society he lives in he must clear his mind of the ideological trappings which are part of the equipment for worldly success of the class to which he belongs. In his renunciation of the commonplaces taken for granted by his class he will find himself faced with the question that comes resounding through the centuries, Pilate's anguished question: What is the truth?

It is a question to which humanity has found many answers. It has been involved in all the casuistries and sophistications and the proliferations of verbiage the human mind is capable of. I believe it can be best answered in the form of a creed. I believe that there are certain simple realities which are universal to all men, no matter how diverse their backgrounds or their environments or their social customs. The man who humbly seeks out these realities is on the firm path which will lead him to the truthful observation of the world about him.

Man's great achievements come when he examines reality without preconceived ideas. The man of letters who will be useful to humanity in our day will examine the social conflicts with the cool and eager eye of young Darwin examining a cuttlefish or an insect. Lies and delusions are an inevitable part of the human mentality so the truth can never entirely prevail, but a tiny flash of truth is seen a long way. Small illuminations have farreaching consequences.

When I say that the man of letters must avoid preconceptions I do not mean that he must be without standards. The human mind can no more function without the conviction of right and wrong than a mammal can exist without a skeleton. Without firm belief that good is good and evil is evil where can we find the inner fortitude needed to explain to the masses of men, whose minds have been befogged by endless selfserving propaganda, what we mean by civilization?

The terms we have to use have been so mutilated in the mouths of politicians that one can hardly pronounce grand old words like "liberty" and "democracy" without an apologetic blush. The ideas behind these terms have lost all urgency for the populations that benefit most from them. It sometimes seems as if the only people who have any understanding of civil liberty are the people in the Communist states who are deprived of it.

In fact the best description I have seen in some time of the sort of thing I want to defend came from an escaped Russian sailor. The man jumped overboard from a Soviet freighter anchored in the bay off Calcutta. He swam to another ship and finally made his way to the shore. The Russian authorities tried to snatch him back by claiming he'd stolen a sum of money, but the Indian law court wouldn't give him up, and he finally made his way to the United States. On being asked why he risked his life to escape to the free world, he answered that, first, he was tired of being ordered around by stupid people who knew nothing about navigating a ship and, next, that he thought people, in America at least, really were equal before the law, and that here "each person is able to build his own life without directive from above, and that each citizen through his own development brings good to society."

The story of that Russian sailor makes the problem concrete. The question before us is what can we do to preserve and improve the sort of society all these refugees from the Communist slavecamps hope for when they risk their lives to escape to freedom.

I do not believe that the values the conservatives want to conserve can be furthered by a static resistance to change. The problem is to find ways of adapting the institutions of modern industrial society so that they will serve the purposes of civilization. That this sort of adaptation is no philosopher's dream is proved by the success of United Europe. Those nearest to it probably see more defects in the foundations than we do from the other side of the Atlantic, but the fact remains that in fifteen years progress has been made towards uniting the peoples of Europe whose wars first put our civilization in deadly jeopardy.

Turning for a moment to my own country the tasks which I would urge on the conservatives are equally arduous, but success would be equally rewarding. At home in the United States the same sort of shrewd and patient work which produced the framework of a new Europe is needed to resolve two great mass conflicts. Methods must be found to keep the agitation for Negro rights from degenerating into racial warfare. That is a very special situation that demands tact, forbearance and social inventiveness on both sides instead of the fanning up of hatreds by politicians and professional troublemakers.

The other mass conflict we don't hear so much about. The

rise to power of empirebuilders among the labor unions has brought about a sort of schizophrenia in American industry. Management and labor have become two warring camps, with government, in the hands of votehappy politicians, usually on the side of the labor leaders. While the financial gains of the workers have been so immense as to throw large sectors of the economy off balance, very little has been done to carry out the original aims of the old nineteenth century labor movement.

The original impulse came from the need factoryworkers felt to assert their human dignity. In modern industry the wageworker is starved for a feeling of participation in work well done. As the situation stands today the worker in the massproduction industries can have no feeling of belonging to the productive enterprise that affords him his livelihood. He takes almost no part in the government of the labor union that takes such a large slice of his pay. Although useful solutions have been tried out, and some with great success, our politicians can only see in the labor unions a means for delivering regimented blocks of votes at the polls. The social engineer who talks directly to both the man at the bench and to the man at the desk and manages to bring about a rational integration of management and labor in some form of cooperation will have deserved well of his country.

One of the tasks of the conservatives as their influence grows will be to suggest reasonable solutions for social problems. Ideas don't depend on victory at the polls. Politicians are notorious for snatching at ideas proposed by the opposition. Practical measures to humanize industrial society are in my opinion more important than neat ideological statements or political victories. The trend towards a totalitarian society can only be stemmed little by little by practical measures which change the alignment of institutions. There is no way of saving civilization by a formula like the Communist Manifesto which has done so much to destroy it. The great political slogans of the past have tended to come out of the application of general ideas to specific situations, so now the vocabulary of a new conservatism will come into being gradually out of the workaday struggle to remedy specific abuses.

One of the weaknesses of conservative theorists has been that their diagnoses of social and political trends have been so pat and plausible that they have tended to stick to them too long. Some of the diognoses applied marvelously five years ago, but they don't apply today. Even under the rigid shell of Communist dogma changes have occurred. Many free world positions have been so badly defended that for the time being at least they have become indefensible. It is time to look at social and political phenomena with a fresh eye. Only after the naturalist's calm and dispassionate evaluation will it be possible to use your humane standards as a measuring stick and to decide which trends you want to back and which you want to discourage or oppose.

The field is certainly open to fresh ideas. In spite of their successes against the looselipped liberals of the free world the Communists are still struggling in the straitjacket of Marxist dogma. Among the crowd of little Stalins and ersatz fuehrers and spurious duces that have climbed to power out of the debris of the European colonial system, the socialist ideology has become a cloak for the most aboriginal forms of personal dictatorship.

In western Europe there have certainly been developments, some hopeful and some discouraging. At least there the effort to apply brains to the difficulties created by the last war has had tangible results. The Englishspeaking countries, after some brilliant early successes for the cause of civilization, such as the generous treatment of Germany and Japan and the aid the Marshall Plan gave to the rebuilding of Europe, have had very little to offer.

The chief strategy of our leaders in the ideological war has been a refusal to face facts, and a strange inability, once the facts were admitted, to take the action the facts demanded. The world is waiting for a renovation of its political and social theories.

The conservatives must come up with invigorating new ideas. The other ideologies have come to a dead stop. It's a time of stalemate in a number of directions. A sort of calm has descended on the world. The peoples under Marxist rule seem to have run out of enthusiasm for ideological warfare. One is reminded of the sudden calm that descended on Europe when the wars of religion began to peter out. Perhaps fresh voices can make themselves heard. They must speak up fast because the calm can't last very long.

On the whole it is an interesting time to be alive. Five years ago the triumph of Communist dictatorship seemed almost certain. Now, in spite of the threat of nuclear extermination and the equally fearsome prospects consequent on the population explosion, it looks as if civilization might still have a fighting chance. It makes me wish I were a great deal younger.

A Protest Protested: Please
Mr. Rip Van Winkle
Wake Up Some More

Edmund Wilson's protest (*The Cold War and the Income Tax: A Protest*; Farrar, Straus and Company, Inc., 1963) is a document of no mean interest. The author has one of the best literary minds of our generation. He has developed a limpid and casual prose in the great tradition of essaywriting in English. His criticism exhibits a rare combination of qualities. He has humor and a very personal sensitivity to whimsical human nuances. Besides being a historical critic and an able journalist of literature he is a scholar; as John Adams said of Jefferson: "a great rubber off of dust."

There can hardly be a subject more appealing and timely than the misadventures of a man of talent caught in the bureaucratic web of the Internal Revenue Service. It is one of those situations that Kafka prophetically foresaw. Vivian Kellems told the story from the point of view of small business. Now we have it from the point of view of the absentminded professor who is also one of our ranking men of letters.

He tells the sad tale of lese majesty towards the bureau-

National Review (1964).

cratic state and of the retribution that followed. The recital is clear and brief, uncloyed by selfpity. I kept thinking what a waste of a hardworking man's time and energy. Perhaps I was influenced by personal affection for the author, whom I have known off and on for many years. Knowing and admiring the man I found the wrecking of his odd little ivory tower extremely poignant. There are times when one is reminded of the adventures of the nearsighted Mr. Magoo. There's a charm to such heedless innocence. I too can remember the house on East 53rd Street.

Like many of us of the particular literary generation which came of age during the first world war, Edmund Wilson was profoundly influenced in his intellectual formation by the French and English literature of the nineteenth century. We came away from that reading with a much higher opinion of the social rating of the man of letters than was general in the American society we grew up in. To tell the truth, though the more discreet of us kept the conviction to ourselves, we thought the writer was tops. You can feel the pang of disillusionment when Wilson writes: "My lawyer on one occasion had evidently tried to persuade a Utica official that the Internal Revenue Service ought to show consideration to a distinguished man."

The revenue agent answers sourly that Mr. Wilson will be treated "like any ordinary man on Water Street." Water Street is more or less the Skid Row of Utica, so the comparison was hardly intended to be flattering. Wilson hastens to point out, with great justice, that the ordinary man on Water Street with no money to hire lawyers to fight back for him, fares even worse than offenders who consider themselves more distinguished.

Wilson's crime was that for one reason or another he had neglected to file income tax statements for nine years. It wasn't until 1958 that Internal Revenue woke up to the situation and started their hue and cry. They made up for lost time. As he describes his ordeal, he was threatened with jail, fingerprinted, crossquestioned by probation officers, and condemned to pay a large fine. To make things worse publishers' royalties, magazine payments, and all other sources of income were garnisheed at the source. The revenue agents who handled the case were deaf to pleas for a reasonable settlement which would give him an opportunity to pay off his debt over a term of years. The worst feature of the situation was that the culprit hardly ever saw the same agent twice. Each of them had hurriedly run through the files, but none of them seemed to have taken the trouble to get a real grasp of the various aspects of the case.

Eventually an agreement was rather suddenly reached between the culprit's lawyers and the taxcollectors. One can imagine some member of the Kennedy administration, friendly to the profession of literature, getting wind of the affair and reaching Commissioner Kaplan on the phone to tell him for God's sake to call off his bloodhounds. How would the "American image" look abroad if the Internal Revenue Service reduced our best known literary critic to destitution or sent him off to die in a prison cell?

The levies and liens were lifted, but the eminent author was left at sixtyeight loaded with debt to the government and to his lawyers. His own damn fault you'll say. Maybe, but isn't the system a little bit to blame? And doesn't a man who has worked hard all his life in the public service deserve some special consideration from the community? I don't think it is pressing too far the claims of the literary fraternity (a bunch of swelled heads I'll admit) to say that an excellent writer, like an excellent physician or a first rate productive worker in any field performs what should be recognized as a public service "above and beyond the call of duty." It is reported that Edmund Wilson has retired to lick his wounds in some European capital. I hope it won't be for good, as he threatens. A writer belongs in his own country.

This protest is a cry from the heart. "We are not concerned with hardship," the taxcollectors kept telling Wilson. His discovery of the untrammeled power of the federal bureaucracy came as a shock. Personal experience brought home the old adage: the power to tax is the power to destroy.

He speaks of himself as Rip Van Winkle waking up, but I find it regrettable that Rip Van Winkle didn't wake up all the way. His mediations on the subject of taxation never transcend his own private problems. He might have let his mind roam a little over the social consequence of our tax structure. He might have hit upon some fresh and useful observations.

Hasn't our tax structure become a dominant factor in the development of industry? The shape of business and industrial enterprise is continually being conditioned by whether expenditures for various activities are tax deductible or not. Tax regulations mould men's careers. The expense account carnival is one example. Another is the inordinate growth of advertising and publicity. Don't tax regulations force money, which might better be spent on profitsharing for employees or in improving the methods of production or the product, into unproductive channels? I suspect that it is not so much the amount of taxation but the confused system by which it is administered that hampers growth and invention and fosters a bureaucratic lethargy in American enterprise. These are subjects on which a man of brains and diversified reading should have formed opinions. Taxation is too important to leave to the economists.

Personal as it is, this account of one man's struggle with the tax authorities should be recommended reading for members of Congress who deal with tax matters. Taxation is reaching a degree of oppressiveness incompatible with personal liberty.

So far these protests seem to me to be in the right direction. It is when the eminent critic starts to itemize his complaints about the way the United States government is spending money it takes from him, that I begin to wonder whether much of Rip Van Winkle's intelligence isn't still fast asleep.

I am not objecting to our eminent critic's private opinions. I often don't agree with them, but they are always arguable. It is when he allows his private opinions to be lost in the group obsessions of the liberal intellectuals that I feel like scolding. My complaint is against the whole substratum of preconceptions on which a large majority of our academic and literary people base their thinking on current affairs. I'm not scolding at any particular man. I'm scolding at the intellectuals as a tribe. Again *la trahison des clercs.* Their motions seem to me to be based on unexamined propaganda, or hearsay, and on emotion instead of on fact and experience. They are not producing a useful analysis of the dangers that face mankind. Their obfuscations are useful only to the propaganda of the Communists.

This particular Rip Van Winkle starts off disarmingly with an apology. He admits that it is paradoxical that an erstwhile Socialist should complain about state power: "I must confess with compunction that I was naïve enough at thirty-one to take seriously Lenin's prediction in his pamphlet *State*

and Revolution written in 1917 before his return to Russia—
[Let me interrupt: that is before Lenin had any experience
with the realities of governing]—that the clerical work of
a socialist government could easily be attended to in the
spare time of the ordinary citizen . . . and that the state
would wither away and cease to harass the individual. . . . It
was assumed that the working class could maintain an international solidarity and that it did not want horrible wars.
But both these assumptions were incorrect. The working
class . . . has to be recognized today as a Marxist fiction."

Among all the farewells to delusion penned by the dis-
enchanted Socialists of my generation this seems to me one
of the clearest and simplest. The trouble is that having dis-
missed the basic delusion, Rip Van Winkle's slumbers are
still haunted by that host of ancillary delusions which have
become the commonplaces of "liberal" thought.

From the moment when, on page 45 there appears the
rubberstamp reference to the "dubious evidence" on which the
Rosenbergs and Alger Hiss were convicted, it's as if, instead
of the voice of a first rate intelligence, we were hearing another robot of the ventriloquists of Communist propaganda.

Though there may be room for difference of opinion about
details, the Communist conspiracy by which the formulae
for atomic explosions were filched from the American labora-
tories and transmitted to the Soviet Union is a fact. It is part
of the established history of our times.

It is hard to understand how a writer as wellversed in
Marxist history as Edmund Wilson showed himself to be in
To the Finland Station should have neglected to study the
military communism which resulted from the stress of the
Russian civil war and gave an aggressive cast unforseen dur-
ing the early days of the revolution to every Soviet institution.

Our Rip Van Winkle writes as if the Communist Party's organization for world conquest did not exist, as if Cuba had not been occupied as a Communist outpost and as if the terrorism and sabotage of democratic institutions which are the preliminary skirmishes of an invasion of Venezuela were not daily occurrences. It is perfectly possible for reasonable men to disagree about what measures should be taken to meet this situation, but any man who writes as if the situation did not exist is deep in the slumbers of delusion.

Our Rip Van Winkle complains bitterly of the military purposes for which the government spends the money it extorts from him, but he never brings up the question of who started the contest that made all this expenditure necessary.

Stalin starts it towards the end of the second world war. The moment the American landing in Normandy and the lavish supply of American warmaterials relieved the German pressure on the Soviet armies, Stalin's propaganda began to din in every Communist's ears that the next enemy to be overthrown was the United States. The destruction of the United States has been project number one of the Communist apparatus for nearly twenty years. If the writer had felt doubt about the truth of these facts, an hour or two reading in any wellstocked library should have offered him conclusive proof.

So far from opposing Russian expansion it was American policy during the nightmare twilight of the Roosevelt administration to turn over half the world to the Communists. In an access of folly, which can only be compared to the errors in leadership which brought about the ruin of Athens in the Peloponnesian War, American troops were pulled back and every facility was offered the Russians to occupy eastern Europe. In the case of Prussia and Austria the theory was promulgated that Russian occupation would punish the people for their war crimes. If it hadn't been for the presence of mind of General MacArthur Japan would have gone the way of East Germany.

I know that the abandonment by the Western Powers of the Esthonians, the Latvians, the Lithuanians and the Poles and later the Czechs to Stalin's police state is ancient history and that it is considered bad taste to bring it up, but I don't see how it is possible for a wellinformed man to indulge in diatribes against militarism in Washington without taking account of the situation which brought it into being in its present form.

Let me say here that I can't help feeling sympathy with antimilitarists even in their most crackpot manifestations. For better or for worse the uselessness of war has been basic in my political thinking all my life. As a young man I was opposed to our taking part in the first global massacre and I was bitterly opposed to Franklin Roosevelt's policies which led to our involvement in the second. I've always had fellow-feeling for the isolationists. I should like to have seen the United States develop into a great neutral nation, like Sweden or Switzerland.

If anybody had consulted me about the atomic bomb I would have said "drop it on Iwo Jima." Having been around the Pacific as a war correspondent, my opinion was that the Japanese were already defeated. All we needed to do was to tighten our blockade and wait for their peace proposals.

Naturally, nobody asked my advice. Plenty of other men, in a better position to make their opinions count, felt the same way but their opinions were overruled.

This is all water over the dam. We live in the age of

atomic warfare and we have to deal with it. Hasty denunciation by literary men of army and navy and airforce officers who are conscientiously trying to do their duty by experiments with new methods of warfare won't help us, not a little tiny bit. We need all the arms we can dream up. We need, even more, cool and clear and wellinformed thinking.

Almost anybody who keeps up with the progress of events would agree with some of Wilson's protest against the State Department's foreign policy. The trouble is he doesn't go far enough. He leaves out the most important parts of the story. He slurs over the realities, upon which useful analysis must be based, of the disasters for the cause of civilization which have resulted from American folly. To blame all the "cold war tensions" which have been the journalistic commonplaces of the last few years on "American encirclement of the Soviet Union" is to fall into a trap set by the Communist propagandists and to do their work for them.

The fallacy into which this sort of thinking falls which is to my mind the most dangerous to the cause of peace is the spreading of misapprehensions about civil defence. Anyone who was in England during the last war must remember the magnificient power of resistance shown by the noncombatant population through their organization of teams to put out incendiary bombs and to fight fires and to dig the dead and wounded out of the wreckage left by the German bombings. Civil defence did as much as the courage and skill of the young fighter pilots to win the Battle of Britain. It did more. It gave the British noncombatants a feeling of heroic comradeship that saved them from moral collapse during the unimaginable stresses of the bomb attacks.

This fashionable attitude of jeering at the attempts, which

I admit have been distressingly feeble, to get civil defence organizations started and shelters established in this country is based on ignorance of the realities of war, of any war.

Ignorance in the active intellectual is much more dangerous than the ignorance of the man in the street, because the intellectual can turn his ignorance into printed phrases which become implanted prejudices in the popular mind and serve to block people off from learning by their own observation and experience.

I don't know anyone who had experience with civil defence during the last war who doesn't think it essential to the morale of the population. The European neutrals like Sweden and Switzerland have welldevised plans for protecting their population from fallout at least. From the reports of careful observers we know that a great deal has been done in that respect for the population of Moscow. Why should so many American intellectuals show an almost frantic objection to offering similar protection to the people of their own country?

One of the most effective deterrents to the use of nuclear bombs against American cities would be the knowledge by a possible enemy that we had an alert civil defense based on efficient community shelters. Another would be the successful development of antimissile missiles, or of methods of disrupting the electronic controls of hostile rockets.

The technology changes almost daily. Men who write to influence the public mind should try to keep up with the little driblets of information which occasionally seep through the scientists' veil of secrecy. The news isn't all bad. Anyone who saw the results of the firestorms that accompanied the thousand plane raids towards the end of the last war knows that atomic destruction could hardly be worse. Quantitatively, it is true that individual bombs will destroy larger areas, but qualitatively the results would not be so different if proper shelters removed the possibility of death from fallout. Spreading hysterical terror of atomic warfare solves none of its problems. It is equivalent to crying fire in a crowded theatre.

"Now how is one to struggle against this situation?" asks Edmund Wilson. He describes in touching terms the persecution of men whose consciences have as he puts it driven them to acts of personal defiance.

He cites the case of the Major Eatherly who has been celebrated in England and France and throughout the Communist countries by the ban the bomb propagandists as the American Dreyfus. He expounds the Eatherly myth in such touching terms indeed that when I reviewed this book for *National Review* in 1963 I, for one, swallowed the story without checking on it. It now turns out from the carefully documented work of William Bradford Huie in *The Hiroshima Pilot* (Putnam's, 1964) that the true history of Major Eatherly is different indeed. From the transcripts of his trials the history appears to be that of a compulsive swindler and of softheaded V.A. psychiatrists who tried to save him from himself. Interesting reading indeed, but the moral is far different from that enunciated by Bertrand Russell and his claque. The answer to Edmund Wilson's question is that before we "struggle against this situation" we must try to learn what the situation actually is.

Be that as it may, it is true that conscientious objectors against paying taxes have no standing with Internal Revenue. They are stripped of their possessions and, if particularly unlucky, serve terms in federal prisons. You can't help admiring the courage and dedication of those selfimmolated martyrs but you wonder whether, as a way of influencing events, their sacrifice is much more effective than the sacrifice of the poor bonzes in Vietnam who pour gasoline on their saffron robes and burn themselves up.

"What is the author of this protest to do?" Wilson asks again. "... Our country has become today a huge blundering power unit controlled more and more by bureaucracies whose rule is making it more and more difficult to carry on the tradition of American individualism. ... I have come to feel that this country, whether or not I continue to live in it, is no longer any place for me."

He turns back nostalgically to the nineteenth century he was born in. The confident reformer of the past always saw himself confronted by an enemy who would represent for him a release of the forces of life, the "dawn of a new day," the beginning of a "better world." Today he finds no such adversary. "Not 'capitalism,' not 'communism.' Simply human limitations so general as sometimes to seem insurmountable, an impulse to internecine destruction which one comes more and more feel irrepressible." These elements "plus our runaway technology" have produced what he considers the frantic militarism of the Washington bureaucracies which are preparing "the demise of our society" under the mushroom cloud.

The final note is of a despair that seems unnecessarily helpless. One is reminded of the black nihilism of some of Mark Twain's last writings. In the face of such massive unbelief an answer may seem presumptuous.

It is true that history is irreversible. You can't turn back the timestream; but, if tendencies toward the good didn't survive interwoven with the forces of destruction in the flow of events we wouldn't have had any civilizations to lament the passing of. When institutions are shattered some of the good in them seems to remain in men's consciousness. All through history intelligent and courageous individuals have been picking up the fragments and piecing them together again. If this weren't true mankind would hardly have survived the tussle for food round the mouths of the caves in the ice age.

In spite of many terrible events and many reverses suffered by the cause of civilization, in this winter of 1963-64 the prospects of the power struggle in the world do not seem quite so threatening as they seemed a few years ago. The machine for Marxist supremacy is less united than it was. There appear to be relaxations behind the barred frontiers. The Communist-controlled populations may even be losing some of their enthusiasm for the regimented militancy that has swept over so much of the world. The danger of war is less immediate than it was. Though it is hard to see how the western powers can regain the ground they have lost for civil liberties and for civilized methods in general, it looks as if they might be granted a breathingspace to reconsider their follies.

It is a time for taking stock. Perhaps some critical voices can make themselves heard. Instead of throwing down their cards in a fit of pique it is the duty of men of intelligence and learning to get to work, as they always must, patiently piecing together civilization's broken fragments, dissecting the generalized commonplaces that obscure realities, sorting out truth from falsehood, extolling the good and decrying the evil. Even if it were possible at any time, this particular moment would be the wrong time for a man of letters to resign from responsibility. Suppose you did shake the dust of Idlewild off your feet would the dust of the new Roman airport be so different? Though many of us sometimes would like to think there was, there is really no sense to the cry of the clown in the English musical: "Stop the world I want to get off."

Lincoln and His Almost
Chosen People

The story of that day has been so often repeated it is etched in the American mind. You have read it or heard it told so often it is as if you had been there yourself. It's as if all of us actually remembered the neat streets of Gettysburg jingling with horsemen and carriages that Indian summer morning, the ladies in hoopskirts and shawls, the bearded Amish in their flat black hats, the hobbling convalescents in weatherstained blue from military hospitals, and the gleam of the Marine band that led the cavalcade of blackcoated dignitaries out the Taneytown road to Cemetery Ridge.

Right behind the band President Lincoln's dark gangling frame, topped by a tall silk hat, towers above the dumpy figures of cabinet members and secretaries. For once he rides a horse that suits him, a fine big chestnut. Even his most querulous critics admit that day that he sits his horse well.

A square wooden plaform has been erected at the cemetery. It bristles with state governors and congressmen and diplomats interlarded here and there with a general in uniform. The speakers face the multitude of raw graves and the shallow valley and the ridges where nearly forty-five

Written in 1963.

thousand men fell dead or wounded in the three day battle which ended Lee's invasion of the North. Beyond the ridges and the russet woods of late autumn smooth blue hills smoke in the distance.

Delivered at a celebration of the centenary of the Gettysburg Address in January, 1964.

The opening prayer, which was described as touching and beautiful, was also remembered for its extreme length. Then the band played "Old Hundred" and the stately figure of Edward Everett, ex-senator, ex-secretary of state, four-time governor of Massachusetts, the first American to win a doctorate in a German university, the apostle of Hellenic studies, the ex-president of Harvard College, brahmin of the brahmins and fashionable orator of the day, advanced to the podium with a sheaf of papers in his hand.

"Standing beneath this serene sky," he began, in the voice which had been described as melodious as the prodigious Webster's, "overlooking these broad fields now reposing from the labors of the waning year, the mighty Alleghenies towering before us, the graves of our brethren beneath our feet, it is with hesitation that I raise my poor voice to break the eloquent silence of God and Nature."

Dr. Everett's voice broke the silence for something like two hours according to the reporter from *The New York Times,* who went on to describe the sightseers wandering over the slopes in search of souvenirs, and the great number of carcasses of dead horses which had been left to rot in the fields.

Listeners on the edge of the crowd, too far away to follow the learned Bostonian as he led them, in measured periods, through human history from Pericles' funeral oration to the Union successes of the past summer, may well have been regaling each other with fresh tales of the President's oddities. When he had been called to speak to one throng waiting at a train stop the day before he had smiled at them wryly from the back platform. "Well you've seen me," he said, "and according to general experience you have seen less than you expected to see."

When a military band came out in the moonlight to serenade him at Judge Wills' house in Gettysburg, he appeared tall and grim at a second story balcony and told the people thronging the street below he was sure that they would listen to him if he did make a speech but that tonight he had no speech to make. He added that in his position it was important for him not to say foolish things. "Not if you can help it," came a voice from the crowd. "It often happens that the only way to help it is to say nothing at all." The President made his bow and retired. Some people appreciated this kind of humor, but a great many didn't.

It was hard for people to understand that Abraham Lincoln was not an off the cuff speaker. Every sentence he uttered had to be phrased and rephrased, and written out in his careful hand. He had worked long and hard over the scant two pages he was planning to read as his share of the dedicatory remarks.

We were most of us brought up on the story of the notes scribbled on the back of an envelope, but unfortunately the record proves that Lincoln started drafting the Gettysburg Address at the Executive Mansion in Washington, and finished it at Judge Wills' house before going to bed the night he arrived in Gettysburg.

He was never quite satisfied with it. His invitation to speak had been an afterthought on the part of the Cemetery Commission. The press of executive business left him little time to arrange his thoughts for the address. He was preoccupied with the message to Congress he was preparing for early December. In spite of two great victories for the Union cause that had ushered in the summer's campaign, Gettysburg and Vicksburg, it had been a heavy year. Draft riots in New York. Copperhead agitation in the Middle West. At that very moment Bragg's Confederates had a federal army bottled up in Chattanooga. Grant was on his way to the rescue. After having allowed Lee to make good his retreat across the Potomac, Meade was facing him along the Rapidan. Again Meade had let the wily strategist choose his own ground: Lincoln trembled for the result. As if he hadn't enough public worries, his dearest little Tad had taken sick. He had left Mrs. Lincoln, who had never recovered from their son Willie's death the year before, in a state near hysterics.

Just before starting for the cemetery the President was handed a cheering telegram from Secretary of War Stanton. Grant had things in hand at Chattanooga. Mrs. Lincoln reported the boy was better.

Even this late in his career Lincoln was a nervous speaker. His voice was shrill and his delivery mechanical at the start. Sitting with an air of respectful attention on his face through Edward Everett's oratorical set piece, which a Philadelphia reporter described as like Greek sculpture, "beautiful but cold as ice," Lincoln had time to collect his thoughts. He even made a couple of last minute changes in the order of words. A hymn, specially composed for the occasion and sung by the Baltimore Glee Club, rose out of the "thundering applause" that greeted Edward Everett's patriotic peroration. During the singing Mr. Lincoln was seen to put on his eyeglasses. He ran his eyes hastily down the two sheets he'd brought out of his pocket. His strapping young friend and junior partner

Ward Hill Lamon, whom he'd appointed United States marshal and who acted as a private bodyguard, rose to his feet and introduced "The President of the United States."

Accounts differ as to the immediate effect on the audience of the Gettysburg Address. Young John Hay, then one of Lincoln's secretaries, thought "the Ancient," as he called him, acquitted himself well. Others found his delivery high-pitched and tremulous with taut nerves. A reporter wrote of his "sharp unmusical treble voice." The speech was over so soon that a photographer who'd meant to photograph the President delivering it didn't have time to focus his lens. There was applause but Lincoln felt it perfunctory. "Lamon" he is reported to have whispered to his friend as he stepped back from the edge of the platform, "that speech went sour. It is a flat failure and the people are disappointed."

The address stuck in people's minds. The more they remembered it the more they were impressed. Edward Everett wrote Lincoln handsomely next day: "I should be glad, if I could flatter myself that I came as near to the central idea of the occasion in two hours, as you did in two minutes." *Harper's Weekly* in New York found the speech "simple," "felicitous," "earnest." Even among New Englanders who had been so scornful of the railsplitting attorney from backwoods Illinois the address was spoken of as "one of the wonders of the day."

As the years went by, memorized by every schoolchild, the Gettysburg Address became, along with the Declaration of Independence, one of the showpieces of the American heritage.

Why should these few words have rung so true? Why should they have evoked such response from so many different kinds of Americans? Wasn't it that Lincoln, by birth and education, was the man of his time best fitted to speak from the main stream of the national culture? The great underlying fact which motivated the history of the United States throughout the mid nineteenth century was the migration westward. As a boy and youth Lincoln lived that migration. The inner spirit and the external ethics of the nation were based on the Protestant Bible. The Bible was the mould of Lincoln's intellectual formation.

In that sense Lincoln was the besteducated man in the United States. The college trained gentry along the Eastern Seaboard were thrown off by his canny use of the ignorant countryboy pose which he found such an asset politically. They couldn't see that education was a profounder matter than college courses. The bulk of literate Americans were still shut up too tight in their provincial backwater of the English literary tradition to appreciate the energy or the depth of the national culture then forming. Based on the Bible and on the tradition of the Scotch-Irish borderers it was part of the main stream of the culture of the English speaking peoples. As a wielder of words Lincoln was among the forerunners of the great American tradition. Lincoln. Walt Whitman, Mark Twain.

Born in Kentucky, where his father and grandfather had moved from Rockingham County, Virginia, as part of the first wave of settlers across the Appalachians, his earliest memory was being told how his grandfather Abraham was killed by an Indian while clearing the forest behind his cabin. Lincoln described his father Thomas as "a wandering labor boy . . . who never did more in the way of writing than bunglingly write his own name." The family legend had it that it was Abraham Lincoln's mother who taught his father that much; certainly she seems to have started young Abraham reading the Bible at an early age.

Thomas Lincoln worked as a carpenter and odd job man. He drifted westward with the tide. Having trouble getting title to the land he'd cleared in Kentucky, he moved the family to Indiana where the homesteader had a better chance. Lincoln wrote of himself as a boy as large for his age . . . "and had an axe put in his hands at once; and from that till within his twentythird year he was almost constantly handling that most useful instrument."

When he was nine his mother died of an epidemic known as "the milk-sick." Thomas Lincoln, who seems to have been luckier with the ladies than with crops or landtitles, went back home to Kentucky and picked himself a new wife. Abraham and his sister needed a woman's care.

This was a competent widow with three children, said to have been a childhood sweetheart. Children were an asset to a pioneer family. Many hands made light work. She was tolerably well furnished with this world's goods in the shape of housefurnishings and farming equipment and Abraham Lincoln affectionately remembered her care and kindness. Perhaps she encouraged him to pay attention to his schooling when he could get it, "by littles," he described it.

Abe grew up with a reputation for great strength. The neighbors thought he was lazy. Most of them agreed with his father that reading a book never cleared an acre of land. A cousin, John Hanks, told Herndon, reminiscing about the days when he and Abe worked together in the field as shambling teenagers: "When Abe and I returned to the house from work he would go to the cupboard, snatch a piece of corn bread, sit down, take a book, cock his legs up as high as his head and read. We grubbed, plowed, mowed and worked together barefooted in the field. Whenever Abe had a chance in the field while at work, or at the house, he would stop and read."

Outside of the famous "school of hard knocks" Lincoln got his early education almost exclusively from the Bible, from *Pilgrim's Progress* and *Aesop's Fables.* The shrewd and salty comments of the Hebrew chroniclers made more of an impression on him than the miracles. He instinctively recognized that the Old Testament encompassed an entire literature, mythology, the poetry, as well as the traditional history and the religion of the tribes of Israel. Lincoln once remarked that, compared with other books that came into his hand, it was the truthfulness of the characterization that impressed him. Saul and David were real men. The chronicler did not gloss over their sins and weaknesses. The boy could compare them with men he knew.

The border life of the Lincoln and Hanks families wasn't too different from the life of the Israelites. Though there had been some improvement in tools, their technology had not advanced too far from the technology of the days of Abraham the patriarch. Though the machine age was imminent, the first twenty years of Lincoln's life were spent in the age of handicraft.

Pilgrim's Progress and *Aesop's Fables* fitted in with pioneer culture where storytelling was an art. When he came to *Robinson Crusoe* it fitted in perfectly: that was how young Abe lived most of the time. Added to that were the scraps of oratory and of quotations from the classics he found in his school readers. From these quotations and from the Biblical teachings, he could assemble a body of standards to judge the world by. Then, when he read Parson Weem's *George Washington,* his whole soul kindled with the thought that there were nobler things to do in the world than hoe corn.

Ambition started to stir him to do something grander than split rails.

His reading broadened when he moved to New Salem and, later, to Springfield. Gibbon gave him a touch of the ironic and Augustan view of history. Volney and Tom Paine disparaged the Biblical miracles that the revivalist sects he was brought up with based their faith on. For a while he fancied himself a freethinker. Eventually the inconsistencies of the freethinkers struck him as forcibly as the inconsistencies of the Biblical mythmakers. He was never a churchmember and had no interest at all in sectarian dogmas, but in the last analysis he was as profoundly imbued with the religion of the Bible as any man who ever lived.

Lincoln was bound he'd push out into the world for himself the day he turned twentyone. Before he could leave home he had to help his father's family in one more migration, this time into the black loam country of Illinois. He helped his father build wagons and load them with the plows and the hoes, and the bedding, and the pots and pans, and the furniture the second Mrs. Lincoln had brought from Kentucky, and they set off for a new location further west.

When he described the journey for John L. Scripps, who was getting up a campaign biography in 1860, his words naturally fell into the Old Testament cadences: "March 1, 1830, Abraham having just completed his twenty-first year, his father and family, with the families of the two daughters and sons-in-law of his stepmother, left the old homestead in Indiana and came to Illinois. Their mode of conveyance was wagons drawn by ox teams, and Abraham drove one of the teams. They reached the county of Macon, and stopped there some time within the same month of March. His father and family settled a new place at the junction of the timberland and the prairie," Lincoln's narrative continued. "Here they

built a log cabin, into which they removed, and made suffi-
cient of rails to fence ten acres of ground, fenced and broke the
ground, and raised a crop of sown corn upon it the same year."

Compare the cadence with this passage from Chronicles:
"And they went to the entrance of Gedor, even unto the east
side of the valley to seek pasture for their flocks.

"And they found fat pasture and good, and the land was
wide and quiet and peaceable; for they of Ham had dwelt
there of old."

These were probably the last rails Abraham Lincoln ever
split in his life. He was on the lookout for better ways of
making a living. He once told a friend that his father had
learned him to work but he had never taught him to like it.
While he still lived at Pigeon Creek, he worked as helper
with the ferryman and occasionally brought passengers ashore
from the Ohio River steamboats in his own skiff. At nineteen
he made his first trip down river to New Orleans as a hired
hand on a flatboat.

The family had hardly settled near Decatur before Lincoln
began to show interest in public affairs. His signature appeared on a petition to the county commissioners to change
the location of the polling place. It was during the political
campaign that same fall that he made his maiden speech
when the candidates for the legislature came to Decatur.
"Pictured out the future of Illinois," noted a listener. He
added that one of the candidates said "he was a bright one."

Young Lincoln was an enthusiast for "internal improvements." Steamboats were taking the place of flats and bateaux.
The difficulties of another trip poling a flatboat down the
Sangamon and then drifting down the Illinois and the Mississippi to New Orleans brought home the need for quick and
cheap transportation to open up the western country. When

he was the Civil War President years later, no one had to explain to Abraham Lincoln the importance of the Mississippi. The knowledge had come with the callouses on his hands as he tugged at the steering oar past the settlement at Nogales which was to become Vicksburg.

The trip was in the interest of a storekeeper named Offutt. On his return Lincoln clerked in Offutt's store and helped him run his mill at New Salem. Clerking in a store gave him leisure to read and to exchange droll tales with the customers. Already he had a local reputation as a storyteller. Lincoln used to figure that his whole schooling barely covered a year, but he could write read and spell a great deal better than most of his neighbors. He was in demand to draft public documents.

For a while he couldn't decide whether to study law or blacksmithing. The law won out. Oldtimers told Herndon that Lincoln was hardly ever seen in those days without a book under his arm. He devoured the newspapers.

When Offutt's business showed signs of going on the rocks Lincoln decided he had made enough friends around New Salem to take a fling at running for office. The lineups were forming for the presidential contest between Andrew Jackson and Henry Clay. Though Lincoln's family and friends were all Jacksonian Democrats, reading Henry Clay's speeches convinced Lincoln he ought to be a Whig. It was as a Whig he decided to run for the legislature.

His appeal to the voters was disarming. He discussed the feasibility of constructing a railroad across the state. (This was 1832. The first line of the Baltimore and Ohio was still in course of construction. New Salem wasn't such a backwater as people have tried to make out.) Right at the present, reflected young Lincoln, a railroad would cost too much to be financed in Sangamon County. The aspirant legislator presented a detailed scheme for canalizing the Sangamon River.

He spoke up for public schools. His argument in favor of universal education was Jeffersonian: "That every man may receive at least a moderate education and thereby be enabled to read the histories of his own and other countries, by which he may duly appreciate the value of our free institutions"; and he noted furthermore "the satisfaction to be derived from all being able to read the scriptures."

He apologized for his youth and ended on a very characteristic note: "Every man is said to have his peculiar ambition. Whether it be true or not, I can say for one that I have no other so great as that of being truly esteemed by my fellow men, by rendering myself worthy of their esteem." (The phrase still smacks of the copybook: he was just turned twenty-three. That copybook phrase was to become the imperative of his career.) . . . "I am young and unknown to many of you. I was born and have ever remained in the most humble walks of life. I have no wealthy or popular relations to recommend me. My case is thrown exclusively up on independent voters of this county, and if elected they will have conferred a favor upon me, for which I shall be unremitting in my labors to compensate. But if the good people in their wisdom shall see fit to keep me in the background I have been too familiar with disappointments to be very much chagrined."

This was a busy summer. Besides running for the legislature Lincoln hired out to a certain Captain Bogue who was trying to establish a steamboat service from Beardstown on the Illinois to the fastgrowing settlement of Springfield about twenty miles above New Salem on the Sangamon. This was internal improvements put in practice. Lincoln's job was to hew with a longhandled axe, cutting away snags and fallen trees that impeded the passage of the good ship *Talisman*.

The *Talisman* never reached Springfield. She stuck on a dam on the return trip on account of the falling water. The enterprise was a failure. Steamboating on the Sangamon proved unprofitable. It was probably the experience of this trip that caused Lincoln a few years later to dope out and patent a contraption for easing boats over sandbars.

Back in New Salem with forty dollars in his pocket, and at loose ends, Lincoln enlisted in the militia. The occasion was an expedition to drive Black Hawk and his Sauk warriors back across to the further side of the Mississippi River. Lincoln was elected captain by his company. Describing his part in that campaign in a sardonic speech he made in Congress many years later he said he hadn't seen any Indians but had had some bloody struggles with the mosquitoes. He was mustered out in time to lose his election, but he had the satisfaction of carrying New Salem by a large majority. "The only time," he stated with some solemnity in his autobiography "that Abraham was ever beaten by a vote of the people."

Wellwishers got him appointed postmaster as a consolation. He picked up a little income as assistant to the county surveyor. Reading the surveyors' manual interested him in geometry. When he was finally elected to the legislature he took Euclid along to study in slack moments. One of his colleagues lent him law books and eventually took him into his office, when Springfield became the state capital, as a partner. About that time he discovered Shakespeare and memorized scene after scene. Shakespeare's people, like the characters in

Chronicles and Kings, were flesh and blood men and women like the people he knew.

According to Herndon, his partner in later years, Lincoln ceased to do much reading when he took up the practice of law. He absorbed more information from talking to people than from reading books.

By the time he became a successful lawyer and married a lady of upperclass breeding, Lincoln's own education was complete. From the experience of pioneer life and canoeing on the Sangamon and flatboating on the Mississippi and drawing plats for Illinois boom towns and passing the time of day with all comers at the postoffice, and from absorption in the Bible and from reading Shakespeare's plays and the speeches of Henry Clay he had already assembled the moral and intellectual tools with which he was going to cope with events and problems for the rest of his life. His outlook was tinged by the crackerbarrel humor of the country store and by a peculiar note of melancholy best expressed by the stanza of his favorite poem which he found in a newspaper and quoted again and again in all sorts of contexts:

> 'Tis the wink of an eye, 'tis the draught of a breath
> From the blossoms of health to the paleness of death,
> From the gilded saloon to the bier and the shroud.
> Oh why should the spirit of mortal be proud?

The classics of this particular mid American mid nineteenth century culture formed the mental bank which Lincoln could draw upon whenever political life demanded that he put his notions into words. They had to be words people could understand. They had to be words people would feel.

His phrases quickly reached the understanding of his hearers because their education too was based on the King James Bible.

When Lincoln, in the Gettysburg Address, described self-government as "government of the people, by the people and for the people" he touched his audience to the quick. The words aroused something more personal than the rubberstamp response to a political slogan. They aroused unspoken memories of marking the ballots at the polling place, serving on jury duty, petitions to the legislature, political debates in the grand manner, such as the still freshly remembered oratorical contest between Lincoln himself and Stephen A. Douglas which had done so much to polarize Republican opinion during Lincoln's losing campaign for the Senate. Behind the first meanings of the words he used were resonances that struck deep chords of feeling among storedup recollections out of Bible reading and hymnsinging in church. To many he seemed a minor prophet come back to life out of the Old Testament.

Lincoln never denied that he was a professional politician. He was a professional of selfgovernment. Implicit in many of his speeches was the effort to explain the paradoxical relationship between the leader and the led which was buried deep in the phrase "government of the people, by the people and for the people." He felt that this balanced interplay was something the people of the United States had that nobody else in the world had. It was easy to feel but hard to pin down in a precise statement.

He came very close to saying what he meant in an address he delivered before the New Jersey state senate in the course of his extended speaking tour on his way to Washington for his first inauguration in the winter of 1861. He had been engratiating himself with the assembled legislators with reminiscences of what the name "Trenton" had meant to him: "May I be pardoned if upon this occasion I mention that away back in my childhood, the earliest days of my being able to read, I got hold of a small book, such a one as few of the younger members have ever seen, Weems' 'Life of Washington.' I remember all the accounts there given of the battle fields and struggles for the liberties of the country, and none fixed themselves upon my imagination so deeply as the struggle here at Trenton, New-Jersey. The crossing of the river; the contest with the Hessians; the great hardships endured at that time, all fixed themselves on my memory more than any single revolutionary event; and you all know, for you all have been boys, how these early impressions last longer than others. I recollect thinking then, boy though I was, that there must have been something more than common that those men struggled for. I am exceedingly anxious that that thing which they struggled for: that something even more than National Independence: that something that held out a great promise to all the people of the world to all time to come; I am exceedingly anxious that this Union, the Constitution, and the liberties of the people shall be perpetuated according to the original idea for which that struggle was made, and I shall be most happy indeed if I shall be an humble instrument in the hands of the Almighty and of this, his almost chosen people, for perpetuating the object of that great struggle."

In using the phrase "his almost chosen people" Lincoln was picking his words with care. He was saying that the application of the principles laid down in the Constitution and the Declaration of Independence was a continuing process, not yet completed. This was the theme he resumed in those great phrases in the Gettysburg Address that toll like a bell: "It is for us the living rather, to be dedicated here to the unfinished work

... that these dead shall not have died in vain ... that this nation under God shall have a new birth. . . ."

A hundred years later what do the words of the careworn national prophet who spoke at Gettysburg mean to us?

An uncommitted observer from an alien culture, say a wellread Arab journalist, might well search in vain, under the opulence, the crime, the daily exploitation of everything that is worst in human nature which forms the surface of our national life, for any of the deepseated responses that Lincoln relied on to give meaning to his phrases.

Lincoln was no sectarian, but his outlook was profoundly Christian. Our uncommitted observer might well discover that the bases of Christian conviction were so eroded away in the United States that there was little left but the compulsive dogoodism of social service. He might well find that the only people who understood what the word "liberty" meant were refugees from the Communist countries where liberty had ceased to exist.

He would find the Bible, which was the fountainhead not only of individual Protestant Christianity, but of the literary tradition of the English speaking peoples, not only neglected at home but chased out of the schools. He might suspect, that if the atheists carried their victory to its logical extreme, the Testaments might soon be removed from the public libraries.

He'd find that many Americans had so lost faith in the concept of nationality they didn't care whether the United States were chosen or not. He would find it hard to see how Lincoln's words could meet with anything but a perfunctory or ritual response if they were spoken for the first time today.

This uncommitted observer might well discover, against the background of a sort of widespread material wellbeing which the human race has never had to cope with in its history, that the concept which for Lincoln was embodied in the expression, "the people," had been so disfigured by the manipulations of mass communication as to be unrecognizable. He might even suspect that the very technological advances which so changed the shape of society as to raise hob with the ethical norms of the population, were in danger of bogging down through a failure of the inventing and improvising imagination. Having read Mene Mene Tekel Upharsin off the walls of the banquet hall, our uncommitted observer might well hasten to shake the dust of these states off his shoes. Babylon too was prosperous in its day.

But we are not uncommitted. "This nation under God" is our country. "His almost chosen people" is our people. As Americans we are irrevocably committed to that "something more than common" that Washington's Continentals fought for when they surprised the Hessians at Trenton.

"That something that held out a great promise to all the people of the world to all time to come" is the cement which reunited the nation when Lincoln won his war against the Confederacy. It is that something, added to the political and religious and literary traditions of the English speaking peoples, which has bound together these congeries of immigrants of various origins through the hundred years since Lincoln spoke at Gettysburg.

At Trenton Lincoln had proclaimed his anxiety "that this union: the Constitution and the liberties of the people shall be perpetuated according to the original idea for which the struggle was made." This idea was based on individual liberty and individual responsibility. It depended upon the belief that there was a divine spirit in man which ever strove for the good. The truth of this conviction can't be tested by logic or proved by scientific experiment, but the contrary can't be proved either. Inevitably the moment comes when we have to take the leap of faith.

"Faith" is a big word. Lincoln wouldn't have needed to explain it, but today it has become one of those bugle words that leave an emotional blob in the mind instead of a sharp definition. By "faith" I mean today whatever conviction produces a feeling of participation in a common enterprise. A civilization is a common enterprise. When faith is lost civilizations coast along on their inertia for a while but soon they start to rot and disintegrate. Much more than on material wellbeing or on technological successes their survival depends on an inner imperative which causes men to reach for what is good for them instead of what is bad for them. Selfgoverning institutions particularly depend on individual responsibility for the choice between what is right and what is wrong.

If Americans cease to be dedicated to "that something more than common" which Lincoln spoke of, the republic he gave his life for has no more reason for being. The continuing process that faces the generations alive today is the adjustment of the methods of selfgovernment and of the aspirations of individual men for a full life to the changing shape of mass-production institutions.

There is nothing easy about such an assignment. The alternative is the partisan despotism that pervades two thirds of the globe. Even partial success will call for the rebirth of some sort of central faith as strong as Lincoln's was. Only then may we continue to entertain the hope that "this government of the people, by the people and for the people shall not perish from the earth."